LOST GOLD
OF THE REPUBLIC

LOST GOLD
OF THE REPUBLIC

*The Remarkable Quest for the
Greatest Shipwreck Treasure
of the Civil War Era*

PRIIT J. VESILIND

:: SHIPWRECK HERITAGE PRESS ::

Books and other publications by Shipwreck Heritage Press celebrate the adventure of deep-sea exploration around the world.

Our books are distributed to the book trade by Continental Sales, Inc. (888-327-8537) and to individuals via your favorite bookstore — online or around the corner. Please visit our website for further information or to request a catalog. For all other inquiries, contact us at Shipwreck Heritage Press, 1555 E. Flamingo Road, Las Vegas, Nevada 89119.

Shipwreck Heritage Press
www.lostgold.net

Lost Gold of the Republic, © 2005, Shipwreck Heritage Press, LLC

Publisher's Cataloging-in-Publication Data
(Prepared by The Donohue Group, Inc.)

Vesilind, Priit.
   Lost gold of the Republic : the remarkable quest for the greatest shipwreck treasure of the Civil War era / Priit J. Vesilind.

      p. : ill. ; cm.
   Includes index.
   ISBN: 1-933034-06-8

1. Republic (Steamship) 2. Odyssey Marine Exploration (Firm) 3. Shipwrecks — North Atlantic Ocean. 4. Underwater archaeology — North Atlantic Ocean. 5. Numismatics — United States. 6. Coins, American. 7. United States — History — Civil War, 1861–1865 — Antiquities. I. Title.

G530.R47 V47 2005
910.91758

First Hardcover Edition
10 9 8 7 6 5 4 3 2 1
Printed in Canada

Cover design by Jim Tobey and Rebecca Hagen
Text design by Chris Long, Mighty Media, Minneapolis

Acknowledgments

THIS BOOK BEGAN AS an assignment to write about the search and recovery of the SS *Republic* for *National Geographic*, a story that the magazine published in its September 2004 issue. I am grateful to *National Geographic* editors Bill Allen, Bernard Ohanian, and Peter Miller for allowing me the latitude to pursue the subject deeper, and to researcher David Wooddell for his tireless pursuit of accuracy and detail in chasing down the stories of Louis Caziarc, Benjamin Ryer, William and Henry Nichols, and other survivors of the shipwreck.

My thanks to Odyssey Marine Exploration's founding fathers, Greg Stemm and John Morris, for their hours of interviews, and for giving me full access to the company files. In their zeal to identify every fact about the shipwreck, Odyssey researchers had compiled a formidable file of old news clips, articles, and papers that formed the base of my historical research on the sunken steamship. I am especially grateful for the support of Guy Zajonc, Odyssey's corporate counsel, and shipmate on a previous underwater adventure. Thanks also to Ernie Tapanes, George Becker, Laura Barton, Mike Barton, David Morris, and Ellen Gerth of Odyssey, and especially to resident writer and historian Lange Winckler, who shared his notes and resources with me. And, Kathy Cunningham, thank you for making me feel at home in Tampa.

As part of my research I spent several weeks at sea on the *Odyssey Explorer*, a bracing experience made easier by the professional skill of Captain Mike Paterson. A special thanks to Chief Officer George Renardson, who patched me up when I tumbled from the top bunk one morning during rough weather and badly bruised my leg. I also sailed on the RV *Odyssey*, ably captained by Sterling Vorus. Thanks to archaeologist Neil Dobson, the self-described "Oatmeal Savage," and conservator Herb Bump for the good company and the dark humor while watching endless hours of underwater video on the monitor.

My gratitude to Roy Truman, Bob Leedy, Jim Starr, James Andrade and other ROV pros for helping me understand the technical operations of the ship, and to Gerhard Seiffert for his unfailing good humor and quiet competence. And to Eric and Gary Peterson, Ewan Bason, J.J. Jackson, Jose Rodriguez, John Vorus, Jacques de Rahm, Hague Palmer, Chris Saturley, Terry Snyder, Jim Gibeaut, and others on the team for their support and friendship. My friend and bunkmate, photographer Jonathan Blair, was a constant source of support and good advice.

Jason Williams and his crew of JWM Productions, especially Lucy McDowell and Nick Gardner, shooting for National Geographic Television, generously shared their research to help complete the full story of the ship.

In New Orleans I got generous help from Alecia Long, historian at the Louisiana State Museum, as well as Greg Lambousy, the museum's director of collections and an expert on the New Orleans Mint. Geoffrey Footner helped me find my way through the streets of Fells Point, Baltimore.

I relied on some key secondary sources, especially Cedric Ridgely-Nevitt's *American Steamships on the Atlantic*, which included the classic and perhaps only historical account of the *Republic*'s career. I owe a great debt to Chester G. Hearn, who wrote the colorful and absorbing account of occupied New Orleans in *When the Devil Came Down to Dixie: Ben Butler in New Orleans*. *New York Times* writer William Broad's book, *The Universe Below: Discovering the Secrets of the Deep Sea*, was invaluable, as was William MacLeish's charming *The Gulf Stream: Encounters with the Blue*

God, which inspired me to cast the powerful current as a major player in the *Republic* drama. Thanks also to George Bass at Texas A&M's Institute of Nautical Archaeology, who kindly reviewed key sections of the book, and to Bob Ballard, who has shared his vision of ocean exploration with me over many years and voyages.

My warm appreciation to Thyrza Nichols Goodeve, great-great-granddaughter of Colonel William Nichols, one of the heroes of this book, who opened up her family archives and mementos to me, to *National Geographic*, and to Odyssey. She is now the keeper of the flame for a great American family.

A special thanks to my editor, Philip Martin, whose skill and enthusiasm led him to contribute much substance and direction to the book project.

And finally, to my loving wife, Rima, who has had the thankless task, for more than 30 years, of reading my raw text and telling me what's wrong with it. Somebody's got to do it.

Priit J. Vesilind

Contents

An Odyssey Begins

GREG AND HIS GRANDFATHER ate scrambled eggs and Vienna sausages for breakfast on Halloween morning, 1964, then decided to go fishing together. The eight-year-old from Michigan had come to visit his grandparents in the warm, green panhandle of Florida, and could not wait to get on the water. And "Papa Shell," as Greg called him, had a plan.

"Hey," the 58-year-old man said to his grandson, "you want to go to the pond and get some bass? Or should we go out to the bay and do some shark fishing?"

"Are you kidding, Papa Shell? Let's go shark fishing!"

So the two of them packed a lunch, bought some bait, and headed out from the little town of Lynn Haven to St. Andrews Bay, a wide inlet leading to the Gulf of Mexico. They climbed into Papa Shell's 18-foot wooden boat, pushed off from the dock, and fired up the outboard motor. Slowly they chugged past the pine flatwoods and the marshes, then past the white quartz sands of the barrier beach. Soon they were edging their way out toward the Gulf Stream, that powerful current that sweeps past Panama City on its way southeast to the distant Straits of Florida. That's where the sharks were likely to be found.

1

As the morning slowly progressed, they talked a little about fishing, about the fine day. But mostly they relaxed and enjoyed the peaceful surroundings. After a while, they found a spot and silenced the motor. Soon they were rocking on the waves and concentrating on their fishing. Their first task was to catch some good-sized jack crevalles to use for shark bait. "Jacks" worked well as bait because they bled profusely, creating tendrils of blood that attracted sharks from a considerable distance.

Around eleven o'clock that morning, the fishing buddies were drifting along a deep channel near the entrance to St. Andrews Bay as an oversized yacht approached. Papa looked up too late. The huge vessel was passing close by — far too close. He started the motor and scrambled to get away, but the wake of the passing yacht caught the stern of the small fishing boat and washed over it. In an instant, Papa Shell's little vessel was swamped and tipping precariously on the large swells. Just before it rolled over completely, the grandfather managed to wrap Greg in a life jacket. In the next moment, the two of them were tossed into the sea.

They came up treading water beside the overturned hull. An air pocket beneath the boat kept it afloat, but with its weight and shape, it was impossible for the 58-year-old and the boy in the water to turn it back over. They were shipwrecked, floating slowly into the Gulf of Mexico, away from the Florida panhandle, in shark territory.

Paddling over to the eight-year-old boy, Papa Shell took off his belt. He slipped it under Greg's arms, then tied the belt to the towring on the bow of the fishing boat, so the youngster would be held up out of the water. Grandpa surely knew this was a calculated risk. As long as the boat was afloat, it would keep his grandson's head above water, possibly attracting attention from a passing vessel. But if the tiny boat were to sink, it would drag the boy down with it.

Greg's memories of the rest of that day are glimpsed only in fitful, dream-like moments, in brief, stark visions with great gaps in between. "Grandpa was floating alongside of me for a while, and then he started coughing. And then . . . he was there beside me . . . dead.

"And I knew that he was dead, but I remember holding his body for hours and hours, just holding on to it to keep him from drifting away.

"I remember he had a red-and-white checked shirt on. And his face was white — just white as white can be.

"I remember seeing boats in the distance, and yelling, holding on to my grandpa, yelling for these boats until I was hoarse."

Hours passed, first filled with terror, then with an overwhelming thirst. Hanging by his grandfather's belt to the side of the boat, his throat thick and dry with salt, Greg held on, even as boats came and went in the distance in that terribly real dreamscape, without noticing the little overturned hull riding low in the water.

The fishing floats they had set out in the water were still intact, bobbing beside the boat, dangling baited hooks intended to lure in sharks. Visions of slashing teeth and bloody water terrified the young boy. But eventually fatigue overcame him, and he closed his eyes and lapsed into semi-consciousness as the whole assemblage — upside-down boat, with a frightened boy attached, holding onto his lifeless grandpa — drifted off into the vast flow of the Gulf Stream, a little shipwreck.

Just before dark, two local men returning from a fishing trip came upon the capsized boat miles from shore. A small head bobbed beside the boat; a small hand reached up and gave a feeble wave. Greg barely remembers the men untying him and lifting him up into their boat. He remembers only that the cooler on the rescue boat was filled with "specks" (spotted weakfish), and that his grandfather was dead. Papa Shell's body was recovered the next day, after an 18-hour search, near the bridge that spans St. Andrews Bay.

Some ships go down big: thousands die, grand staircases and crystal chandeliers collapse as a dance band plays bravely on. The world shudders. Other ships go down small. A cargo of cotton and

3

molasses is lost, or a hold full of terra-cotta jars of olive oil disappears. A few sailors here and there are washed overboard by storms on an indifferent ocean. Thousands of boats capsize. A man drowns and is found floating face down off the Florida panhandle.

But this man was Clifford "Papa Shell" Shelkofsky, a respected man from the town of Lynn Haven. And his grandson was Greg Stemm, who would grow up to become co-founder of Odyssey Marine Exploration of Tampa, one of the world's most successful companies in the field of deep-water shipwreck recovery.

The ordeal at sea and the death of his beloved grandfather must have been too heavy a memory for the eight-year-old boy to bear. Vaguely, Greg remembers living through the funeral in a sort of trance, then he must have tucked the accident into his mind's deep storage. He passed through his school years back home in Michigan without thinking of the tragedy, perhaps not even remembering it in any conscious sense. But the growing child also developed a fascination for shipwrecks. He watched every Jacques Cousteau special, popular on TV in the early 1960s, and pored over each issue of *National Geographic* that took readers beneath the sea. He dreamed of growing up to be an underwater explorer and archaeologist.

At school, like many a young boy looking to discover himself, he challenged his teachers with a rash of rebellions and little mischiefs. On his family's farm, however, he worked long hours — and learned to keep equipment working with baling wire and ingenuity. He was, he discovered, also a natural salesman and entrepreneur. He bought, repaired, and sold cars, and in high school did well as part owner of a lucrative cherry-harvesting company that pioneered the use of huge mechanical tree-shaking equipment.

But the sea had stirred something vital in him that could not be ignored. In 1974 he headed off to New College in Sarasota, Florida, to study marine biology — a field that brought him as close to his true interests as possible, since underwater exploration and archaeology programs were few. Then, remarkably, one evening in a dorm room, all the memories of that awful shipwreck suddenly came back. His mind flooded with memories of his ordeal with his grandfather, Papa Shell — thoughts that he had suppressed for more than a decade. And in that instant, the pieces of his future began to coalesce.

Greg never graduated; he had no patience for pedantry. He dropped out of school to hit the road as a front man for comedian Bob Hope, which led to a swift and successful career in advertising and promotion. He knew he could make money, whatever the product. By the late 1980s, from his new base in Tampa, Greg finally found himself entering the world of deep-water research.

On a whim, he and his business partner, John Morris, had branched out in 1987 from real estate development to buy a ship, a research vessel that could be outfitted with remotely operated vehicles (ROVs): robotic submersibles with mechanical eyes and arms that could delve into the depths far beyond the reach of human SCUBA divers. Their timing was good. Specialized tools for deep-ocean work — often cobbled from espionage electronics and cable-company hardware — had begun to be widely available to private customers, though the equipment was still extremely expensive. Only a handful of researchers, Greg and John knew, had applied such tools to shipwreck excavation. Florida was awash with professional and amateur treasure-hunters, combing the sandy beaches, shoals, and shallow waters for wrecks. But few had the financing or desire to put together long-term projects to search for sunken vessels far out at sea and in deep water.

Maintaining a serious deep-ocean recovery capacity consumed a tremendous amount of capital. Underwater exploration was no hobby for Greg and John; it would have to be a business. And why not? The ambitious partners were convinced that they were as able as anyone to find shipwrecks and tell their stories of disaster at sea. They would bring the artifacts to the public — and sell some of them to support more expeditions. It was a dream that could come true.

But they quickly found themselves treading on the territory of a long-standing cadre of academic archaeologists and scientists, many of whom dismissed the two newcomers to the field as "treasure hunters." But Greg and John refused to be so easily categorized. A Midwest sense of fair play and decency fueled their dreams: to develop a pioneering approach to commercially viable marine archaeology that could win the respect of all. Persistent to the point of stubbornness, they dedicated themselves to placing their brash new company at the leading edge of deep-ocean exploration.

Today Greg Stemm is a tall, nearly lanky, sandy-haired man with a trim beard that cannot hide a quick, friendly grin. He's a devotee of the Grateful Dead, yet he looks more like television's Opie grown tall. But the boyishness barely disguises a mind percolating with angles and possibilities. He is quick with words, a good PR man, and business comes naturally to him.

John Morris is the yang to Greg's yin. Born in Flint, Michigan, he is a former contractor and land developer who cut his entrepreneurial chops working with his father and brothers in the family construction firm. He moved to Florida in 1973 as a 24-year-old to manage a branch of the family business for a few years, then returned to the Sunshine State in 1979 for good. John is a soft-spoken man with strong opinions who suffers fools very, very poorly. Things somehow clicked between these two men. Together they ventured into a world where they were not especially welcome and, eventually, found the ultimate target: a shipwreck of lost gold.

It was the late summer of 2003 when Odyssey Marine Exploration, after a search that spanned more than twelve years, zeroed in on the shipwreck of the SS *Republic,* a twin-paddlewheel steamer from the Civil War era that had reportedly carried $400,000 in specie (coins of gold or silver). The steamship had been en route from New York City to New Orleans in 1865, intending to bring supplies and cash to the suffering city that had once been the economic colossus of the South. The shipment of coinage had been not a humanitarian act but a business venture, promising great profits to its 19th-century investors who had hoped to use the cash to gain even more wealth. But profits were not always so easily ledgered when a sea voyage was involved. Instead, the steamship *Republic* foundered in a hurricane. Pummeled for days by the fierce storm, powerless when her boilers failed, and finally abandoned by her passengers and crew, the ship disappeared in an instant beneath the waves, spiraling down to rest somewhere in the rushing currents of the Gulf Stream, many miles off the coast of Georgia.

The SS *Republic*, originally launched as the SS *Tennessee*, would remain hidden in those deep and very dark waters for the next 138 years, forgotten and beyond the grasp of any technology. Its remains, if discovered, surely would offer a unique time-capsule of one of America's least understood eras. But the two partners, Greg Stemm and John Morris, also were aware of the potential treasure of the *Republic:* its reported cargo of United States coins, undoubtedly many of rare vintage, perhaps some freshly minted and in pristine condition. Such coins would be worth vastly more than their original $400,000, the face value of the specie according to the ship's captain. This lost steamer had the potential to be the most profitable shipwreck ever found and excavated in the deep sea. It was the dream of every ocean explorer.

With an estimated three million shipwrecks scattered around the world, according to United Nations' estimates, it is said that the ocean bottoms hold more history than the museums of the world combined. They also hide an incalculable amount of wealth and treasure. Adventurers have always dreamed of finding sunken ships, whether Spanish galleons from the New World that foundered in storms or treasure chests of pirates and privateer raiders lost at sea. But for centuries, recovering a ship in deep water was the stuff of fantasy; lost gold, if sunk far out at sea, was forever lost. The bottom of the deep sea seemed as remote and hostile as the outer planets.

While the history of shallow-water exploration goes back hundreds of years, deep-ocean exploration has a much shorter timeline. For only a few decades, military commanders, academic researchers, and a narrow range of industrial enterprises have tested deep waters by voyaging down in manned submersibles or dispatching robotic vehicles. During the Cold War, between 1950 and 1990, the prime source of funds and technology for deep-sea exploration was the U.S. Navy, as it vied with the Soviet Union to build sophisticated submarines and listening platforms. On the commercial side, oil and gas firms learned to build gigantic, island-like platforms far offshore from which to tap the earth's crust below deep waters, such as in the North Sea between Norway and Great Britain. And in the era before the satellite link, companies succeeded in binding together continents by laying thousands of miles of deep-sea wire and cable for instant overseas communication. To support these government and commercial needs, a handful of private ocean-engineering companies sprang up to provide specialized hardware and technology.

As technologies improved, research efforts became increasingly interested in the natural riches of the deep sea. Marine scientists made stunning geological and biological discoveries, journeying in manned submersibles to deep oceanic rifts between tectonic plates, discovering — in tales reminiscent of Jules Verne's *Twenty Thousand Leagues Under the Sea* — unimagined communities of amazing plants and animals that live without oxygen, synthesizing chemicals from their strange surroundings to survive.

Subsequent geologic research led to another tantalizing discovery: an abundance of strange metal nodules present on the deep-sea floor. Fantastic wealth was lying down there, strewn about like river stones, if someone could devise a method to harvest it. Since the 1960s, deep-ocean mining for those nodules — manganese, cobalt, nickel, and other metals — has held enormous promise. Yet that promise has flickered because of daunting engineering challenges, the fickleness of global metal prices, and politics.

In the 1980s, another possibility fired up the imagination: that a wealth of valuable sulfides and other minerals might be mined from "hot chimneys" in the sea-floor crust around volcanically active areas. But that scheme also fell by the wayside as the risks were found to outweigh the rewards.

In this dangerous and speculative realm, serious seekers of cultural materials in the deep ocean were few. The expense of exploration was daunting and sources of funding limited. In the past several decades, Robert D. Ballard, working first with Woods Hole Oceanographic Institution and later for his own Institute for Exploration, succeeded in locating famous historic ships such as the *Titanic* and the *Bismarck,* as well as wreck sites of ancient ships in the Mediterranean and Black Seas. But the payoff from these projects for Ballard has been limited to articles, books, films, and lectures; the cost of his expeditions usually exceeded any financial gain.

Private projects to recover deep-water historical wrecks have usually been intimidated by technical demands and the lack of institutional support. In the 1990s, for example, a spate of expeditions to find the lost airplane of aviator Amelia Earhart fizzled out because of equipment failures and severe funding challenges.

Despite the romantic possibility of finding shipwrecked jewels, coins, and bars of gold and silver spread across the sea floor by centuries of seafaring misfortune, deep-sea exploration is still a costly venture. Even with excellent research, it can take years of painstaking exploration, of dragging sonars or magnetometers back and forth across vast areas of ocean. The projected expense generally defeats most plans on the drawing board.

Only a few entrepreneurs have found riches in the deep. One was marine explorer and inventor Tommy Thompson, whose team located and excavated the SS *Central America*, a Gold Rush–era sidewheel steamship carrying bullion, coins, and gold dust back from the El Dorado of California. Others have been left in a morass of legal problems and debt, notably researcher Paul Tidwell, who made a foray into the deep Atlantic in 1999 to search for the gold cargo of the Japanese transport submarine *I-52*. He found the sub, but the gold still lies entombed within the hull.

Recently, with better equipment available, private underwater salvage companies have silently managed to locate and haul up the cargoes of a small number of wrecks for their booty. But until Stemm and Morris came along, no one had made a sustained effort to establish a privately funded company to find, recover, and conduct archaeological investigations of shipwrecks in the deep ocean on an ongoing basis. Certainly no company had tried to straddle the worlds of science and salvage so thoroughly.

Archaeology in the deep ocean, however, can have several advantages over projects conducted in shallow water, starting with politics and legal issues. First, it is generally easier to secure a title to a shipwreck located in international waters than one that came to rest near the coastline of a country whose politics and laws dictate complex ownership issues. Second, deep shipwrecks tend to remain intact; they are more likely to stay where they first hit the ocean floor rather than being scattered across the sea bed or buried under shifting sands by each subsequent hurricane, as can happen with shallow-water wrecks. And since they are inaccessible to casual divers — folks with a boat, some basic diving gear, and time on their hands — deep-water wrecks are far less likely to have been disturbed by today's looters or amateur collectors (or by ancient salvors sent out to recover a valuable lost cargo soon after a ship's sinking). Finally, artifacts from deep-water sites tend to be in remarkable physical condition, as the low oxygen levels and absence of light prohibit the growth of coral and other corrosive material.

Odyssey's success addresses a critical question in the world of ocean exploration: can commercial excavation be done responsibly, with respect for the need for scholarly documentation? Odyssey brings together cutting-edge equipment and broad goals; it combines archaeology and public education with new models for financing and management. Depending on the success of the model — and limitations that would be imposed on commercial work if an international convention advocated by UNESCO (United Nations Educational, Scientific, and Cultural Organization) were widely adopted — deep-sea exploration stands at the beginning of a bold new era. Many will be tempted; only a few are likely to succeed. But given that estimate of three million shipwrecks resting on the ocean floor, there would seem to be enough promising sites to go around for everyone from archaeologists to divers to commercial explorers like Odyssey.

The story of the *Republic* and its discovery is a sequence of amazing tales, a nautical version of *The Arabian Nights*, beginning with the shipwreck of the tiny boat in which Papa Shell met his maker. In a fairy-tale twist, his grandson, Greg Stemm, has become one of the men at the core of the world's leading shipwreck company. He knows all too well the powerful forces of the sea, as well as its utter lack of sentiment. His intuition tells him that within each shipwreck, large or small, is a narrative of suffering, courage, and loss.

And he knows that the ocean can severely punish little mistakes. "When you're out at sea," he says, "a beautiful day can quickly turn into death."

Death surely came to the SS *Republic,* but she steamed from New York harbor on her last voyage as a ship of buoyant optimism. She carried the hopes of her passengers for a return to a normal life after the fratricidal bloodletting of the American Civil War. She carried the hopes of the city of New Orleans to regain its vigor and *joie de vivre* after the Yankee occupation. And she symbolized the hopes of a nation that had just begun to heal. When she sank to the bottom on that fateful day in October 1865, none who read the news of her sinking could have imagined her re-emergence more than a century later into the bright world of open air and renewed dreams. That was left for others to envision.

This is the story of the steamship *Republic,* first named the SS *Tennessee,* and the decade-long search by Greg Stemm and John Morris for her resting place. At its heart it is a story about the dreams of adventurers and entrepreneurs, always looking forward to the next opportunity, beginning with those climbing aboard a side-wheel steamship in New York harbor, ready to embark on a sea voyage in that year of renewed hope, 1865.

CHAPTER 1

Riding the Blue God

EIGHT DAYS HAD PASSED, and two men still clung to the raft, a flimsy triangle of broken spars and boards. At least 12 other sailors — perhaps as many as 16, the count is uncertain — mostly firemen and deckhands, had been washed off, or had leapt into the hurricane-swept Atlantic, mad with thirst. Of those who had started out on the crowded raft, only Oliver Martin, the quartermaster of the sunken steamship *Republic,* and James Noolan, a waiter who had been working his way to New Orleans, still survived.

Days earlier, most of the *Republic's* crew and all of its passengers had reached safety on four lifeboats, picked up one by one at sea. But the crude raft had not been found. Three steamships had been persistently searching for the low-riding piece of flotsam since October 31. "When last seen," reported the *New York Herald*, "she had 18 persons on it, and the sea breaking over it, some three feet high. As it is said to have been very poorly constructed there are little hopes entertained of the above vessels being successful on their mission."

Early on the morning of November 2, 1865, the barkentine USS *Tioga* spotted something bobbing among the whitecaps only 20 miles off the Cape Hatteras lighthouse. The *Tioga* took in all her sail, lowered a boat, and delivered Martin and Noolan from the sea. "The men cannot tell the names of any of their companions on the raft," wrote the captain of the *Tioga,* W.D. Whitney, in a report to Sumner Welles, Secretary of the Navy. "They are both doing well, and I shall land them at Port Royal."

The storm that sank their ship was one of those tropical cyclones spawned in the vast North Atlantic Ocean, when air and water are empowered with violent energy by seasonal heat. The storms gather strength as they are blown westward by trade winds, then are bent north with the spin of the planet. Sometimes, bloated with power like an angry god, a storm will intensify into a raging hurricane, blasting its way across the islands of the Caribbean and traveling up the North American shoreline, raking shipping lanes, flooding shoals and barrier islands, pounding winds and rain on coastal towns, sometimes striking far inland.

But these baleful storms that sweep each fall from the tropics are merely part-time actors in the vast theater of sky and sea. The storm that struck the *Republic* would build in wind strength, throw mounting waves against the ship, pound the hull and superstructure for several days, wreak its havoc, and then pass on.

When the hurricane departed, a less visible but equally powerful force had continued to pull on the raft from below. Carried along by its invisible motion, the castaways had traveled on their raft, without any means of control or self-propulsion, to a point some 300 miles north of where the *Republic* had foundered. Martin and Noolan had not only been drubbed by the winds, they had also been reduced to helpless flotsam in North America's most powerful current. They were awash in the ocean river called the Gulf Stream, a place of reckoning for many of man's follies and ambitions, a rushing current dubbed in modern times the "Blue God" by William H. MacLeish, former editor of *Oceanus* magazine, a leading publication for the study of the marine environment.

The Gulf Stream is the invisible backdrop for the story of the *Republic* and its recovery. It is a constant, intimidating presence for mariners. For those who enter its flow, it is a force of nature as ubiquitous and omnipotent as the moon or the sun.

The powerful current is a planetary force, a movement of the ocean sustained by the heating of the earth at the Equator, part of a great wind-driven swirl that circles the North Atlantic Ocean. As deep, cold water flows south from the Arctic, it is warmed by the sun and rises to the surface at the Equator. Here, where the earth spins most furiously, hot tropical winds blow back toward the North Pole, dragging warm surface water with them.

At the same time, the earth is rotating, moving beneath the atmosphere. Accordingly, the winds and currents appear to drift sideways as they move north, a sense of motion called the Coriolis force. Together, these factors set up a clockwise rotation of waters and trade winds around the Atlantic basin.

The Gulf Stream flow is also abetted by the Sargasso Sea, that weed-choked oceanic swamp in the mid-Atlantic where dead sailors and ships are said to float eternally suspended. The circling hot winds drive warm water toward its center, and the water actually bulges up, so that the middle of the Sargasso, like a gently sloping hillock, is some six feet higher than its edges. Because of this slope, pressure beneath the center of the Sargasso is greater than around the edges, and water from the center continually flows outward. That flow, too, is bent in its movement by the Coriolis force. It joins the Gulf Stream, which then forms a boundary between the warm Sargasso and the colder waters of the coastline. Mariners know this temperature-gradient border as the West Wall, a place of rich nutrients that fishermen expect to deliver schools of menhaden, shrimp, and bluefin tuna.

Pushing up from the Equator toward the coast of North America, the northward current slips into the Gulf of Mexico, loops around it like a river oxbow, then pours back out through the straits between Florida and Cuba at a surface speed of five to six knots — as fast as a kayak can travel. At that stretch, the Gulf Stream is 100 miles wide and hauls more than 30 million cubic yards of tropical water per second.

On the sea floor below, at depths of 1,500 to 3,000 feet, the current usually eases to one or two knots. Although this is only the velocity of a brook, it carries sand and grit, sends debris scudding, and sculpts wooden objects into streamlined shapes resembling fish.

Ships and other objects lost in the Gulf Stream tend to end up far from where they disappear beneath the surface waves. In 1985, the Stream swept away the wreckage of the space shuttle *Challenger,* leaving salvagers to chase pieces of the craft along the sea floor like pedestrians pursuing runaway hats on a windy street. In the 1860s, the Gulf Stream might have taken a ship sunk by a hurricane for a fierce underwater ride as it dropped to the bottom of the ocean.

As it surges north, the Gulf Stream keeps its distance from the coastline, anywhere from 50 to 100 miles offshore, roughly following the line of the underwater precipice where the much shallower continental shelf drops into the deep ocean. Off the coast of Georgia and South Carolina, the rapid current washes across the Blake Plateau, an ancient coral reef of ridges and deep gullies scoured by the moving water. As it continues north, the Gulf Stream literally rolls off the Blake Plateau into the North Atlantic, passing Cape Hatteras. It grows broader and gathers power, until it courses with 200 million cubic meters of water a second off the Grand Banks of Newfoundland — like 20 Niagara Falls or 200 million bathtubs simultaneously emptying into the northern ocean.

Then, the Gulf Stream swirls out into eddies to the east. Although no one has demonstrated exactly how, Europeans believe that the Gulf Stream carries tropical warmth to England and the Scandinavian coast, soothing what would otherwise be a much colder climate. London, after all, is on the same latitude as Labrador.

Off the coast of North America, the strength of the Stream and the volatility of the weather have tested shipping lines and trans-Atlantic sailors for hundreds of years. Even before the Civil War, an armada of lost ships — from Spanish galleons to Baltimore clippers to clunky steamers — had come to rest in watery graves on the Gulf Stream floor, stretching in a thousand-mile line from Havana to Cape Hatteras.

On October 25, 1865, the SS *Republic* spiraled down to join them. But castaways Martin and Noolan, shaken and shivering in the early morning on the deck of the USS *Tioga*, had managed to ride the Blue God to safety.

CHAPTER 2

The Adventures of the *Tennessee*

OR THE FIRST 150 years of the North American colonies, until well past the mid-1700s, settlers seldom ventured beyond the accessible latticework of rivers, streams, bays, inlets, and barrier islands that fringed the Atlantic. Their world was the eastern seaboard and the Piedmont east of the Appalachian Mountains, and most folk stayed put as much as possible. Cross-country travel was difficult and sporadic, something not lightly undertaken. A few carriage roads connected towns and settlements, but they were rough or muddy, and truncated unpredictably. Inns and taverns along the way were often seedy and crawling with petty thieves. In comparison, water routes were smooth and generally safer, so they bore the weight of travel and commerce.

Gradually, though, the nation expanded beyond the mountains, and the old inland waterways could not follow. Canals closed some gaps, and sailing vessels carried cargo along the coast, but such travel remained at the whim of winds and weather, as it had since antiquity, and movements were unpredictable. Steam-powered ships, introduced in the 1820s, began to tie port cities and Mississippi Valley settlements together with some consistency, but for many years those early steamships did not round Florida to connect the East Coast to Gulf Coast ports.

In 1830 a trip from New York to New Orleans was an epic undertaking. Travelers setting out from Manhattan faced a convoluted itinerary with weeks on the road and the water. They had two practical choices. One was to take a series of coastal steamers, canal boats, and stagecoaches to Pittsburgh, then descend the Ohio and Mississippi Rivers to the Gulf. The other equally convoluted route was to catch a steamboat across the bay to New Brunswick, New Jersey, find a stagecoach to Trenton, travel by river steamer down the Delaware to Philadelphia, take another stage to Baltimore, and book a steamship to Norfolk. From that Virginia seaport, travelers could find a land route to Savannah or Charleston, then sail to Augusta, Georgia, hop a stage to Mobile, and take a final steamer to New Orleans.

Connections improved rapidly after 1832 when pioneers in Charleston launched the nation's first steamship packet line to carry U.S. mail. The mail contract meant that the ships departed on a regular schedule, whether fully booked with passengers or not. The Charleston investors, it seemed, were counting on the rapid development of steam railroads from southern ports into the interior. If so, they could regularly get manufactured goods into Charleston to send by train into the Piedmont and beyond to be exchanged for agricultural products.

Their gamble paid off. Indeed, these coastal traders with their links to the railroads became the prime carriers of bulk goods and passengers between the states. Southern cotton, grain, and tobacco headed north to sure markets, while manufactured goods and lumber from the great forests of the Northeast headed south. The railroads distributed the goods inland, creating such new interior hubs as Atlanta, and the frontier pushed ever westward as the largely waterborne transportation web developed sufficiently to support new settlers.

A remarkable burst of commercial and mercantile energy followed in the 1840s. The shipyards of America's coastal cities — Boston, New York, Philadelphia, Baltimore — churned out wooden sailing ships as well as wooden-hulled steamships. Timber — white pine, locust, oak — was readily available, so construction costs were low. The ships of the day were increasingly specialized. There were swift packets for passengers and premium freight. There were slow but massive bulk carriers for commodities such as cotton. There were nimble schooners that could slip down to the tropics for fruit and coffee. And there were trans-oceanic clippers built to carry waves of immigrants from the Old World to the New. Over the years, ship-building, once done by small gangs of workers in improvised yards, became an industry that needed a heavy outlay of equipment and a permanent space for machinery.

By the middle of the 19th century, sailing ships had evolved into creatures of billowing beauty and undeniable romance. Eastern ship-yards were still fashioning slim, compact clippers with raked-back masts, the fastest ships ever made. "Skimmers of the sea," the clippers were called, ships that were said to "start before the wind has time to reach their sails and never allow it to come up with them."

But the wind was as erratic as it was romantic, and sailing ships flew only at the whim of the winds. Steam power was replacing sail, a transition that must have saddened shipbuilders as much as it excited others. Steamships made a lot of noise and stank of burning coal but didn't wait on the weather. They provided regular, scheduled service, offered luxurious staterooms and dining halls, and gave travelers a sense of being engaged in something revolutionary and thoroughly modern. Americans were in a hurry, and steamships were the airlin-ers of their day. By 1870 the age of large wooden sailing ships was over.

Packet steamships soon ventured beyond serving the seaboard cities. They soon rounded Florida for Gulf of Mexico ports such as Mobile, New Orleans, and Galveston, even as smaller steamers churned up the river arteries of the Mississippi as far as they could into the continent. The opening of a steamship line between New York and New Orleans, with stops in Charleston and Havana, began in April 1847 when the U.S. Department of the Navy granted a mail contract to A.G. Sloo. After the discovery of gold at Sutter's Mill in California in 1848, shipbuilding and passenger service exploded the next year as would-be prospectors and adventurers headed off to the West Coast on any route they could find — mostly through Central American ports and the Isthmus of Panama. The East Coast routes of the United States were suddenly packed with gold-fevered passenger traffic, plus great quantities of supplies needed to sustain such exploits.

An article in the *New York Daily Times* of February 17, 1852, outlined the clamor for more steamships:

> Our city is rammed, crammed, and jammed full of passengers for California, our hotels are full, our streets are full, and in fact we are full all over, with only one steamer in port to take them away. The *Oregon* leaves this afternoon with over 400 passengers. The *Christiana, Margaret, Amphytrite* and *Philena* are all full, and will be off to-day or to-morrow. These four sailing vessels carry about 600 passengers, leaving a balance of 800 or 1,000 on the Isthmus to wait for the next steamer. . . . In ten days, however, if the steamers which are expected make their appearance, we shall have abundance of steam conveyance for all passengers.

Entrepreneurs who were adroit enough to anticipate the steamship boom fashioned mercantile empires and built fortunes. But with the Gulf Stream their major highway, it was risky business. Each fall the shipping lanes along the coast were battered by tropical storms and hurricanes that rose from the equatorial heat pump. Winds and waves ravaged ships at sea and slammed into port cities, splintering wharves and warehouses.

The SS *Tennessee,* the ship later known as the *Republic,* was built in 1853 at the apex of this American shipping boom — an era that

ended only a few years before the Civil War. She was built at Fells
Point in Baltimore, Maryland, on a rowdy waterfront that bulged
aggressively into Baltimore harbor. Behind this tight warren of brick
homes and factories rose a bluff called Federal Hill and the walls of
Fort McHenry, whose defense during the War of 1812 had inspired
the writing of "The Star-Spangled Banner." In that 1812 war, the
Fells Point shipyards became renowned for their fleet of privateers:
privately owned clipper ships that harassed and captured some 500
British merchant vessels for the benefit of the United States.

But when depression hit in the 1820s, the shipbuilders sought
revenue from more unsavory enterprises. They began to construct
opium schooners for the China trade; they outfitted slave ships for
human cargo from Africa to Cuba and Brazil. The slaver *Amistad,*
famous for its rebellion when a cargo of slaves aboard overpowered
its Spanish crew off Cuba in 1839, was a grim product of Fells Point
shipyards.

By the 1840s, the district had recovered and was becoming a
proud and busy mercantile port. Its steam-driven flour mills and factories hissed and rattled alongside a crammed harbor cross-hatched
by the spars and masts of gaff-rigged schooners, loading and hauling
passengers and cargo. The slave trade routes had opened up commercial ties between Baltimore and South America, and a fleet of
Baltimore schooners was hauling wheat and flour on a regular basis
to Rio de Janeiro, bringing back coffee, sugar, and copper. Runs to
Peru and Chile returned with loads of guano: bird droppings used
for fertilizer — a cargo that let off a foul yellow dust that clung to
clothes and calcified into a hard shell when it rained.

The cobbled streets of Fells Point were overrun with pushcarts
filled with fruit, barrels of oysters, and burlap sacks of grain. Immigrant children scooted between buggies and hackney cabs pulled by
teams of sweating horses. The odor of manure and guano mingled
with coal dust, the tang of the fish market, and the warm ambrosia
of coffee-grinding houses. Fells Point fully reeked with prosperity.

In the 1850s, Baltimore was truly one of America's workhorses. Even as shipwrights formed and pounded out the iron steam-engine of the *Tennessee,* the city was celebrating the completion of the B&O — the Baltimore & Ohio Railroad — which stretched from Baltimore harbor to Wheeling, West Virginia, on the Ohio River. Fells Point was one of the terminals of a new industrial age. It was also a gritty rat's nest, filled with German and Irish immigrants and foreign sailors looking for a good time. Fueled by its many taverns, this town was developing a reputation as a place to "drink, dance, and fornicate," according to Baltimore historian Norman G. Rukert. And it was just recovering from an epidemic of yellow fever.

Baltimore in 1853 was also a hotbed of growing Southern sentiment in the buildup to the Civil War, only seven years away. The city lay on the fault line between North and South, and its citizens were in turmoil. Twelve percent were black, for the most part free men; a portion, however, were owned as slaves. The clannish immigrant groups were vociferously Northern in their political views and mostly abolitionist, except when it came to sharing their own jobs with African-Americans. Baltimore was nonetheless a Southern city. The belles of its high society flaunted secessionist ribbons on their ball gowns. The streets of Fells Point teemed with thugs intent on political warfare. Extremist "clubs" such as the Plug Uglies, the Rough Skins, the Blood Tubs, the Red Necks, and the Butt Enders raided each other's meetings with fists and cudgels.

But gold had been discovered in California in 1848, and the United States, exploding to the west, needed Baltimore-built ships. The city's entrepreneurs tried to straddle the fence and focus their energies on profits. At his Fells Point shipyard, John A. Robb had been building mid-sized steamships for the ambitious Atlantic coastal merchant trade, one of the nation's prime commercial arteries. Robb's latest vessel, readied in August 1853 for its dramatic slide down the skids into Baltimore harbor, was the SS *Tennessee.*

Robb was born in Nova Scotia. He had come to New York with his family at the age of twelve and fought in the War of 1812 as a teenager. He was sent to Baltimore by famed New York naval architect Henry Eckfort in 1826 to help supervise the building of a large Brazilian navy frigate, the biggest ship built in Baltimore to date. Robb stayed to become one of the city's most prolific and versatile shipbuilders.

By coincidence, the launching of the South American naval vessel was also witnessed by ten-year-old Frederick Douglass, who grew up to become one of the nation's greatest African-American statesmen. As a child, young Frederick had been sent as a slave houseboy to the Fells Point home of Hugh Ault, another local shipbuilder. Douglass would return later, still as a slave, to work as a caulker for Gardner's shipyards.

The Fells Point shipyards, like the rest of Baltimore in the years before the Civil War, were hotbeds of bitterness and ethnic resentment. Low pay and competition for jobs between newly arrived immigrants, native-born white Americans, and black workers led to ferocious disputes. Douglass, the future diplomat and civil-rights leader, became one of many victims of that rancor. He wrote about the experience in his autobiography:

> Until a very little while after I went there, white and black ship-carpenters worked side by side and no one seemed to see any impropriety in it. . . . Things seemed to be going on very well. All at once, the white carpenters knocked off, and said they would not work with free colored workmen. Their reason for this, as alleged, was, that if free colored carpenters were encouraged, they would soon take the trade into their own hands, and poor white men would be thrown out of employment. . . . My fellow-apprentices soon began to feel it degrading to them to work with me. . . . They commenced making my condition as hard as they could.

... They at length combined, and came upon me, armed with sticks, stones, and heavy handspikes. . . . The one behind ran up with the handspike, and struck me a heavy blow upon the head. It stunned me. I fell, and with this they all fell to beating me.

Douglass eventually escaped home, and his master queried a lawyer about possible recourse. He was told there was none — unless they could get a white man to testify on behalf of Douglass — because the testimony of a black man was not permissible in court. Since no white man would risk taking the stand against another white on behalf of a slave, the case was dropped.

Other victims of racial injustice may not have survived to tell their tales. But prosperous shipbuilders of booming Baltimore trade hardly noticed. Their sights were set far off to sea in all directions of the compass.

Fells Point shipbuilder Robb was considered one of the maritime innovators of the age. He enjoyed an international reputation and demonstrated a prescience for the future of mass production. One of his designs was for an all-purpose schooner, a sort of basic shell. Geoffrey Footner, a Baltimore historian, recently found the drawings for this prototype in an archive in Vincennes, France. "He [Robb] would distribute the schooner to various buyers, depending on their trade," observed Footner. "It was adaptable for the slaving trade, to the general coastline trade here in the States, or as a pilot ship." The entrepreneurial Robb also built two ships in 1839–40 — the brigs *Brazos* and *Galveston* — for the navy of the Republic of Texas.

But the most pressing need for Robb's business was to supply ships for the Atlantic coastal trade. The SS *Tennessee* was one of those. She was a twin-paddlewheel hybrid; that is, she combined the boxy muscularity of steam with the grace of mast and sail, although the latter features were included only to provide a degree of extra power. Oak-hulled, her decks were of white pine, fastened with copper and iron. Two decks lay below the engine room and super-structure, with cabins for 100 passengers and enough space for 5,000 barrels of cargo.

The *Tennessee's* steam-driven power plant of boilers and engine was built in Baltimore by Charles Reeder and Sons. The side-wheeler burned coal, and her vertical-beam engine was powered by a massive single piston. This gargantuan piece of tooled metal was six feet in circumference and nine feet long.

Behind her boilers rose a 30-foot tall, 15-ton, diamond-shaped iron structure known as the "walking beam." This contraption was engineered to teeter like a seesaw with every stroke of the powerful piston, seeming to swing from one leg to the other, pulling the ship in a series of powerful steps.

The walking beam connected to a crankshaft that in turn drove the great pair of side-mounted paddlewheels. Those distinctively curved shapes, offering an endless succession of broad paddles to churn and pull the ship through the water, were mounted amidships. Built of a combination of iron and wood, each wheel towered to 28 feet, the height of a three-story house.

The *Tennessee* weighed some 1,500 tons. She was 210 feet long and nearly 34 feet across the beam. That was mid-range for the steamships of the day — a size that would prove both flexible and economical. She was "schooner-rigged," which meant she had two masts and a bowsprit (a large horizontal spar). This rigging offered just enough sail to mollify traditionalists. But the sails were merely supplementary; the ship was far too heavy in the water to be pulled by wind alone. To make headway, her engines had to be working.

The steamer had been ordered by James Hooper, president of the Baltimore & Southern Packet Company. She was to be launched on August 13, 1853, but the vessel got stuck midway down the ramp, disappointing those on hand eager to see her enter the water. It turned out that the tallow used to grease the skids had squeezed out. Workmen had to block her up, reconstruct the launch frame, and re-grease. It wasn't until August 31 that the new steamer slipped easily and unceremoniously into Baltimore harbor.

For unknown reasons, six months passed before the *Tennessee* ran her first sea-trial with passengers and cargo between Baltimore and Charleston. Records are sketchy; there may have been a major flaw in her construction; there may have been business snags. In any event, when she left Fells Point bound for Charleston under the command of Lewis Parish on February 7, 1854, both company president Hooper and engine manufacturer Reeder were on board. She returned safely home again, taking just 54 hours for the speedy return trip, with a cargo of rice and cotton and carrying 88 passengers — 59 traveling first class and 29 in steerage. It was the inaugural voyage of a steamship line between Baltimore and southern ports.

For the first chapter of the *Tennessee's* extraordinary career, she was a packet ship. She steamed along the Baltimore-Charleston circuit every two weeks, completing 28 voyages as part of James Hooper's West Indies & Venezuela Steamship Company. Passenger fare was $17.50 for a first-class cabin, $8.00 for second-class. Meals were provided. The *Tennessee* was comfortable, fast, and reliable. But the ship apparently wasn't making enough money for Hooper, who took the steamer out of circulation and put her up for auction on March 22.

All spring she sat, with no takers. Discouraged, Hooper decided to send the steamer on a speculative mission to Southampton, England, to see what business he could work up. Oddly, today's research historians have found no announcements or advertisements for that outbound voyage, unusual if the steamship owner was hoping to make a profit both ways. The *Tennessee* simply up and left port one day in June, with Hooper and Company still registered as her agent.

Across the English Channel from Southampton, Hooper struck a deal. Mortimer Livingston of the Havre Line needed an extra steamer to help carry freight that had been sitting on the wharf in Le Havre, France. The *Tennessee* left Havre with the load on August 19, 1855. The Atlantic return crossing to New York was arduous for the comparatively slight vessel, which had been built for coastal work. She spent eleven days being roughed up in heaving seas, but managed to sputter and sail through it, straggling into the first available port, Halifax, Nova Scotia, damaged and out of coal. It was the ship's first encounter with a heavy-hitting ocean hurricane, but it would not be her last.

Three days later she limped back to New York, where she would remain in port and out of work until a new owner could be found.

As the beleaguered steamer rocked gently in the harbor waters quayside, little did anyone walking by suspect that the vessel would soon embark on an eleven-year stretch of risk and adventure and play a role in the manipulations of the era's most audacious steamship tycoons. In the coming ten years, the *Tennessee* would uncannily become involved in a series of significant events — the California Gold Rush, a bizarre "filibuster" occupation of Nicaragua, and the Civil War. Like the film character Forrest Gump in the movie of that name, the SS *Tennessee* just seemed to show up at the moment when history was being made.

The strange adventures of the SS *Tennessee* began in late 1855 when Hooper finally found a buyer — S. de Agreda Jove and Company. The ship became part of the first American steamship service to South America, pioneering trade with Caribbean and Venezuelan ports in a series of first-calls. The steamer left New York on January 8, 1856, bound for La Guaira and Porto Cabello, Venezuela, with interim stops at San Juan, Puerto Rico, and St. Thomas, Virgin Islands. Thus she became the first steamship to establish a regular route to South America.

But there were only five such voyages, because the enterprise again proved unprofitable. Although the *Tennessee* could carry 100 passengers or more, on her last trip for de Agreda Jove she carried only 56 passengers and a modest amount of freight. The most lucrative steamship routes, it seemed, were still those that serviced the Gold Rush, and the *Tennessee* soon found herself swept into the middle of that madness.

In the nation's westward explosion, thousands of prospectors, opportunists, and young men deserted the teeming East Coast cities to try their hand panning for gold in the fabled mountain streams of California. Some of the most adventurous or foolish struck out cross-country to travel through a still mostly uncharted wilderness on trips of many months. Some made it; others fell prey to disease or injury, or simply disappeared, never to be heard from again. Others, itching for adventure and advantage, took passage on steamships to Galveston, Texas, then followed a trail pioneered by Edmund Fitzgerald Beale, an army lieutenant who had dashed across the Mexican desert with samples of gold nuggets when the news first broke. But the Beale trail was a hard, pitiless route that crossed deserts, and many greenhorns perished on this route as well.

As always in America, businessmen knew a market when they saw one. They quickly produced "guidebooks" to the West for gold-hungry dreamers and sold newspaper ads purporting to offer select routes and accommodations. Most were frauds that left travelers stranded, abandoned, or dead, but the excitement and promise of instant wealth nonetheless spurred on the movement.

Alternate routes to the Pacific had always been by sea, but they were slow in comparison. Wealthier entrepreneurs could catch a gloriously-sailed clipper ship down the eastern coastline, around distant Cape Horn, and back up to San Francisco, a three-month journey. The same trip on an ordinary merchant ship was less expensive but took twice as long.

A number of these "Forty-niners," or "Californios," as they were sometimes called, sought to discover a shorter way that led logically — on the map at least — through the isthmus of Central America, a narrow strip of land between the oceans. In the early years of the Gold Rush, the overland route, from sea to shining sea through the mountainous rainforests of Panama, was an adventure in exhaustion. Forty-niners would step from the relative luxury of steamboats into heated chaos, to discover that the way to the Pacific was crawling with malaria, yellow fever, and unsympathetic *banditos*.

From the port of Chargres at the mouth of the Chargres River, the Californios hired natives with dugout canoes called "bungoes" to transport them to the vicinity of Cruces. There, mules awaited to take them on a slow ride to Panama City on the Pacific coast. Those with financial means might instead hire a "sillero," a kind of chair that the natives lashed to their backs. Either way, it was an ignominious trip. The Panama Railroad Company, through a concession deal with Colombia, did not cross the span with trains until 1855.

Waterways seemed potentially more civilized, so the hunt was on for a practical route that linked rivers and lakes through the isthmus. The Panama Canal would not be built until 1904, but it had a predecessor. William Henry Aspinwall, a shipping merchant from New York, invested heavily and with great risk to forge a continuous water route through Panama. But travelers often felt they were being gouged by the fees involved. One would-be prospector, Matthew Scott, wrote of his experience aboard the SS *Crescent* on February 15, 1849: "We found that but few boats were unengaged & they could not be had but paying the most exorbitant prices say from $15 to $20 per passenger." Scott advised no one "to undertake to come to California this route with less than $500 & then with as little baggage as possible."

The struggling government of Nicaragua saw a chance to cash in on America's gold fever. It figured that prospectors could cross Nicaragua, mostly on water routes, if a safe, expeditious system was developed. The Nicaraguans soon found a willing partner: Cornelius Vanderbilt, the prototype of the American shipping entrepreneur, an investor willing to seek bold solutions and take risks that would daunt lesser men.

Scheming to undercut Aspinwall's Panamanian route, Vanderbilt had been studying maps of Central America and was primed for such a venture. In 1849 he paid Nicaragua $10,000 for the exclusive concession to ferry passengers from the Caribbean to the Pacific, as well as to develop a canal in the following twelve years. In early 1854, self-styled "Commodore" Vanderbilt, in an amazing display of the entrepreneurial spirit of the day, decided to personally lay out the initial route for his Accessory Transit Company steamers. Arriving in Nicaragua, he and his entourage boarded a small steamboat that chugged off into the jungle.

The following year the new route opened for business. It began in the area of Nicaragua known as the Mosquito Coast, a district controlled by Great Britain's economic empire builders. The Commodore's large steamships would drop travelers off in the port of San Juan del Norte, or Greytown, as the British called it, located at the mouth of the San Juan River near the border with Costa Rica. A smaller steamboat would take them upstream to the village of San Carlos on Lake Nicaragua, a large body of water conveniently situated in the middle of the isthmus. Lake steamers would cross to drop their passengers off in Virgin Bay, only twelve miles from the Pacific. Finally, mules or coaches would haul the tired travelers over a road that Vanderbilt constructed for this last leg of the route to the Pacific. There his company had constructed a new port city, San Juan del Sur, where his western fleet of steamships stood ready to transport passengers to San Francisco.

This road of gilded dreams leading to the coast is described memorably, in convoluted "Spanglish," on the official website of today's city of San Juan del Norte:

> From the virgin to San Juan of the South twelve miles of
> forest in diligences painted of blue and white distances by

32

mules were crossed on a highway done of wood planks. Way that crossed Mark Twain in a fresh and Iloviznosa atmosphere lead by coachmen armed of machetes, between barefoot soldiers with mosquetes and a procession of riders and jamelgos, cutting oranges and banana trees, eating hot tortillas and drinking brandy and coffee in jicaras fallows ground, until arriving at the bay of San Juan of the South, clear a small semicircle locked up between green hills.

The allure of the Nicaraguan alternative was obvious to all: the 600-mile-long trip was two days shorter and $200 less expensive than any other way to California, including Aspinwall's Panama route. To build up his route's traffic and political appeal, Vanderbilt even offered to carry the U.S. mail through Nicaragua at no charge.

Soon, however, a new breed of passenger appeared on the Nicaraguan run, intent not on traveling to gold fields beyond but on more nefarious schemes. They were mercenaries, men called "filibusters." (Originally derived from a Dutch word for *pirate*, the term evolved to mean those intent on disrupting the workings of government.) This scruffy, swaggering lot followed the ambitions of one of America's most enigmatic and nettlesome prophets, William Walker. A small, cocky man from Tennessee, Walker dabbled at first in a number of slightly more legitimate professions and callings, from medicine to prospecting. Failing in most everything, he grew to embrace one of the grand, seductive delusions of the times: the "Manifest Destiny" of America to control other nations and peoples. In addition, although at first he had espoused anti-slavery views, he switched to champion the "benefits" of slavery.

Walker first tested his nation-grabbing theories in an abortive attempt to seize Baja California in 1853 with an army of pro-slavery followers called the Knights of the Golden Circle. His subsequent arrest and jail term only fanned the dedication of his followers. One year later, Walker decided to lead American mercenaries on expeditions to Central America, with intent to gain control of these underdeveloped nations and add them to the United States — again, as slave-holding territories.

The charismatic Walker had no dearth of volunteers, as antislavery pressures had already polarized attitudes in the States. Hundreds of disaffected and rootless soldiers of fortune, mostly from the American South, took up the dubious cause. The popular press came up with the term "filibusters," and the name stuck.

Walker's reputation brought him to the attention of the Nicaraguan government. Liberal and pro-U.S., the Nicaraguans were facing a conservative insurrection at home; at the same time, they wanted to dilute the power of the British. In a grave error of judgment, they invited the charismatic Walker and his minions to come in and swing the balance of power back to Tegucigalpa, the nation's capital. The Nicaraguans woefully underestimated the hubris of the man that they invited into their midst.

On May 4, 1855, Walker set sail from California for Nicaragua on "a leaky old brig" called the *Vesta* with just a handful of followers (56–58 soldiers of fortune, according to various accounts; "The Immortals," admirers called them). Landing a few weeks later at San Juan del Sur, Walker and his men seized a steamer on Lake Nicaragua and used it, with reinforcements from California and local factions, to attack and capture Granada, the seat of the conservative opposition to the government. A year later, rather than retreating gracefully from the internecine intrigues, Walker declared himself president of Nicaragua in a farcical election. He declared English the official language and petitioned the U.S. Congress to have Nicaragua join the United States as a slave-holding territory. In this age of global empire building, Washington quickly recognized Walker's new government.

The wary Vanderbilt had at first supported Walker, hoping to stabilize Nicaragua's internal feuding, but the tycoon soon realized

Walker had more grandiose schemes. As much as Vanderbilt hated losing ground to any competitor, he loathed slavery even more.

But the potential wealth from the shorter Nicaraguan route across the isthmus was at stake, and Vanderbilt's business partners were more open to Walker's megalomaniacal vision. Behind Vanderbilt's back, several of them had been plotting with the leader of the filibusters to seize control of the transit route and cut Vanderbilt out. Walker was quite willing to do this for the sum of $20,000, and once in power, quickly transferred the Accessory Transit Co. concession to Vanderbilt's less squeamish associates, Cornelius Garrison and Charles Morgan.

Morgan had been a major figure in the steamship trade between New York and Gulf of Mexico ports. With a feeder line from New Orleans to Galveston, his ships hauled passengers, provisions, and light merchandise to the Lone Star Republic of Texas in return for cotton and hides. During the Mexican War, he chartered his vessels to the government and pocketed four million dollars. Where profits were to be had, Charles Morgan was on hand. Moral questions apparently played little part in his business plan.

Now the ebullient Morgan set his sights on Central America. He purchased more ships to enlarge his Nicaraguan fleet, including the twin-paddlewheel SS *Tennessee,* which cost him $70,000. As part of Morgan's new Nicaragua Steamship Company, that once-elegant liner was refit as a troop ship for adventurers and soldiers of fortune. Boisterous roughnecks and callow youths crowded into the extra berths jammed into her staterooms. *Tennessee's* first Nicaraguan voyage for Morgan set out from New York to San Juan del Norte on October 6, 1856. She carried 300 men, three times the intended passenger capacity, but Morgan had apparently made a deal with John McKeon, the New York district attorney, that mitigated any objections or interference from marine regulators.

The second load of adventurers set out on the *Tennessee* from Manhattan on Christmas Eve, but the weather turned on them. A northeastern gale swept along the East Coast and broke the vessel's paddle shaft, leaving her with power on only one side. Crippled, she was forced into Norfolk in the wintry storm, where the recruits and Californios boarded a Charleston liner, the *James Adger*, and proceeded to their destination.

Quickly repaired, the *Tennessee* hauled her next load in January 1857, this time with 300 paying passengers and 250 "immigrants," as the filibusters were euphemistically designated. Many must have slept on her decks, bundled in blankets through the brisk winter passage.

When an escalation in fighting closed the Nicaraguan port of delivery, the *Tennessee* was forced to drop off its passengers instead in nearby Panama.

On one of the *Tennessee*'s return voyages to New York, she carried the survivors from one of the filibusters' most incendiary and tragic episodes. A contingent of 145 Texas recruits had arrived in Nicaragua to hitch up with Walker on March 11, 1857. They had taken two steamers, the *Scott* and the *Rescue,* up the San Juan River as far as the Machuca Rapids. There they met other mercenaries and formed a small army of some 400 filibusters, who intended to attack the Nicaraguan fort at Castillo, a stronghold of the nation's conservative faction. But the drafts of both steamers were too deep for the shallow river.

After a council of war, the little ragtag army decided to retreat and attempt to join Walker by way of Panama. On their way back to the coast the next morning, at 9 A.M., the boiler of the *Scott* mysteriously exploded. The sudden blast carried away the entire upper deck and wheelhouse and gouged an immense hole in the bow of the boat. Some 60 men were killed and 25 injured. One or two were blown onto shore by the force of the explosion.

Witnesses identified a possible "miscreant" who had tossed gunpowder into the furnace of the ship, but nothing was proven. The shocked survivors, nursing their wounds, were loaded onto the waiting SS *Tennessee* at Greytown and returned home. In the *New York Herald* of April 7, some described their ordeal:

> The groans of the wounded were heart piercing. . . . I was lying there among the wounded . . . some of whom ran about the boat after the explosion with the skin of their arms and hands hanging in strips, shrieking and groaning and begging to be put out of misery.

Still, Walker's power increased, and conservative politicians across Central America grew alarmed. Vanderbilt was also bitterly eager to get his revenge on the two partners who had betrayed him. With British goading and Vanderbilt's considerable resources, a new mercenary army was hired to expel the filibusters from Nicaragua. A Costa Rican force seized steamships on Lake Nicaragua and gained control of the transit route, shutting off the flow of finances, men, and supplies to Walker's maverick government. In the end, Vanderbilt got his revenge on both Walker and the liberals.

Gracious in victory, Vanderbilt offered any contrite filibusters a free ride home, and many took him up on it. On May 1, 1857, Walker and his forces were force-marched by an escort of U.S. Marines down the coast and onto ships headed back to the United States.

But hundreds of Walker's followers were trapped, likewise needing passage to flee back to the United States. In the late summer of 1857, the SS *Tennessee* brought home 275 soldiers in Walker's woeful army, the final shipload. The "immigrants" were now labeled "deserters." The ship stopped in San Juan, then steamed to New York City, arriving on September 18, ending the story of the filibusters' preposterous and meddlesome role in Central America. Not long after, steamship service from the East Coast of the United States to Nicaragua came to a halt.

The grand adventure of Southern boys abroad was over. Walker was exiled from Central America, but the man's lust for power was insatiable. He staged four more coup attempts, all before the Civil War. In 1860 he was captured by the British navy, which turned him over to authorities in Honduras, who in turn promptly stood him up against a wall and shot him.

The resourceful Charles Morgan, who had betrayed Vanderbilt and sided with Walker in hopes of taking over the Nicaraguan route with his own steamship company, realized his luck had run out in the failed Central American gambit. He shifted his steamers back to the Gulf of Mexico. The SS *Tennessee* was redeployed to a twice-a-month run between the vibrant city of New Orleans and Vera Cruz, Mexico.

The *Tennessee* was in her prime during her tour of duty in Morgan's commercial fleet. Always fast and sturdy, she delivered a host of immigrants onto the streets of a growing New Orleans, along with shipments of California gold and Mexican silver needed by the New Orleans mint to be stamped into bright new coins.

Steam technology was continuing to advance rapidly, and Morgan wanted to outfit his ships with the latest and most economical equipment. In an 1859 visit to New York, the *Tennessee* got her engines repaired and boilers refit, as well as a slick coat of copper sheathing applied to protect her from fouling and corrosion. Sporting her improved power and shiny casing, she returned to the Gulf.

That's where the Confederate navy found her in 1861, tied up to a wharf in New Orleans, already a storm-lashed veteran of swashbuckling adventures and lost causes.

CHAPTER 3

Seahawk

REG STEMM, WHOSE MIND throws off more ideas before breakfast than most men have in a week, would have enjoyed the rough-and-tumble of the steamship tycoons. He also thrived in that same Caribbean environment of warm waters, quick money, and entrepreneurial risk. Greg had come to Florida from Michigan for his education but left Sarasota's New College after a few semesters, lured away by a chance to join the advance team for comedian Bob Hope. He parleyed that experience into a concert- and event-promotion business, then established a marketing firm that focused on large public events. Greg learned how to convince and coordinate people, how to deal with everything from inflated egos of star performers to mountains of supplies needing to be delivered on time. He learned to bounce back from surprises dealt by the weather, from the fickleness of the media and the public. Those were heady, chaotic days of pulling myriad details together to make each new project work — good training for shipwreck expeditions.

In 1984 he found his love. It took only one dance at Uncle Guerney's bar in Bradenton, near Sarasota, for him to know. Laurie DeFrain was also from Michigan. She had been a student at the nearby campus of USF, the University of South Florida, and was now running her own graphic design firm. "I taught Laurie in school," remembered Dan Bagley, a communications professor at USF, "and I got to know Greg through her, when she got serious about him." Bagley recalled his thoughts when Laurie first brought Greg to meet him, her favorite professor and mentor: "Laurie was so special, I said, 'Lord, let him be magic.'"

Husband and wife joined forces to build a successful advertising agency. It was Laurie who introduced Greg to a client named John Morris, the man who would become his longtime business partner. The two men hit it off quickly, both enjoying the way they could bounce ideas off each other, often just sitting together with friends at a pleasant waterfront bar, looking out at the sun setting on Tampa Bay, tossing thoughts back and forth and scribbling on napkins. They quickly learned to respect each other's way of thinking.

Laurie and Greg's ad agency quickly grew; they began to explore side ventures that edged the versatile firm back toward the sea. For their part, Greg and John began to work real estate deals together in earnest; among a variety of projects soon underway, they hoped eventually to build a marina.

In yet another venture, with some partners in Jamaica, Greg and Laurie bought into a 400-passenger boat used for dinner parties and began to charter boats from Montego Bay and Negril. And in a pivotal moment, Greg found himself in December 1986 in the Cayman Islands, where he ran into a man named Ronnie Steiner in the infamous, pirate-infested Holiday Inn bar on Seven Mile Beach.

Greg told Steiner about his dinner-boat operation and casually mentioned an interest in expanding into additional charter-boat markets in the Caribbean.

"I got a ship for you," said Steiner, a boat-building broker from Alabama. "It would make the ultimate dive-charter boat. It's got a decompression chamber and lots of other equipment."

Steiner saw he had Greg's attention, so he continued. "It's an 85-foot research ship, owned by the University of North Carolina."

The ship, it turned out, had been operating mostly under grants from the National Oceanic and Atmospheric Administration. NOAA was the federal agency involved in deep-ocean research, with interests from marine-life conservation to hurricane forecasting.

Steiner delivered his punchline. "And it's going to be auctioned off this month."

Something clicked inside Greg — something intuitive rather than rash, he said later. He suspected the ship could be worth a half million or more, if Steiner's description of it was reliable. On a handshake, he agreed to submit a rock-bottom bid of $100,000 to buy the vessel.

Four weeks later Steiner phoned. "Come get your ship."

To purchase the ship, Greg wrote the check on the account he shared with John Morris for real estate projects; John was unavailable at the time to discuss the deal. Now, he had to go and explain his purchase to his business partner. Did he want in or out?

"John, I just bought this ship," Greg telephoned. "You interested? Do you want to be involved?"

From the very beginning, a productive tension existed between Greg and John. As Lange Winckler, Odyssey Marine Exploration historian, observed: "John plays the *eminence grise* to Stemm's firefly. You can't pin Greg down to any position. And he reserves the right to change direction at the drop of a pin. They have had epic disagreements. It's caution versus risk. John keeps him grounded."

But the conservative one was intrigued. Something about this decision had the ring of the inevitable. John Morris had spent a lifetime sailing for pleasure, having logged thousands of miles in many ships. All of a sudden, in a flash of serendipity, he was being asked to turn his hobby into a business. Why not?

While the differences between the two partners were obvious to all, including them, they were also developing immense trust in each other. Both shared a common bond: a willingness to travel unconventional paths. John had left college after three semesters for lack of interest. As he put it, they didn't have anything to teach him that he wanted to know.

John had served in Vietnam in the Seabees, the naval command that goes into combat areas with the Marine Corps to set up camps. Even in the navy, John had cultivated a maverick reputation that put results ahead of nuance. He played the military procurement system like a harp, once swiping a truck for his unit from another outfit, practically right under their noses. He carried a variety of military collar insignia in his pocket, putting on what was necessary to get things done. Sometimes he was a second-class petty officer, but often a lieutenant or captain.

Ocean exploration? Sure. Count him in. Morris agreed to put up half the money. It was a new challenge, and it seemed clear to both men that there must be far more to find in the deep ocean than what treasure hunters had gleaned from the shorelines.

Their new ship had an appropriately colorful history. Christened the *Shady Lady* as an offshore shrimp trawler, on her first voyage she had been confiscated by the Coast Guard in a drug bust. NOAA had granted a million dollars to convert her to a research vessel. Then, just a short time later, inexplicably the university that owned and operated her put the ship on the auction block.

Greg and John kept the more respectable name the University of North Carolina had bestowed on the vessel for research activities, the RV *Seahawk*. They also decided to name their new company, formed to own her, after the ship.

"We really didn't know for sure what we were going to do with it," Greg admitted. The two partners knew one thing for sure: she would make a grandly ostentatious party boat.

So they invited 30 of their best friends for a trial run in a Tampa parade of boats at the annual Gasparilla Festival, an event named for legendary buccaneer José Gaspar who reputedly had roamed western

Florida waters in the late 1700s to early 1800s (at least, according to the local Chamber of Commerce). Gaily decorated with ribbons, the new floating acquisition made quite an impression on Greg's and John's friends and clients. Sure enough, the *Seahawk* was a heck of a good party boat!

But parties wouldn't pay for her upkeep. The two partners needed something more substantial — a business opportunity to match her capabilities. In the next serendipitous moment on which their world seemed to pivot, they got a phone call from a Cajun deep-sea techie named Bubba Guarino. Bubba was a sales rep for a company called Deep Ocean Engineering (DOE), which was looking for a platform to test some ROVs. Designed for deep-water projects, ROVs (remote-operated vehicles) need a surface support vessel, like the *Seahawk*, equipped with control equipment and big enough to transport the ROV to an offshore site and lower it with a crane into the sea. (On his desk blotter, Greg still keeps the original pink "While You Were Out" note with the fateful message he returned.)

So it was that Bubba, Greg, and John found themselves on the Gulf of Mexico with a little red ROV strapped to the deck of the *Seahawk*, moored about 300 feet above a site where a Madeira Beach fisherman named Bobby Spaeth had recently snagged a mysterious large anchor. This might be the resting place of a Spanish galleon, they had been told.

Excited, they huddled around the monitor screen and watched the ROV using its thrusters to scoot around the sea floor, lighting up coral masses and the occasional curious grouper. There was no galleon to be found. But Greg caught John's eye across the room. They each could see the same light bulb popping in the other's head. They were hooked! The amazing capability of the underwater robotic technology had captured their attention. And they had the right ship for the job.

Only a week after the experimental trip, John called Sylvia Earle and Graham Hawkes, the underwater pioneers who owned DOE.

Deep Ocean Engineering, Inc. was *the* ROV company designing and manufacturing equipment for applications ranging from military use to deep-sea film-making projects. John and Greg invited Earle and Hawkes down to Florida for a visit. The four of them spent a week aboard a friend's yacht, along with Greg's wife, Laurie, Bubba Guarino, and Professor Dan Bagley and his wife, Ann. The topic was the emerging field of deep-ocean technology — and how Greg's and John's marketing and financial expertise could be used to assist DOE, which was also a relatively new company formed in 1982.

Shortly after, John and Greg purchased their first deep-sea vehicle from DOE and created a new company, called Seahawk Oceanographic Services (SOS). They hired Bubba Guarino as its chief ROV pilot and technician. John Morris was CEO; Greg Stemm was operations officer and chief visionary.

Seahawk purchased several more ROVs from Sylvia and Graham, then branched out into search technology with the acquisition of side-scan sonars. Side-scans are small torpedo-like sonar devices, designed to be towed by a long cable just above the sea floor. They send out a sonar signal to each side. The signal bounces back off sea-floor obstructions, creating a sonic reflection that is transmitted through the tow cable to a visual monitor on the support vessel pulling the side-scan through the water. These ghostly outlines of images can be recorded and studied, in real-time or later, for the characteristic shape of a shipwreck or other sea-floor anomalies.

Seahawk was in business to help others locate and inspect things lost at sea. The company leased its gear in turn to the U.S. Navy, the Coast Guard, insurance companies, and other clients. At first this was a side business, occupying a few offices in Greg and Laurie's advertising agency. But it soon consumed their passions; eventually, it dragged them away from advertising. "In a sense," said friend Bagley, who later became director of corporate communications for Seahawk, "it was a hobby that got way out of control."

Not content with using their technology to service others, Greg and John wanted to initiate their own projects. They began to develop a strategy to use their team and equipment to mine that portion of the ocean's wealth that really intrigued them – the shipwrecks that littered the deep-sea floor around the world. John began to raise money among like-minded true believers, and Greg set out to learn everything possible about the latest technologies and what opportunities were out there.

Shallow-water archaeology had developed into a battleground between archaeologists, sports divers, and treasure hunters. But deep-water exploration was still in its infancy. Only a handful of companies or institutions possessed the full range of capabilities that John and Greg were assembling. Oil, mineral, and cable industries owned the same hardware and had the money, but had little interest in shipwreck artifacts. Why not, asked Greg and John, combine commercial techniques with cultural targets?

On the face of it, the potential was staggering: 99 percent of the ocean had never been explored; traditional archaeology had merely nibbled around the fringes. The knowledge and wealth from some 2,000 years of shipwreck disasters just lay out there, waiting for the capable and courageous.

"It's mind-boggling," marine explorer Robert D. Ballard, Ph.D., was fond of saying. "We've gone to the moon. We're probing the moons of Jupiter, but an American submarine hasn't even dived to the ocean floor in the southern hemisphere of our own planet."

The overriding obstacle for most underwater archaeology projects was money. And the higher the academic aspirations, the less money was available. Funding for ocean exploration had traditionally come from only a few sources: university programs, a few rare nonprofit institutions such as Woods Hole Oceanographic Institution, and of course the military, with its considerable investments in Cold War espionage. Therefore, to get research grants, deep-water explorers usually had to cut deals with academic programs or cultivate political connections. Even the few luminaries in the field, men like Bob Ballard, were always scrambling for enough money and enough time on the water. Much valuable time was spent instead on fund-raising visits and lecture tours.

However, with better equipment available on the open market, the field suddenly was wide open for private companies that had enough funds and moxie. But the opportunities for abuse were equally huge. If a wreck was found in international waters, salvage companies could do virtually what they wanted with it, even dyna-mite the hull to get at a treasure trove or rip the entire wreck to shreds with giant grab-buckets to conduct a quick and low-cost recovery. Several companies, operating beyond the strictures of the respectable ocean-research community, had in fact done just that.

With Seahawk, John Morris and Greg Stemm proposed a new vision: a shipwreck-recovery firm supported by private investors and commercial funding, seeking profits, yet prepared to conduct serious archaeology and create educational programs for the public from its finds.

The early years of Seahawk witnessed some notable blunders of murky research and technological operations. The company's found-ers quickly learned harsh lessons about the might of the Gulf Stream and the fragility of human beings. In 1987, Seahawk was engaged by a group of researchers convinced that they had located the wreck of the *Elizabeth Massey*, a torpedoed World War II freighter that had carried millions of dollars worth of copper.

Working in deep water on the edge of a strong four-knot Gulf Stream current, DOE founder Graham Hawkes joined the technical team, as they tried to squeeze a new-generation "Super Phantom" ROV through a narrow slot in the sunken ship's hull to locate the copper. But the vehicle got wedged in the opening. In the shifts of the rushing current, the ROV's tether snapped, leaving the piece of high-tech equipment, worth $100,000, lost in the depths.

Still convinced by the researchers that the copper horde was worth the effort, Seahawk contracted with a dive company to send a diver down to the wreck site in an open bell. This is a contraption like an underwater elevator outfitted with communications gear and toolbox. An operation of this type involved more risk than the loss of an ROV; to send a human being down on a tether to the deep-ocean floor was a mission on another moral plane. Especially in the surging current, a person could die from one small mistake or miscalculation. There was no room for error.

Once the diver reached the shipwreck, Seahawk's remaining ROV was launched and sent down to join the diving bell beside the hull. The plan was that the ROV, like a seeing-eye dog, would guide the diver in an attempt to penetrate the hull. Communications were difficult, and the diver's voice had the bizarre Donald Duck effect of a man breathing helium.

On the second day of probing, the high-pitched duck-voice from below stunned the team at the control consoles above with news: "Guys, you aren't going to believe this, but this is no freighter. This looks more like a tanker."

The puzzlement of those listening on the ship above grew as the high-pitched voice continued. "There are no decks in here — just giant baffles that look like this thing was carrying oil."

The realization sunk in; this ship was not the *Elizabeth Massey*. There was no hope of recovering copper. Gloom spread over the control room. Then John, who had been mapping the current, announced more bad news. His computations suggested that the Gulf Stream was about to surge. If they didn't get the diving bell up quickly, the operation could lurch into the danger zone.

It was all happening too quickly. First they had to bring up the ROV. Only then could they begin to hoist the diving bell, stopping periodically to take it through the compression stops needed if the diver was to avoid getting the bends, a serious condition caused by rising too rapidly. But the *Seahawk* was being pulled off station by the surging currents. The anchor wires were stretched to their limits. A terrifying hour passed before the bell was safely hoisted to the deck and the diver hustled into a decompression chamber.

Within minutes of the diver's retrieval, one anchor cable snapped. The team barely recovered the other two cables before the powerful current swept the *Seahawk* away from the recovery site.

Greg and John sat on the bridge and looked at each other in stunned silence. They had come within minutes of possibly killing a man — and for a load of copper that wasn't even there.

Later, they discovered the truth. Incredibly, the *Elizabeth Massey* had never sunk. She was actually the rescue ship that had saved the crew of another sinking ship, an oil tanker named the *Pan Mass*, which had caught a well-aimed torpedo from a U-boat. In the government paperwork filed on the accident, an inattentive clerk had switched the names of the two ships. John and Greg were the victims of faulty information supplied to them by the research group.

From this travesty came two operational tenets that would guide John and Greg for the rest of their careers. One, they would never again send a human being into the sea in a dangerous recovery operation; nothing on the ocean floor was worth a life lost. Two, they would insist on complete and irrefutable research before launching any operation.

In the winter of 1987, just a year after buying the *Seahawk,* Greg headed off to Reno, Nevada, for the annual meeting of the Society for Historical Archaeology. He wanted to offer the Seahawk company's services and wares to scientific researchers. But he quickly discovered that none of the conference-goers could afford those services, and even fewer trusted anything that smelled of a profit motive. It seemed to him that to gain respect in the discipline, you were expected to take a vow of poverty. "Their annual budgets were often what it would cost to run our equipment for one day," he noted.

As always, Greg had been optimistic; he and his partner owned a great new ship, some ROVs, and other sophisticated technology that clearly could benefit the underwater archaeologists assembled at the conference. He and his partner were ready to explore the seas. But in the tradition-bound fraternity of underwater archaeology, Stemm was an outsider, a fast-talking, earnest young man from the wrong side of the academic tracks.

The trip to Reno was not a complete strike-out, however. That is where Greg met Robert Marx, a veteran of many shipwreck campaigns and expeditions. Marx was a prolific writer of popular books about shipwrecks, a man who had been knighted by the king of Spain for his underwater exploits. Like Greg and John, Marx was largely self-educated. He had similarly been discounted by the archaeological establishment because he advocated the sale of artifacts and refused to denounce commercial operations. But of greatest interest to Seahawk, he also had a map that might as well have come out of *Treasure Island*. It was a chart that showed, he claimed, where a 17th-century Spanish galleon lay, probably loaded with treasure.

Marx had heard of the site originally from shrimp fishermen who had pulled up earthen Spanish "olive jars" in their nets. The nets had been dragged in very deep water near the Dry Tortugas, about 80 miles west of Key West, an area known for its deadly combination of spectacular hurricanes and shallow reefs. In the 1622, this deadly combination of nature's elements had decimated a heavily laden Spanish treasure fleet sailing back to Spain with New World loot. Fishermen, Marx argued, know where a lot of wrecks lie — they just don't know how significant they are. They think of wrecks as places where their gear gets hung up.

Marx had explored the site years ago with legendary deep-ocean pioneer Willard Bascom; they had almost managed to get an immense Spanish anchor into their boat. To Greg, it all sounded credible. So,

Marx mused, Greg and John had a ship and an ROV? Maybe they could do business. But Marx wanted $10,000 for the map, plus ten percent of any profits.

To raise cash for a new ROV, search equipment, and Marx's map, the Seahawk partners invited a likely investor to Dan Bagley's house for dinner. (Bagley claims he was chosen host because he had the most presentable house at that time. John and Greg were living a more "free-wheeling" lifestyle, he recalled.) The guest of honor was a man named Dan Derfus.

Derfus delivered the needed capital. Weeks later, the partners drove to Marx's house in Melbourne, Florida. They agreed to buy the map, and were convinced as well to also offer Marx ten percent of the value of any artifacts recovered from the wreck.

What happened to their dictum on research, research, research? As they were driving home, John turned to Greg: "This may be the low point in my career. We just paid ten grand for a three-dollar fishing map with an X in the middle of it."

But they were in the game now, taking the next step in their rapidly coalescing business plan. The Seahawk partners agreed that they wanted to avoid the tainted phrase "treasure hunters." Key West's famous Mel Fisher, discoverer of the Spanish treasure galleon *Atocha,* was the most famous shipwreck explorer who claimed that title with pride. Unfortunately, his flamboyant marketing methods and tendency to challenge authority had alienated many of the nation's leading marine archaeologists, in spite of some valuable work he pioneered in the field.

No, if Seahawk found something, it was going to implement a new model for commercially driven deep-sea explorations. It would conduct serious archaeology: pre-disturbance surveys, conservation, interpretation, the works. The company was also going to undertake an active outreach program to try to mollify the many concerns of bureaucrats and policy-makers. Only then would Seahawk bring up the valuables. Economically, the timing was opportune. Oil prices were down, which meant oil-industry winches and ROVs could be bought or rented relatively cheaply. Seahawk already owned a ship. And now they had Bob Marx's map.

Seahawk ventured out to the Dry Tortugas in the spring of 1988 with its operational platform — the RV *Seahawk*. The map they had purchased gave no specific coordinates for the wreck, just a general indication based mostly on anecdotes Marx had collected from shrimpers, plus some strings of Loran A data (Loran was a method to navigate at sea by comparing signals from low-frequency radio transmitters). With Marx's hearty encouragement, Greg and John were about to learn their next lesson in ocean recovery conducted in the Gulf Stream.

Greg's brother, Scott, was heading up the search operation, having recently quit his job as an Emergency Medical Technician and fireman to join the team. Quick with electronics and with a natural talent as a pilot, Scott had replaced Bubba as the company's chief ROV pilot and technician.

The RV *Seahawk* at that time had no Global Positioning System (GPS). The research team had to gauge every sonar line using a combination of imprecise Loran, dead reckoning, and eyeballing. Nonetheless, they tackled the arduous task of "mowing the lawn," as the search operation was called: guiding their ship back and forth, back and forth, in a tight, slightly overlapping pattern, while towing a side-scan sonar. This torpedo-shaped device dangled on a cable, many hundreds of feet below the ship, pulled just above the vast, invisible sea floor.

For weeks, the RV *Seahawk* wove its way across a ten-square-mile area, criss-crossing the predicted location of the site, just off the main route of the Spanish treasure ships. In all that time it spotted only one anomaly — an indistinct shadow on a sonar printout that looked as likely to be a pile of rocks as an intact Spanish galleon.

The disappointing results were reported by Scott: nothing but that one small anomaly that looked nothing like a shipwreck. It looked more like a smudge of coffee spilled on the side-scan paper. While not overly promising, the smudge could not be dismissed either, because no one had ever seen a Spanish galleon on side-scan. The team was truly in uncharted territory.

Unfortunately, the depth of the anomaly — nearly 1,500 feet — required a different ROV than the one they had planned to use, as well as other equipment needed to operate in the swift current of the Gulf Stream loop. Deciding to take a shot at this potential target, they brought in a group of investors who supplied them with enough money to buy a new ROV and equipment — but budgeted only enough cash for a week of offshore operations.

On April 15, 1989, the *Seahawk* steamed out of Tampa, bound for the Dry Tortugas, with their newly acquired deep-water Phantom ROV, purchased from Deep Ocean Engineering and nicknamed *H2D2*. Jan Ricks, who had been aboard the previous year during the search, was now captain. The team included John, Greg and Laurie, and Greg's brother, Scott. To provide technical advice, Graham Hawkes and one of Hawkes' ROV technicians from DOE, John Edwards, came along. The captain's brother, Tim Ricks, was employed as chef.

The close-knit team was short on time but prepared to give it a go. They figured if they couldn't find the wreck in a week, it probably wasn't there.

Once out on the site, just getting the ROV down to the bottom was a challenge. The site was on the periphery of the Gulf Stream; it was not unusual to encounter two or three knots of current. This proved difficult for even the new ROV to manage.

So the team improvised. They developed a "clump weight" arrangement; this used a heavy weight to drag the ROV down to the bottom, but left about 100 feet of umbilical free. This allowed the ROV to cruise around the clump weight and inspect a given area.

It was crude but worked reasonably well to get the ROV down to the bottom where it was needed.

They also had no sophisticated underwater positioning system to tell exactly where the ROV was relative to the ship. Although they could put the ship directly over the spot where the anomaly had been recorded, there was no way to accurately determine where the ROV was after it was launched. Consequently, the ROV was flying almost blind, except for a small scanning sonar that could "look" about 100 feet in front of the ROV.

Scott, the best ROV pilot aboard, spent hours at the control console, "flying" around the area trying to locate anything that looked like it might be the target. He was given an occasional rest when Graham Hawkes took the controls, but after two days with no results, the team concluded there must be something wrong with their navigation. They could find nothing on the sea bottom that looked like a shipwreck.

Graham had another idea. Instead of flying the ROV around, they rigged it so it could be towed by the ship in a search pattern. Two more days were spent in this operation, towing the ROV around on the bottom. Still nothing appeared, and their tight budget allowed only one more day's work on the site. Prospects were dimming rapidly.

As a last-ditch effort, they re-rigged the ROV to fly once again on its own power and began a methodical search in a box pattern. Everyone was exhausted from five days of 24-hour operations, and the stress on the helmsman trying to hold station manually, using a Loran chart plotter, was taking its toll. John Morris, acknowledged to be the best at keeping the boat positioned in the right place, had been primarily responsible for doing so, but the stress of fighting the current, wind, and waves had really worn him out. The fatigue showed on his face and in his stiffening shoulders.

Their last night arrived. John and Greg agreed that if they found nothing that afternoon the ship would head back to Tampa — empty handed. The wind was kicking up, making it even harder to maintain the boat's position. An exhausted John needed a short rest; he turned the helm over to Jan, who proved even less successful at keeping the *Seahawk* from drifting off-station. The wind increased in intensity.

Scott wouldn't give up, however. As he continued to fly the ROV around the ocean floor, he kept his eyes glued to the tiny ROV monitor. On earlier projects, Scott often half-jokingly referred to his "special technique" for locating wrecks. As an ROV pilot, he would look for a big fish, preferably a grouper, and spook it with the ROV. Then as it swam away, he followed it — hopefully to a shipwreck, where the fish naturally might head for protection.

As Jan drifted farther and farther off course, Scott yelled for him to try to hold his present position. He had just seen a huge grouper, and he wanted to try to follow it to see if it would lead him to the target.

Jan struggled to hold station against the mounting wind, and Scott fought against the current to follow the huge fish. Minutes passed. Suddenly, a piece of wood came into view, and everyone heard Scott let out a yell. The team rushed to crowd around the tiny monitor. Scott continued past the piece of wood, still following the grouper. Then something bigger came into view on the screen.

More bits and pieces of wooden wreckage appeared. Then, without warning, the screen showed a huge pile of what looked like big, round pieces of pottery. John and Greg instantly recognized what they had found: Spanish olive jars. Were these from the target shipwreck? Greg scrambled to their small library onboard to hunt for Marx's reference book on shipwrecks that included a chart of types of olive jars and their respective dates.

He opened it to a bookmarked page to see a line drawing of the same jars that now appeared on the monitor screen, littering the sea bottom. These were indeed "middle period" olive jars, which placed them squarely in the period that they had hoped their target ship might be: a contemporary of Mel Fisher's treasure-laden *Atocha* and the other vessels of the famous 1622 fleet sunk in a hurricane en route to Spain with New World riches.

The exhausted team stood in stunned silence. Greg and John caught each other's eyes and nodded. Although the exact identity of the sunken vessel was still not known, they had found the world's first deep-ocean Spanish Colonial shipwreck.

The shipwreck rested in nearly 1,500 feet of water, just 50 miles from the resting place of the *Nuestra Señora de Atocha,* made famous by Mel Fisher's discovery of its immense treasure, a site awash with gold, jewels, and other valuable artifacts. The *Atocha* — and likely, from its proximity and the date of the olive jars, Marx's mysterious X — were part of a flotilla of Spanish galleons that foundered in the Gulf Stream in 1622. The sizeable fleet, including some smaller supply and dispatch vessels, was carrying cargo on its way back to Spain. It had first headed northeast, intending to catch a free ride on the Gulf Stream for the initial leg of the voyage before veering east across the Atlantic. But it had been caught by a hurricane and thrown onto the treacherous shoals of the Florida Keys. In the years since, the wrecks were repositioned by successive centuries of storm or partially buried in shifting underwater sands.

The ship John and Greg had found, her name unknown, lay beyond the territorial waters of the United States. To gain exclusive rights to the ancient shipwreck, they had to bring an artifact from the site into a Federal Admiralty Court. A few weeks later, after returning to Tampa to reprovision the *Seahawk,* they returned to the site and sent *H2D2* down again. A retrieved artifact presented in court would clearly establish the age and nationality of the sunken vessel, and the desired "arrest" order from the court would prohibit competitors from poaching on the find.

The little ROV was able to locate a key object, a small flared dome: the ship's bell. They raised it using a Rube Goldberg contraption built by Greg's childhood friend, Jim Cooke, now a doctor; he found the offshore operation so fascinating that he played hooky for a few days from his job as an anesthesiologist to help his buddies. The bell was too encrusted to reveal any ship's name, often engraved in the bronze. But it was clear proof that they had found an early 17th-century Spanish galleon.

Predictably, the competition began to circle like predators. Seahawk got wind of another firm trying to raise money to excavate the site with grab buckets. Greg wasn't sure if it was piracy or fraud that the competition was contemplating. Fraud was the more likely possibility. An unscrupulous company might use the allure of a potentially lucrative site to attract money from investors; after the money was spent, the operation would be declared a failure and the investors would lose their funds.

"It's much easier," Greg noted, "to promise treasure than to find it. The Dry Tortugas site is much too deep for any diver, and even with exact coordinates it would be really difficult to hit with a grab bucket. Besides, whatever they grabbed would be ours because of our admiralty claim."

The Spanish wreck off the Dry Tortugas was Seahawk's first significant find; it represented John and Greg's first potential payoff as deep-sea explorers. Energized, they knew they needed better hardware to excavate the site. In 1989 they ordered a customized 1.8-million-dollar ROV from AOSC, a manufacturer in Aberdeen, Scotland. They called it *Merlin* after the great wizard of Arthurian legend, and they expected it to work magic.

Almost in parallel, underwater explorer Tommy Thompson was developing his own system for working on the deep-Atlantic wreck of the SS *Central America*, a Gold Rush–era steamship that had sunk carrying gold bullion and gold dust as well as coins. As an engineer, Thompson chose to build his own equipment from the ground up; he developed a unique system specifically designed to recover the gold found on his shipwreck. The Seahawk team took a different tack, deciding to utilize commercial equipment and alter it for archaeological use. Unlike Thompson's operation, John and Greg's approach required complex acoustic positioning technology and other special capabilities dictated by archaeological goals. As a result, *Merlin* was the first ROV custom built for deep-ocean archaeology. It was capable of lifting 250-pound loads in its advanced manipulators or tenderly cradling fragile artifacts in its customized claws.

The huge new ROV needed a much bigger work platform, able to support *Merlin* and a team of 40 technicians, archaeologists, and crew. John and Greg located a 210-foot former offshore-oil vessel and outfitted it with four large winches. They also added giant anchors, enabling it to be moored over the deep-water Dry Tortugas site for months at a time. In anticipation of its primary mission, the new vessel was named the *Seahawk Retriever*. It represented a huge leap forward in capability — and in expense.

To raise the cash, Seahawk went public in 1989, through a merger with a blind-pool company called Fox Ridge Capital Corporation. Considered a "penny-stock" company, Seahawk connected with investors excited about ocean exploration. There was no dearth of takers; after all, the company had gained the rights to an intriguing wreck and the media was kind – touting the company's new technology and its amazing find around the world. The prospect of treasure, and of getting involved in adventure and science, was highly appealing to high rollers with available investment money. It was a bold, exciting business; it got people's attention.

Dan Bagley was again part of the team. His job was to help leverage the considerable publicity — to further the interest in the artifacts, to build a brand identity, and to develop a sense of "family" with the investors. As PR professionals, Dan and Greg knew how to make fans of the investors, sending them updates, making them feel as if they had joined a common cause. The company was well bankrolled; now it had to come up with some treasure.

The Dry Tortugas wreck was not the mother of all galleons, as Seahawk at first had hoped and dreamed. It was no *Atocha*. But it did yield over 17,000 artifacts, including 26 gold bars, 726 silver coins, over 6,000 pearls, 80 intact olive jars, a gold-and-emerald ring, and three brass astrolabes — antique navigational instruments worth perhaps as much as $200,000 apiece to collectors. John de Bry, director of the Center for Historical Archaeology, a nonprofit scientific organization based in Melbourne Beach, Florida, appraised the material at $4,797,100. The cost of the operation was three million dollars.

As important as the value of the artifacts recovered, the 10-month operation proved that robots could, in fact, be used for deep-ocean archaeology. In what was hailed as the world's first robotic underwater archaeological operation, the team had proof of its business concept. Even if its first successful shipwreck project didn't make the company fabulously wealthy, a template for finding and recovering wrecks in the deep ocean was being established. It would now be a matter of figuring out how to apply these lessons to develop a real business.

It seemed an auspicious beginning, a discovery with both archaeological and commercial rewards. Greg and John made ambitious plans for the coming profits. They would build a cutting-edge conservation laboratory in Tampa, and a shipwreck museum and visitors' center. The artifacts would attract the public, which was hungry for good stories and dynamic history of the sea and its riches. And Seahawk held a remarkable position in the field as the only shipwreck research and recovery company traded on the NASDAQ stock exchange. "In the long term we believe good science is good business," communications director Dan Bagley told an admiring press.

Nevertheless, the company found a cold shoulder in much of the academic community. In its eyes, Seahawk was an interloper and possibly a despoiler of important historical sites. "It was tough," said Bagley. "We couldn't get archaeologists to take us seriously. For the longest time we had all this data, and we'd say, 'Come on, study the data. Come and see. You've got a doctoral dissertation here waiting to be done. This is not selling your soul to the devil.'"

Skepticism arose more from the reputation of earlier treasure hunters than from anything Seahawk did. "Archaeology by grab bucket" was a major concern. "Everybody says they're going to do the right thing, but often it doesn't work out that way," said John Broadwater, a marine archaeologist for NOAA, the federal agency involved in marine exploration. "Field work and recovery are the fun part. It's the years of analysis and conservation and preparation of a detailed report that usually trip people up. It's hard to get the commitments of time and funds to do all those things."

Clearly, achievement was no guarantee of acceptance. The nautical archaeological community did not like pirates or anything that sniffed of financial profits. Its attitude was that real archaeologists don't finance their work by selling artifacts; it's unethical. As academics, they preferred to seek and wait patiently for funding, rather than let private companies get involved. And if that funding was not forthcoming, they wanted to leave shipwrecks untouched, available for some future day.

In the view of academics, archaeology was best left to them. Archaeology cannot — or should not — be done by "treasure hunters," the summary label and judgment bestowed on Seahawk.

The response maddened Greg Stemm, who wanted very much to do it right — and to be respected for it. He knew that traditional, shallow-water archaeology had not adapted to technology as well as other deep-sea disciplines had. He felt that innovation was at a standstill and that the nautical archaeological community was more of a guild than an enterprise. He knew that a private company, employing good archaeologists, could do the work in less time and with high standards, and do so year-round, not just in frantic, intern-filled summer seasons.

Most deep-water nautical archaeologists, even the most prolific ones, get only limited chances to actually work in the field. Emory

Kristof, the blunt-spoken veteran *National Geographic* photographer and a deep-water technical innovator, offered this perspective: "One of the problems with oceanography today is that if you get your Ph.D. and write to get grant money through peer review, you might go on five expeditions in your entire life. Science and oceanography is like baseball or ballet dancing: it's better if you practice it. The problem with most scientists is that they don't get to play the game very often."

Greg and John wanted to practice their trade without the constraints and the prejudices. "I'd go to archaeological conventions, talk and listen, do presentations on our work. But I felt like I was beating my head against the wall, for years sometimes," said Greg.

So he did what all good business innovators do — he went to work to change minds. He was first to admit that he was no scientist, although he had studied marine biology. But he was no treasure hunter, either. "John and I are here because we're fascinated with shipwrecks," he often explained. "The gold is just the way we pay to indulge our passions."

The Dry Tortugas excavation had set off a spate of publicity for the firm, which in turn uncovered the skepticism of the old, entrenched archaeologists. Who were these amateurs moving in on their territory, academics were asking, and did they know the slightest thing about culture and preservation of artifacts?

The producers of NBC's *Today Show* recognized the popular appeal of this debate. It planned a provocative point-counterpoint session, casting the upstart deep-sea businessman Greg against a traditional archaeologist. Seahawk was contacted; *Today Show* host Bryant Gumbel was interested in an interview — or rather, in a debate between Seahawk and someone who would represent the opposite perspective. Greg agreed to appear, but got a lump in his throat when NBC called back and told him who he would be facing: George Bass, head of the Institute of Nautical Archaeology (INA) at Texas A&M

University. Bass was generally considered the world's most respected underwater archaeologist, the father of the discipline.

"I was only 32 years old," Greg remembered. "I had just gotten into this field, and they were going to set me against my hero, the guy whose exploits I'd followed in *National Geographic* while I was growing up?"

Greg set about reading all of George Bass's books, his articles, and his testimony to Congress about the pending abandoned shipwreck act. He studied Bass's analogies, talking points, and positions. He even engaged in mock debates with Bagley, in which Dan played Greg, while Greg played an acerbic and powerful George Bass.

"We decided to use one of Sun Tzu's primary tactics for dealing with a more powerful foe," Greg remembered, "to focus on becoming one with your opponent. 'George,' I would tell him, 'once you understand what we're doing, you'll understand that we're both on the same team.'"

When the live program began, both men fired their opening salvos about the future of oceanic exploration. Bass suggested that Greg had "good intentions" but that Seahawk was in over its head. Greg replied that Seahawk was a totally transparent enterprise, and that Bass should come to Tampa to review the operation; then he could make a valid judgment. Gumbel, after listening for a while to the back-and-forth debate, eventually stepped in and said, "Well, Dr. Bass, what's your problem? Here's a guy, inviting you to come out, promising he'd do archaeology, letting you be the judge, what's the deal?" For better or worse, the program ended up with Gumbel arguing with Bass. The exchange later provoked a pointed academic paper by archaeologist W.A. "Sonny" Cockrell entitled, "Why George Bass Couldn't Convince Bryant Gumbel."

Greg had mixed feelings about his Pyrrhic victory. He telephoned Bass to express regret that they had had to meet as adversaries. He again invited the professor to come visit Tampa and see how the

Dry Tortugas operation was working. "We do good archaeological fieldwork," Greg told him, "and no one has compelled us to do it." But Bass declined.

Some months later, Bass unexpectedly called back: "Greg, I'm in Florida, and I'd like to drop in on your shop and see what you're doing." Seahawk was given little time to prepare; Greg figured this was to ensure that there would be no special set-up just for the coming visit. He was confident, though, that Bass would be impressed with their technology. Most of the Institute of Nautical Archaeology research studies had been conducted on shallow-water wrecks, where SCUBA divers could set out traditional archaeological grids around the site and excavate with their hands, as if they were on land. Deep-ocean work was not an expertise that INA had developed.

Dr. Bass showed up at the door, and the Seahawk partners proudly gave the academic eminence a tour of their conservation laboratory. At one point in the afternoon, as they were discussing the different types of teeth found in the wreck, Greg remembered that Bass seemed to tune out for half a minute, as if they had lost him. It was a puzzlement to Greg and to the Seahawk archaeologist present, Jenette Flow.

A few weeks later Bass called with a bombshell of a reaction. He told Greg that he was impressed with Seahawk's work and asked if Greg would come and give a presentation to Bass's graduate students at the Institute of Nautical Archaeology. Greg accepted, and as he was being introduced to the classes at Texas A&M, Bass told them to pay close attention — that they were about to see a glimpse into the future of underwater archaeology. It was one of the first real connections between the academic and commercial worlds on the issue of shipwreck exploration.

That night after the class, Stemm and Bass were deep in discussion, working on a pitcher of beer in a bar in College Station, rolling ideas around in their heads, dissecting what had taken place and what it meant. Bass looked at the younger man.

"You know, Greg, I was in your conservation facility, and you guys were talking about this pre-erupted molar. For the life of me, I couldn't imagine it. Your interest in something like that just did not reconcile with what I thought treasure hunters did. And I finally realized that you're interested in the same things that I am. We're just approaching it from different angles."

That pregnant evening helped shape Greg's ideas of how to separate truly significant shipwreck artifacts from ship's cargo — the common trade material that can be salvaged and sold. Bass and Stemm discussed, for example, that significant artifacts should be kept together, as found, to be studied. On the other hand, it might not be necessary to keep hundreds of the same bottle, coin, or brick as cultural artifacts; historical interpretations could be based on just a few examples of multiple items — especially those that were mass produced.

Sitting together, the academic and the entrepreneur, speaking from different worlds but sharing a thirst for knowledge about what lay deep in the ocean, the two found common ground. The conversation was a tentative first step, with cautious words to avoid major mishaps, with care to navigate a slippery slope in search of a new understanding. It was a meeting that could have been put together only by the most unlikely of one-time adversaries, like Nixon in China.

CHAPTER 4

New Orleans & the Civil War

THE STRUGGLE TO HOLD together North and South failed when South Carolina seceded from the Union on December 20, 1860. On February 4 of the following year, in a meeting held in Montgomery, Alabama, six other angry Southern states joined South Carolina to form the Confederate States of America.

Louisiana seceded from the United States on January 26, 1861. After a two-month independent fling as "the Nation of Louisiana," the state turned over all its resources to the Confederacy. Among the prizes was the New Orleans mint, with its nearly $500,000 in gold and silver. The mint had been in the business of striking $20 double eagles, $10 eagles, $5 half eagles, and $2.50 quarter eagles, as well as silver dollars and pocket change.

For a while, financiers, bankers, and merchants on both sides of the split nation continued, cautiously, to do business. In that shadowy time between war and peace, bags of newly struck gold and silver coins, minted in New Orleans under the authority of the State of Louisiana, somehow found their way to the vaults of the Bank of New York in New York City. They would not be seen again until the recovery of the SS *Republic*.

Many Americans held out hope that the secession of the Southern states was all a bluff, and both sides questioned the other's willingness to ask men to die for its cause. But after April 12, 1861, when provisional Confederate forces attacked the Union garrison at Fort Sumter, South Carolina, there was nothing to do but prepare for full-scale war.

The Confederate States of America in 1861 had a ragtag army and no navy at all. After the outbreak of war at Fort Sumter, the new president of the Confederacy, Jefferson Davis, simply called on private Southern vessels to attack and capture Northern shipping. President Lincoln, not wanting to acknowledge Confederate independence, declared this to be illegal privateering. On April 19, 1861, Lincoln proclaimed a naval blockade around Southern ports from South Carolina to Texas, a move intended to strangle their commerce.

The Confederacy desperately needed warships. In New Orleans, it quickly appropriated 14 Northern-owned steamships that had failed to depart before the blockade was imposed, while granting neutrality to the more than 40 British and other foreign vessels tied up at the wharves. Among the ships seized were the SS *Tennessee* and five other ships of Charles Morgan's commercial fleet.

In June, Commander W.H. Hunter wrote to the Confederate Navy Department in Richmond, suggesting that the *Tennessee* be armed to serve as a dispatch vessel on ocean routes, calling it "a very strong and fast seagoing vessel."

The Southern navy actually paid the ships' owners for appropriating their vessels, believing in the inviolable principle of property rights — one of the tenets of their resistance to the Federal government. On January 14, 1862, a letter from Confederate Secretary of War Judah P. Benjamin to Major General M. Lovell, commander of the Confederate army forces in New Orleans, suggested using the $100,000 sale price of the *Tennessee* to judge the offers for the 13 other steamships: "The recent sale of the *Tennessee* will afford a good opportunity for testing their true value."

The SS *Tennessee* was in prime condition; a new set of boilers had been installed in New York the previous year. The Confederates swiftly armed and refitted her as a blockade runner. She was to try to slip through the cordon of Union naval vessels in an attempt to keep commerce moving and bring badly needed supplies back to Southern cities. Within days, port authorities loaded her down with cotton bales to trade abroad; one proposed plan was to send the ocean-going *Tennessee* to France to purchase saltpeter, needed to produce gunpowder.

Intelligence of the blockade runners' preparations reached the Union Consul in Havana, who nervously fired off a telegram on March 12, 1862, to Secretary of the Navy Gideon Welles:

> Dear Sir:
> The Department learns of the arrival at Havana on the 23rd ultimo of the steamer 'Colonel J. Whitmore,' 430 tons, and the steamer 'Florida,' 429 tons, from New Orleans with a thousand bales of cotton, and also of the escape from New Orleans of the steamers 'Magnolia,' 'Tennessee,' and 'Vanderbilt.'

Although the report was premature, as the *Tennessee* and perhaps others were still tied up off New Orleans' Canal Street, Welles quickly dispatched a scathing message to the commanders of his two Gulf of Mexico blockading squadrons, Flag Officers W.W. McKean in the east and David G. Farragut in the west, castigating them for letting Confederate vessels get by.

The SS *Tennessee* was too well known a ship to escape his notice, was Farragut's mild response. "She will never leave the South," he responded confidently.

Farragut was right. The Union blockade had such a stranglehold on Southern ports that few of Morgan's converted liners saw action for the entire first year of their mustering. Because the *Tennessee* was built for ocean traffic, her draft of more than 16 feet was too deep to navigate the back channels in and out of the port of New Orleans. With this draft, she would have to try to pass through the main South West Pass, or "Pass a l'Outre," to the Gulf, a waterway heavily patrolled by Union ships.

Accordingly, to the frustration of her assigned crew, the side-wheel steamship spent three unproductive months tied up in port, her load of cotton moldering on board. On one of several attempts to make a dash through the blockade, the new captain of the *Tennessee* arranged to have Confederate gunships escort her through at night; the plan was to have the gunboats provoke a skirmish; in the midst of the action, the steamer would sneak past. As night fell, the ship slipped from her moorings and took her place near the entrance to the channel. But the gunboats failed to appear at the arranged spot; they had all been sent north for battle on the Mississippi. As the captain of the *Tennessee* paced and peered into the darkness, the idea of going it alone smelled of disaster. He waited at anchor until 3 A.M., then retreated silently back to the wharves.

The Union blockade effectively shut down New Orleans, the Confederate States' most important port, and the impact on the Southern economy was widespread and severe. In the 1830s and 1840s, the city had shipped out most of the agricultural commodities of the entire Mississippi watershed, and in exchange brought in the products of the world needed for the plantation economy. Down the muddy Mississippi and its great network of tributaries had come the bounty of the estates of the upper South and that of much of the farmland on the western side of the Appalachians. From along the Gulf of Mexico coastline, still more barges had arrived with cotton bales from Alabama and Texas. Fully half of the cotton grown in the

United States had been handled on the broad wharves of the cosmopolitan city located on the crescent of the Mississippi River.

Before the Civil War, New Orleans seemed to exist in another world from that of the rest of the South. The city's sophisticates were a spirited mix of wealthy planters, multi-hued Creoles of Spanish and French ancestry, white "Americans," and some 17,000 *"hommes de couleur libre"* or free "men of color," many of whom were well-educated, owned property, and ran small businesses or practiced trades or professions. It was an island of urbanity in a rural region, a pleasure-loving Roman Catholic enclave in stark contrast to the otherwise largely Protestant, Anglo-Saxon South. New Orleans was also the nation's largest slave market. In many respects, it looked, smelled, tasted, and acted more like the exotic capital of some Caribbean nation than a port city in the United States.

Its merchants and aristocrats had strong connections to European cities as well as to the East Coast, and had established an elaborate social structure. Wealthy planters from inland estates owned property in town. All viewed the city as a fine place to come and spend the winter's social season. Parisian dressmakers and German silversmiths kept shops along the Vieux Carre. (It was to New Orleans, after all, where Rhett Butler and Scarlett O'Hara came to shop on their honeymoon.) And pleasure was already a serious business, with a wealth of fashionable bordellos and the beginnings of carnal celebrations for Mardi Gras.

Lady Emmeline Stuart Wortley, a British traveler of the day, remembered the sight of the city's steamships at night, ". . . the floating palaces of steamers, that frequently look like moving mountains of light and flame, so brilliantly are these enormous river-leviathans illuminated, outside and inside." Indeed, behind the trappings of exotica stood the muscle of commerce. A dozen steamers moved in and out each day from the massive wooden wharves that stretched a full five miles along the shoreline. Wrote Henri Huy, a French pianist and composer, of his visit to New Orleans in 1846:

Like all foreigners who visit the great Louisiana city, I was seized with admiration on seeing the activity which reigned on the docks, literally covered with bales of cotton, casks of sugar, barrels of flour, sacks of cereal, lumber, tobacco, salted meat, etc. It is a world of commission men, speculators, and dealers who argue feverishly in the midst of this piled-up merchandise. Horses, wagons, Negroes, and whites bustled about in an area six-hundred feet wide, where half the business of the United States takes place.

In the 1850s, as the *Tennessee* slid on her second try down the skids and splashed into the Baltimore harbor, New Orleans had been poised to pass New York as the nation's prime gateway. Needing to earn money on their return trips, the ships that carried cotton abroad to Liverpool often granted special prices to passengers for the return to New Orleans, and the low fares attracted German, Italian, French, and especially Irish immigrants, a swelling cadre of adventurous newcomers eager to give the New World a go. By the time war erupted, New Orleans had grown to 168,675 people, more than four times the population of any other city in the South.

And that populace was a true *macedoine*, an energetic hodgepodge of people. In a book set in the New Orleans of 1860, Joseph H. Ingraham wrote about the coming of a northern governess to New Orleans by train:

Onward our car wheels bore us, deeper and deeper into the living heart of the city. Nothing but small shops were now to be seen on either hand, with purchasing throngs going in and coming out of them, while myriads of children seemed to swarm about the doors, crawl along the curb-stones, paddle in the gutters, and yell miscellaneously everywhere. I never saw so many children in my life. Some were black, some not so black, some yellow, some golden skinned, some tawny, some delicate milk and gamboges color, and some pure white, at least, such spots of their faces as the dirt suffered to be visible, seemed to promise an Anglo-Saxon complexion underneath. The major part, however, were olive brown, and plainly of French extraction; and I could hear the bright black-eyed little urchins jabbering French, to a marvel of correct pronunciation that would have amazed a school girl. At length the houses grew more stately, the streets more genteel, and crowds more elegantly attired, and the cars stopped, and we were in New Orleans!

In those flush years New Orleans was also the financial capital of the South. The city's 13 banks held more than twelve million dollars in gold and silver deposits. The bankers lent their money readily, financing foodstuffs such as corn and pork and other supplies for the westward movement, and established the credit system that became universal among planters. From 1835 to 1842, New Orleans bank capital exceeded that even of New York City. To further enhance the city's position, Louisiana's Bank Act of 1842 was the first law passed in the United States requiring banks to keep a reserve of specie (gold and silver coinage) against notes and deposits.

In New Orleans the ten-dollar bank note was known as the "Dix," the French word for ten; some think it was the origin of the term "Dixie." The New Orleans mint, established in 1835 by the Andrew Jackson administration to serve the frontier, was one of seven that printed U.S. currency for nationwide distribution. In the opinion of financial analysts of the day, nowhere was the national currency stronger and better protected.

But it was a tenuous prosperity in several respects. First, the city had been built below water level on a flood plain. The ground was perpetually moist and fetid. With no drainage, bathwater and raw sewage puddled in the streets, creating breeding grounds for mosquitoes. Cholera, yellow fever, typhoid, and dysentery took a grim toll. Yellow fever, called "the strangers' disease," killed 7,849 people within four months in 1853. And the shifting, sprawling Mississippi was not as mighty as it may have looked to visitors at first glance. As settlers headed into the plains and agriculture boomed in the Midwest, silt from increased farming upstream quickly built up in the mouth of the Mississippi, closing down shipping channels to the Gulf. In 1852, 40 vessels ran aground on the bar within a few weeks.

Second, the city's geographical position on the outskirts of the country's southern borders, around the long Florida peninsula, and at the end of a sea route swept now and then by powerful hurricanes, had begun to work against her prominence. The completion of the Erie Canal in 1825 had already offered an alternative waterway to points west through the Great Lakes, and the development of steam engines allowed ships to run upriver to other distribution hubs, instead of most cargo being swept downriver to New Orleans. Then came the railroad expansion in the 1840s that built Atlanta into a commercial hub, stealing New Orleans' thunder. By the 1850s, New Orleans had already begun losing trade to St. Louis and Chicago, cities located more directly on routes west instead of tucked away into the coast of the increasingly isolated Gulf of Mexico. In the period leading up to the Civil War, New Orleans had already begun its decline.

The coming of the war seemed to bewilder most New Orleanians. True to its diverse and complex population, the city was torn in its loyalties, goals, and visions for the future. "There was a big ethnic mix here that kept things boiling, and not at all a unanimity of opinion on the war," according to Alecia Long, a leading New Orleans historian. "It was similar to New York in that respect," she wrote. "For many people here it would have made sense to stay in the Union." Along with ethnic tensions there were class differences as well, especially between the city's mercantile class and the so-called

"Bourbons," the elite class of the insular plantations throughout the rest of Louisiana, who strongly supported the Southern cause.

For the business community, the prospect of secession from the Union was anathema; they relied on northern shipping and expertise for their survival, and much of their trade was with the North. On the other hand, the city's outlying aristocracy was enmeshed in the plantation economy and slaveholding, and eagerly embraced secession. Even on the eve of war, the city marked its social season with lavish Mardi Gras parades and balls, sending masked revelers into the streets to spread hope. In December 1860, "One white visitor" wrote to the city newspaper, the *Picayune:*

> The Southern people think the result of the election [of Lincoln] is a sort of declaration of hostility by the North. Nearly every day Lincoln's effigy is hanged in the principal streets and squares. Where it is run up it is saluted with the firing of cannon and cheers. Secession is openly talked of, apparently with increasing confidence in its success.

After its secession from the United States in January 1861 and its brief attempt at independence as "the Nation of Louisiana," the state officially cast its lot with the Confederacy. Having seized control of the New Orleans mint in January, the state transferred the facility to the Confederacy in March. The Confederacy planned to mint coins bearing a new Confederate States of America design, but while a die was being created, many silver half dollars continued to be produced there by the Confederacy, using existing U.S. dies and the captured bullion on hand.

During the month of April, the new design was ready, and the New Orleans mint became the first and only former U.S. mint to strike a Confederate coin. The obverse, or front, used the existing Liberty Seated federal die, while the reverse proudly displayed a

Confederate shield topped by a liberty cap, with stalks of cotton and sugar cane entwined round it.

But it was only an abbreviated test run. The mint struck a grand total of only four coins — four paltry pieces — and no more. The mint was forced to close down operations for lack of bullion. The Union blockade had effectively stopped the flow of silver from the Bolivian mines of Potosi and gold from California. For the remainder of the war, the mint was used as a military barracks.

For the first year of the war, New Orleans remained a major manufacturing center for the South, supplying the Confederate army with clothing, knapsacks, armaments, tenting, and tinware. The shipyards turned out Confederate naval vessels, including the ironclads *Mississippi* and *Louisiana*. But its citizens provided men and supplies to both sides of the conflict, especially as new immigrants signed up to join the ranks of their army of choice. The regiments from Louisiana tended to be a bit exotic; one company from the 10th Louisiana listed soldiers from Austria, Corsica, Greece, Ireland, Italy, Martinique, Portugal, Scotland, Sicily, Spain, and Switzerland. Some men barely understood the rudiments of American life, much less the cause of the nation's internal political strife, but enlistment papers were signed and arms and equipment issued to all who wanted to serve. There was a war to be fought.

The city was used to a certain level of luxury, and if any good will toward the North remained among the citizens of New Orleans, it dissolved as the Union naval blockade, begun in 1861, shut down trade and made life arduous. Coal grew scarce, as did manufactured items such as shoes, dry goods, and soap. To save paper, people wrote letters by first scrawling vertically on a page, then horizontally. When the price of coffee skyrocketed, they made do with homemade brews from roasted chicory, sweet potato, and corn. Newspapers resorted to publishing on the back of wallpaper. The blockade-running ships that squeezed through the naval stranglehold barely delivered enough goods to ward off utter starvation in the city.

Without hard money, inflation spiraled. Banks were unable to pay out in hard currency, and Confederate bills deteriorated to less than 30 cents on the dollar. The Confederacy printed so much paper money that no one knew exactly how much had been printed. One Southern humorist told about the Confederate Secretary of the Treasury being asked how much money was in circulation: "Akkordin to the best of his rekelekshun, thar war six hundred miliyuns or six thousand miliyuns — he waren't sure which."

So merchants and bankers created new ways to conduct business. They began to print their own currency: private bank notes and trade tokens that certain businesses agreed to accept instead of money. This pseudo-money was issued by New Orleans department stores, even by parish governments, with full exchange value often limited to their own clientele. Around the city, a hodge-podge of odd scrips, five-cent streetcar tickets, and drinking-house coupons, called shinplasters, served as small change. The joke on the streets, wrote a citizen, George W. Cable, "was that you could pass the label of an olive-oil bottle as money, because it was greasy, smelt bad, and bore an autograph."

Compounding the problem with the bank notes was that most Southern bank notes were redeemable only in Confederate money. The banks had hedged their bets. So those who staked their future on the Confederacy faced a profound devaluation of their paper currency when the tide of battle changed for the worse. At war's end, they would be out of luck. "As to the ante-war currency of the south," wrote the *Picayune*, "the largest portion of it — in fact, we may say all of it – is out of circulation. Such of the bank notes as have any value, are bought by the Richmond bankers at prices ranging all the way from 10 cents to 95 cents on the dollar."

New Orleans' days as part of the Confederacy were short-lived. In the early morning darkness of April 24, 1862, Flag Officer David G. Farragut's naval invasion force headed into the channel of the

Mississippi River. After days of shelling the Confederate outer defenses with mortars, Farragut had decided to run the gauntlet. Employing a number of clever strategems, including having Mississippi River mud smeared on his ships' hulls and tying tall trees to masts to confuse the enemy, his Union armada surprised and outgunned the outlying bastions, Fort Jackson and Fort St. Philip, and after a fierce fight, slipped by and steamed toward the city. The naval ships were accompanied by a unit of the Union army, sailing in on other vessels in a formidable amphibious attack.

In New Orleans, General Mansfield Lovell, commander of the outmanned Southern forces, decided they would leave no supplies for the Yankees. He sent out a detail to seize wagons and empty the warehouses. The men simply burned whatever raw materials remained in the city, torching tobacco sheds, coal yards, lumberyards, and 11,000 cotton bales on the wharves. They closed the storehouses for the poor, even as 1,940 families came to offer their last donations. They floated the hulls of derelict ships out to sink and choke the navigation channels on the river. Steamship crews deserted and stevedores abandoned the wharf. The SS *Tennessee* was among the few vessels to survive the holocaust.

In the self-inflicted destruction, more than ten million dollars in Confederate assets went up in smoke. Then Lovell withdrew his meager troops to the north as the invasion force neared, forever earning the contempt of the townspeople, who had figured that the general's job was to defend them, not burn their city and abandon them.

The city seemed deserted when the Union fleet threaded through smoldering and half-sunken vessels to reach the wharf by Canal Street on April 25. As the transport ship USS *Mississippi* pulled up, its band struck up the "Star-Spangled Banner," to the cheers of a small gathering of Unionists. But in the middle of the cautious celebration a unit of Confederate cavalry thundered down the street, fired into the crowd of mostly women and children, then wheeled and stormed back into the city.

Farrugut demanded the city's surrender. The mayor stalled for several days, allowing General Lovell to move the last of his men and supplies out of the city. The town capitulated on April 28.

Chaos ruled in those fearful last days. A hungry rabble of looters roamed the streets, breaking into warehouses for sacks of sugar, bacon, rice, and corn. Relates Chester G. Hearn in his book about Union General Benjamin Butler, *When the Devil Came Down to Dixie,* "The maddened crowed seized a man whose only crime was that of looking 'like a stranger and might be a spy.' They located a rope and unceremoniously hanged him from a lamppost on the corner of Magazine and Common streets."

The citizens of the city were stunned by the arrival of Farragut's ships; the city had been believed it was well defended by the outlying forts that Farragut had so boldly bypassed. His fleet's sudden appearance in the port was "Like an electric shock," reported one New Orleans diarist:

> The news soon spread all over the city. Twelve taps from the fire bell spread the alarm — the signal for the town's militia to report to their commands. Merchants closed their stores, teachers suspended classes, banks made hurried requests to depositors to withdraw their valuables, women hid their silver plate and jewelry, and Confederate currency descended to a "perfect state of chaos," many people discarding it. The rumble of heavy guns a few miles downriver drove people wild. Aside from the militia, the men in town consisted mainly of foreigners, blacks, wealthy businessmen, and the elderly. They broke into the Marine hospital, which had been converted into a small arms factory, and made off with all the muskets and ammunition by noon: civil order collapsed.

The women of New Orleans became the most vociferous opponents of the occupation. One of these, Julia Le Grand, wrote of the city's first reaction to the appearance of Union forces: "A pitiful affair it has been. . . . Never can I forget the day that the alarm bell rang. I never felt so hapless and forsaken. After it was known that the gunboats had actually passed, the whole city, both camp and street, was a scene of wild confusion. The women only did not seem afraid. They were all in favor of resistance, no matter how hopeless that resistance might be."

When Farragut's fleet arrived, the *Tennessee* was tied at dock, twin paddlewheels idle, its cotton cargo still on board, gamely flying a French flag. But Farragut easily saw through the ruse. Half the city, he noted, seemed to be French. Practically every shop and service in the city was attempting to hide behind a neutral French identity. But the *Tennessee* was a well-known ship, and a contingent of Farragut's marines promptly seized her, along with others on the wharf.

And so the *Tennessee* was returned to the Northern cause and commissioned as a Union warship. She was quickly fitted with a 32-pounder smoothbore cannon, along with a 30-pounder rifle cannon called a Parrott gun and a smaller 12-pounder rifle cannon. Within a week's time, she was manned by sailors and gunners drawn from the USS *Varuna*, joined by a regiment of occupying army troops. At one point, escaped slaves served among the crew.

On May 8, 1862, Lieutenant C.H. Swasey made the first entry into a pristine logbook: "Put this ship in commission" as the USS *Tennessee*. Noncommissioned officers and more sailors arrived that evening from the SS *Burton*, and the next day he welcomed aboard the ship's new captain, Lieutenant P.C. Johnson.

Johnson's assignment was to support Farragut's attack steamships as they worked themselves upriver toward Vicksburg. It was part of the Union's "Anaconda Plan" — to constrict the South by naval blockade of her ports and by seizing the great Mississippi.

The *Tennessee's* moderate size, relatively light draft (compared to other more heavily-built warships), and high speed made her an extremely useful addition to the Union fleet operating on the river. Soon, the *Tennessee* was busily employed towing coal barges, fresh provisions, powder, and shells upriver, and bringing back to the city fresh dispatches of how the campaign was faring.

As Farragut took his newly augmented fleet upriver to confront Mississippi strongholds, the U.S. Army moved in to occupy the city. Heading the Union forces was General Benjamin Butler, a New England politician, known throughout the South as "Beast" and despised by Southerners to this day.

"His manner wasn't softened by his appearance," Eric Mills wrote in his book, *Chesapeake Bay in the Civil War.* "Unruly hair cascaded down the sides of his shiny, protruding dome. His off-kilter eyes were hooded by pendulous folds of skin. The sagging, frowning countenance was exaggerated by a drooping mustache."

But perhaps his greatest sin in Southern eyes was his lack of deference to the social order: Butler disdained aristocracy. He placed the city under martial law and suspended commerce and industry. He punished violators with severe imprisonment or transport to the nearby prison on Ship Island. But while the upper classes were held in check, the poor and dislocated flooded the streets, including large numbers of plantation slaves who had fled to New Orleans to get behind Union lines.

To quell the possibility of riots, given the recent shortages of food in the city, Butler organized public markets to distribute free food. But with another proclamation, the Union general earned the undying enmity of chivalrous Southern men. After a series of incidents of bold women spitting in the faces of Union officers, and after the rather courtly Farragut himself was bombarded by the foul waters of a chamber pot tossed from an upper balcony, Butler passed the humiliating but cleverly conceived General Order No. 28:

As the officers and soldiers of the United States have been subject to repeated insults from the women (calling themselves ladies) of New Orleans, in return for the most scrupulous non-interference and courtesy on our part, it is ordered that hereafter when any female shall, by word, gesture, or movement, insult or show contempt for any officer or soldier of the United States, she shall be regarded and held liable to be treated as a woman of the town plying her avocation.

In other words, women sassing the occupying army would be treated as whores. As historian Alecia Long noted, "Southern women had been on a pedestal for all their lives, and suddenly they were being treated badly. There was a huge population of prostitutes in New Orleans, so for women to be classed with this group was appalling! They didn't actually think they were going to be raped, but it could cost them their reputations."

No Union soldier was known to have taken advantage of the edict, but the very idea generated new levels of outrage. "There is no more delicate or dangerous subject for the handling of American historians than the character of General Butler," read a passage in *The Standard History of New Orleans*, published in 1900. "He was looked upon so long in the south, and is still looked upon by many, with such loathing, horror and detestation. . . . His order fairly bristled with hatred, and a very unchristian feeling of triumph and pride."

The *Standard History* continued: "As to the order concerning women of New Orleans, that is something no southerner can forgive."

Butler, undeterred, turned to restoring order to the financial mess. Besides scrip and custom notes, the city's banks had been paying their depositors in Confederate bills. At best these were worth only a third of their face value, but they were nonetheless the only legal tender in circulation. However, once the occupation began, Butler ordered the banks to issue one- and five-dollar U.S. Treasury notes. On May

27, nearly four weeks into the occupation, he took the Confederate money out of circulation completely. He also insisted that the banks redeem the questionable scrip and shinplasters they had foisted on the public. Otherwise, said the General, his administration would seize the banks' assets.

And where, he wondered, was all the gold and silver that the city had been known to harbor before the war broke out? One reason for the shortage of specie in New Orleans at the time was that the city's banks, to thwart the impending Union military occupation, had whisked any hard currency they had left to hiding places in the city or to caches upriver, where the funds could be tapped by a starved and retreating Confederate army. Butler knew that the return of the specie would go a long way toward stabilizing the city, and he demanded it back. When bankers confronted him with fears that the returned money would be confiscated, Butler answered that the money would be ". . . inviolate like any other property," but added:

> You gentlemen who have got your gold concealed behind the altars, in the tombs, or elsewhere, better get it back into your own vaults. . . . If I find it elsewhere I shall not recognize it as your property.

Butler promised the bankers he would furnish armed guards for the safe conduct of the retrieval expeditions. Indeed, one cashier returned from a presumptive "supply trip" up the Red River with $350,000 in gold, packed in barrels of beef. Still, hundreds of thousands of dollars of gold coins remained well hidden behind enemy lines and were used to finance the continuing Confederate war effort.

Ironically, the Union military had little cash of its own. It was forced to raid the countryside, confiscating goods and facilities to support its occupation. As needed, the military paid citizens in promissory notes and greenbacks, promising hard cash to the favored few

— when it could be imported. The Union army ruled over a disaffected and skeptical New Orleans; it needed to keep tight control yet avoid outright rebellion. After all, the war was far from over, and the Union needed the city as a staging area from which to send fresh troops to attack Southern strongholds up the Mississippi, as well as a place of extended convalescence for their wounded.

In the end, Benjamin "Beast" Butler proved an efficient but corrupt opportunist who, in the process of ruling the city, enriched himself with Southern wealth. Another of his nicknames was "Spoons," for the silver he allegedly pilfered for himself. He did succeed in cleaning up New Orleans' sewer-clogged streets and wiping out yellow fever and cholera. And in eight months, he stabilized the economy. The availability of goods and services began to revive toward the end of his tumultuous reign, and ships reappeared in port.

But the city was a drab shell of its former splendor. Gone were the days when, as citizen Thomas Dabney wrote in the *Louisiana Historical Quarterly*, "steamboats lined the levee five deep and the masts of high seas traders rose like a forest above the great river." Now, he continued, "The charred warehouses and the occasional arrival of a few steamers made the waterfront a picture of near desolation. . . ."

The old social order, barely intact, was forced to absorb heavy changes. Louisiana was the only region deep within the Confederacy where Union authorities implemented some tentative Reconstruction policies during the Civil War itself. From the capture of New Orleans in the spring of 1862 until Federal troops left 15 years later in the spring of 1877, Washington experimented with programs that might bring the belligerents together without tearing the social fabric apart. Debate raged on racial issues — the nature of the problems and the course of the solutions — and New Orleans was the testing ground.

Abraham Lincoln's Emancipation Proclamation of 1863 freed the nation's slaves, but, as historian Alecia Long pointed out, the situation in New Orleans was more complicated and the impact of Lincoln's act less certain:

> In New Orleans, free people of color were extremely con-
> cerned with losing their status. They had already begun to lose
> privileges even before the Civil War started. They were wor-
> ried that they might be dropped into the same class as freed
> slaves. And there was confusion over emancipation. Even
> after the proclamation there were "Black Codes" put out in
> Louisiana — forced-wage labor that actually re-enslaved freed
> blacks, so a lot was up for grabs — there was an enormous
> social, ethnic, and class transition.

As the Union navy's Mississippi River campaign progressed, the *Tennessee* was elevated from her humble role as a collier. She was fast, and Farragut took a liking to her. His usual flagship was the USS *Hartford,* but after 1863, he became fond of also using the *Tennessee* as a second flagship on the river. He realized that the Baltimore-built steamer was more mobile in tighter conditions and shallower waters than the lumbering *Hartford.* The one-time passenger ship had ample room for his core staff and for the continual stream of officers and couriers who reported to the floating headquarters.

When Vicksburg surrendered to the Yankees on July 4, 1863, an action that split the Confederacy in two, the Admiral was ensconced aboard the *Tennessee,* involved farther south on the river directing the hard-fought naval siege of Port Hudson. When he heard that Vicksburg had finally fallen, Farragut ordered a salvo of guns fired in salute. A few days later, Port Hudson also surrendered.

The USS *Tennessee* was also in the Union fleet that one year later, in August 1864, attacked Mobile Bay on the Alabama coast. The *Tennessee's* role was as one of several guard ships positioned outside the bay as Farragut's main fleet entered and approached the key defenses at Fort Morgan. The city of Mobile, located inside the large bay, was one of the last uncaptured strongholds on the Gulf of Mexico and a popular base for Confederate blockade-runners making runs to nearby Havana, Cuba, so shutting down the port was another key step in the Anaconda Plan.

This was the engagement in which the recently promoted Vice Admiral Farragut was said to utter his famous command, "Damn the torpedoes, full speed ahead!" (Torpedoes were the term of the day for underwater mines. They were first employed by the South, and Farragut himself complained that the weapon was not "chivalrous" as it was invisible beneath the waters.)

Indeed, on that morning of August 5, 1864, commanding from his primary flagship, the *Hartford*, Farragut led his attack squadron of 14 wooden ships and four ironclad monitors into the bay and watched in horror as one of the ironclads, the *Tecumseh*, immediately struck a mine and sank quickly, killing about 90 men. One of his ship's officers later wrote that when Farragut saw the bodies of the casualties of the engagement laid out on his deck, "It was the only time I ever saw the old gentleman cry. But tears came in his eyes like a little child."

After the loss of the ironclad, Farragut gave his order to continue through the minefield, sailing past the fort to capture or chase away the Confederate ships in the bay. It took another three weeks to force Fort Morgan to surrender, an action in which the *Tennessee* continued to play a role. The bay was closed and the noose around Confederate shipping tightened.

Later, Farragut sent the *Tennessee* and his other converted steamers to join the blockade of secondary ports in the Gulf of Mexico to further strangle commerce and prevent the replenishment of Confederate supplies from foreign nations. Ironically, the nimble steamer that had been an unsuccessful blockade runner for the South now distinguished herself in the waning months of the war by chasing down more than a half dozen Confederate blockade busters, including the steamships *Jane* and *Friendship* and the sailing ships *Allison, Annie Verden, Louisa,* and *Emily.*

After the Battle of Mobile Bay, the *Tennessee* was rechristened the USS *Mobile.* The Union navy had captured a tough and well-known Confederate iron-hulled ram ship also named the *Tennessee* and wanted to keep that name on its new prize for its propaganda value, flaunting to the Confederates the turning fortunes of the war.

The old *Tennessee,* now called the *Mobile,* was sent to patrol the mouth of the Rio Grande River between Texas and Mexico. There, in October of 1864, she was caught at anchor by a sudden fierce Gulf hurricane. Pummeled by the high waves, she lost part of her battery of guns overboard and strained her hull.

Full of regret, Farragut sent the *Mobile* to New York for repairs and overhaul. Said the Admiral, "She is so fast and so fine a vessel that I was unwilling to let her go. . . ."

But the years of battle stress and constant steaming had taken their toll on the steamer's boilers. In New York, a Navy board of surveyors examined her closely and found the steamship too badly damaged to fix. She sat out the rest of the war in dry-dock.

Once more the ship had barely made it through a storm, and once again she sat nearly neglected, idle in harbor. But not for long. Once again the impressive cut of her tall paddlewheels — and the promise of some financial gain for investors — pulled her back into the vortex of history. Sitting in the New York dry-dock, the *Mobile,* nee *Tennessee,* caught the eye of mega-merchant Russell Sturgis, whose family fortune had come from the China opium trade. Sturgis was accustomed to buying and selling steamships as if they were horses, hoping to rehabilitate one or two for a few more years of service. On March 30, 1865, Sturgis purchased the war-worn side-wheeler at a New York auction for $25,000, surely a bargain price for a vessel that just a few years earlier in January 1862 had been purchased by the Confederates for $100,000.

To take advantage of the brisk traffic that was resuming between the North and the South, Sturgis's shipwrights quickly refit the old *Mobile* in only three months. They replaced her boilers once again. They completely renovated the musty passenger quarters that for years had served as military bunkrooms for David Farragut's staff. They "civilianized" the deck, removing the guns of war that had seen action up and down the Mississippi.

Sturgis chartered his renovated first-class passenger liner to William H. Robson's New York–New Orleans Line. On May 3, the newly named SS *Republic* was back in action, on her way back to the Crescent City on the Mississippi River, barely 34 days after Lee's surrender to Grant at Appomattox Court House.

Here was a ship that had seen a remarkable slice of history unfold before her bow. She had steamed to England and South America in search of elusive profits. With paddlewheels churning through the waves, she had carried wide-eyed gold seekers and filibusters to Nicaragua and Panama. She had been captured by the Confederates to use as a blockade runner, then recaptured and turned into a Union river gunboat, an admiral's flagship, and a deep-water blockading vessel.

Once again, she was being given new life. Her assignment was the familiar New York to New Orleans run, a route that would once again bind together two great cities of one single nation. The refurbished steamship, now the first-class luxury liner called, perhaps with a touch of post-war optimism, the SS *Republic,* sailed from New York on June 15 and again on July 19 — at this point, her charter had been switched on the same run to the H.B. Cromwell & Company steamship lines. She left New York for her fourth trip on August 20, and once again returned safely.

Her next run was set for October.

CHAPTER 5

The Trial

IN THOSE HEADY YEARS when gold and artifacts from the Dry
Tortugas wreck were coming to the surface, when Greg and John
were successfully holding their own against their academic detractors, they drew up grand plans. The office was thick with drawings and blueprints for a new conservation lab and museum. News
reports in the media painted the future in golden hues.

In 1990, with their new search equipment, Seahawk located a
second Spanish shipwreck, this one in the deep waters of the Atlantic
Ocean, east of St. Augustine. To begin follow-up operations, they
joined forces with Harbor Branch Oceanographic Institution of
Fort Pierce, Florida, to lease an expensive, state-of-the-art Johnson
Sealink manned submersible, to be launched from the RV *Edwin
Link*. They began to shoot underwater images to stitch together a
pre-disturbance photo-mosaic of the site, some 1,200 feet deep.

Enter the Securities and Exchange Commission (SEC), the
federal agency charged with regulating the workings of the U.S.
stock and securities markets. On March 12, 1991, apparently acting
largely on rumor, the SEC launched an investigation of Seahawk.
Eventually, the commission would accuse Seahawk of inflating the
estimated value of the Dry Tortugas gold and artifacts, thus bilking

its investors. As Greg said later, "They came in and pretty much cut the belly out of the company."

The trouble had started with public appearances. Thrilled that Seahawk had found the Dry Tortugas wreck, Bob Marx, the researcher and writer who had sold the treasure map to Greg and John, enthusiastically labeled the wreck as one of the renowned treasure-rich class of Spanish ships called *Galleons de Plata* (galleons of silver), one of the big ships of the twice-a-year fleets traveling back to Spain with gold, silver, and jewels from the colonial New World from the 1560s to the 1730s. In 1622, one such fleet had been struck by a hurricane, resulting in a number of ships lost in the vicinity of the Florida Keys.

Marx based his conclusion on several factors. Gold bars brought up from the site had distinctive stamped markings like those of Mel Fisher's *Atocha,* also from the 1622 fleet. Furthermore, Marx himself had retrieved from the same Dry Tortugas site a large anchor of a size typically carried on the larger galleons of that fleet. The final piece of evidence for Marx was that Seahawk had recovered three valuable astrolabes from the site. Since astrolabes like these had previously been found only on larger ships, this seemed significant. Marx estimated that one of the great treasure galleons could be worth as much as three or even four hundred million dollars — and this was the impressive figure he presented to the media.

Greg and John, new to the business, trusted Marx to know his stuff. Nevertheless, they were cautious in their own press releases, downplaying the potential value and warning investors that the real value would not be known until all artifacts were recovered and appraised. But the public media naturally loved Marx's big numbers. Headlines in major newspapers such as *USA Today* proclaimed the potential riches of the discovery.

Expectations of the Dry Tortugas wreck rose in the public's hopes; speculation grew that it might prove to be the richest deep-water find in history. When Seahawk announced the recovery of the first gold bars from the site, Seahawk stocks soared. Investors were falling in love with the company.

"At the time," Greg noted, "we were a 'small-cap' or penny stock. And it's common that when there's a lot of buying in such a stock, some brokerage firms will sell that stock 'short' — betting that the fast-rising stock is likely later to fall again in value."

In other words, if a million dollars' worth of buying activity suddenly occurs, and a small-cap stock shoots up in value, some brokers will anticipate that the price is likely to drop again soon. They sell on paper an amount of that stock, which they don't even own yet, in essence making a promise to buy that stock by a specified future date. Of course, this works for them only if the stock drops in value soon enough — before they need to complete the transaction.

To the chagrin of those brokerage firms, the Seahawk stock went up and stayed up. It didn't immediately drop back down as so often happened. In this case, explained Greg, the price of the stock wasn't driven by the usual group of brokerage-driven investors.

"Stockbrokers often will take their clients back out of an 'inflated' stock a few weeks after a big rise, and just churn out profits from that." But, Greg noted, Seahawk investors were a different breed. "They were a lot of individuals who were picking up their local papers or *USA Today* and reading about us, then calling up their brokers and saying, 'Buy me some.' People bought our stock because they were sincerely interested in the company. And those kinds of people tended to buy stocks and hold them."

This meant that the brokerage companies that had been selling short had a problem. To cover their obligations, they would soon have to buy the stock — at a much higher price than they had already sold it for. Selling short was always a risky strategy, and considering the amount of Seahawk stock sold short on the marketplace, those investors stood poised to lose millions of dollars.

In the rough-and-tumble of the financial world, one way to avoid such a loss and bring a stock's value quickly down is to discredit the company involved. Greg believes that some brokers circulated rumors about Seahawk that would sully its reputation and thus drive the stock price lower. One such rumor was that the entire Dry Tortugas operation was just a scam — that the company was actually operating in shallow waters in the Bahamas! That's why, according to the rumor, the amazing photographs of the operation were so well lit.

The other rumor suddenly making the rounds was that the gold bars Seahawk was claiming to have recovered from the site were phony — that the company was either manufacturing its own gold bars and stamping them with Spanish markings from the 1600s, or perhaps was buying bars from Mel Fisher and planting them at the site.

"The SEC basically came in and kicked in the sand castle," said Bagley. "And we were guilty of hubris. We thought that we were bulletproof, that as long as we were doing the best job that's ever been done, playing it straight with our investors, we'd be okay. But the SEC really believed we were taking Mel Fisher's bars and filming them in shallow water and faking the whole thing."

Someone in a brokerage firm apparently approached the SEC with those very rumors. And so the agency came to investigate. A central truth is that big money — especially a sudden swell in stock value or trading activity in a highly speculative field — attracts a lot of attention.

Seahawk had already been investigated once before, by the Treasury Department of Florida, to confirm that their company was legitimate. Greg and John had opened up their office and files. "Whatever you want to look at," the partners told the State of Florida inspector, "it's all yours." The investigator spent two days poring through the files and left impressed that all was on the up and up.

"It was a love fest," Greg said. "The state investigator told us, 'You guys are running this company so well . . . good luck, congratulations . . . and by the way, I'm retiring in about six months. I'd love to come to work with you as a compliance officer.'" In retrospect, noted John, the company probably should have hired him.

Based on that experience, Seahawk figured it knew how to handle government investigations: you simply open everything up. If everything's transparent, nothing can go wrong. So when the federal probe began, they cooperated fully, offering to give the SEC space at the Seahawk facilities and access to their files. The SEC sent four inspectors; they set up a temporary office at Seahawk and combed through virtually every document in the company. In all, they requested copies of more than 30,000 documents in the course of their research into company activities.

"This was at an absolutely critical time for Seahawk," said Greg. Expecting a big inflow of capital to follow their promising discovery, Seahawk had negotiated financing to open a tourist attraction featuring the Dry Tortugas artifacts. In fact they had already planned the exhibits and broken ground. But when the SEC began to camp out at the Seahawk offices, the financiers' firm pulled away, worried that the investigation would undermine the company's value. Money began to dry up.

Through the summer of 1991, Greg and John soldiered on, excavating the Dry Tortugas wreck and pursuing leads of other potential sites. Six months, then nine months passed, and although nothing incriminating was reported to the company, the implications of being "under investigation" began to tighten a noose around Seahawk's neck.

One year passed — then a second year, without charges being filed. The SEC raised one question after another; Seahawk answered in turn. The 8,000 shareholders of Seahawk were growing restless and confused. The museum project was put on hold; it had become too difficult to raise the three million dollars in capital needed to continue that project. And Greg and Laurie were expecting the birth of a second child.

"At that point," said Greg, "we made a huge strategic error that we realized only in retrospect." Fed up with the SEC, which would not respond to their worries but had not accused them of anything either, they went to their U.S. senator, Connie Mack, to complain that they were being strangled for no clear reason by a federal regulatory agency. Mack promptly called the SEC for a report, requesting their justification for the tactics being used to investigate the company.

The involvement of an influential senator, Seahawk later realized, gave the SEC a profound reason to find something wrong, if only to justify its actions. It had already spent hundreds of thousands of taxpayer dollars to find a chink in Seahawk's armor; now it had an influential Florida congressman breathing down the agency's neck. Inadvertently, Seahawk itself had turned up the heat.

A few weeks later, when Mack again asked for an update on what the SEC was up to, the agency responded with a list of charges: fraud and insider trading — ten counts each against Greg, John, and Dan Bagley. An additional charge was delivered against John for failure to supervise.

The regulatory atmosphere at that time was tightening up on so-called penny stocks (speculative small-company stocks that sell for a few dollars or less, sometimes for just pennies a share); many investors were being abused, and the SEC held itself out as the victims' champion. In the SEC's view, although it would not comment on the case, Seahawk was on the ragged edge of propriety, a company that didn't seem to do things by normal rules. Even though no complaints had been filed by its own shareholders, Seahawk was developing an unusual business model in an industry characterized by pirates and scammers. The company's directors were minor celebrities, always in the newspapers touting their company. Now they had made a lot of noise with Congressman Mack. Seahawk may have seemed like an easy target, a group of over-confident treasure hunters. Given the complexity of securities law, surely the SEC believed it would find some violation.

The SEC began tossing out quibbles about the real value of the gold bars and the astrolabes, and questioning the propriety of the artifacts market, charging that the directors were engaged in insider trading, selling stock based on "false valuations" given in the company's financial statements (even though the recovered items from the Dry Tortugas wreck had been posted on the books at below the value of actual appraisals). The SEC was determined to prove that Seahawk had known its wreck was not one of the big treasure ships of the *Galleons de Plata* fleet, that it knew Marx was intentionally inflating the potential value. If Seahawk had known this, the SEC theorized, then it had "hyped" the stock by not informing the public early on that it had *not* found a *Galleon de Plata*, thus misleading investors.

The Seahawk team was offered a way out. Sign a consent decree, the SEC said, putting a document in front of John. In the SEC's settlement offer, Seahawk's directors would admit no guilt — but also not claim innocence. And they would have to agree to pay a fine.

Greg, John, and Dan had a crucial decision on their hands. They could pay the $100,000 fine and get the SEC out of their hair. "But if we had done that," said Greg, "we would have been tainted by it for the rest of our lives. We had been accused of fraud and insider trading. If we had signed a consent to a fine, everybody would have said, 'They really did it — otherwise they would have fought it.'"

Their moral indignation arose at the prospect of settling just to satisfy the SEC, a powerful federal agency not used to being rebuffed. In a huge outpouring of support, investors sent some 600 supporting letters to the SEC protesting the agency's actions. Still, most individuals under that sort of investigative pressure would have folded the tent, signed the papers, and moved on. But Greg and John were furious.

"They expected us to settle, whether we thought the case had any basis in law or not," said Greg. "If you study the SEC's track record, you learn that once something becomes a formal investigation, they seldom go away, whether they're right or wrong. It is their feeling that once this has happened, you are going to settle with them."

But the SEC was facing righteously stubborn men who were not willing to settle and go away. "We're going to litigate," the partners agreed. They would fight for their self-respect and the future of their company.

"Given the choice of 'Do this *or else*' . . . I'll almost always do 'or else,'" John added. "I'm just hard-wired that way."

Still, Greg, John, and Dan realized the SEC probe affected more than just each of them individually. The charges were also levied against Seahawk, preventing it from raising money to finish its attraction, search for more shipwrecks, or even to pay its employees. After sleepless nights going over the options with Laurie, Greg finally went to John and told him there was one additional thing they could do.

"When there's a tug-of-war and you're pulling as hard as you can at the end of a rope, and still losing ground, the best thing is to just let go of the rope," he suggested.

"Let's let go of the rope."

It was a difficult decision, but John and Dan agreed. In January 1994, Greg and John negotiated a deal in which they were forced to resign as directors of Seahawk. They also agreed not to serve as directors again in the future. This allowed Seahawk to settle as a company with the SEC, which they did in mid-1994 — leaving Greg, John, and Dan to gird themselves for a personal defense against the charges. Seahawk's day-to-day business was turned over to John Lawrence, a board member of the company, and his partner John Balch, two technology entrepreneurs with backgrounds in manufacturing advanced deep-ocean ROV systems for oil companies.

In one fell swoop, Greg Stemm, John Morris, and Dan Bagley left behind the company they had founded and began to prepare for the long battle promised by their powerful foe.

The pre-trial process moved with agonizing slowness; the next three and one-half years were consumed by growing mounds of legal paperwork, devoured by endless meetings, preparations, depositions, hearings. The cloud lingered over the trio.

Greg described it as one of the most difficult experiences of his life: "The SEC lawyers were sitting up there portraying us as nasty, evil, fraudulent scammers, while our lawyers were trying to get the real story out.

"It's amazing how the SEC guys could spin it. Once the system gets going, it doesn't matter if they know you've done nothing wrong. The SEC lawyer is working for his client. If that client says, 'I want you to go get someone for this or that charge, then that lawyer's going to do everything he can to ruin you."

A determined Morris wasn't going to sit around and wait to be ruined. "Damn it," John said, "I can't stop them from molesting me, but I can stop them from doing it in the dark. I'm going to put a national spotlight on this." They would go to the press.

Bagley, the communications director, sold the media on the story of a brave little group of entrepreneurs under the harassment of a federal agency. He knew what a little illumination could do. "When I showed up with a television crew in the SEC offices," Bagley said, "the lawyers actually ducked out of the rooms and got the hell out of camera view."

But the Commission got its revenge by rescheduling the subsequent depositions in Washington, D.C., in its own offices, rather than in Florida. "It was tit for tat," said Bagley, clearly more philosophical half a decade later at the high-stakes game that had been played.

"When you're young and you think you're right, you take shots that you wouldn't do now. In our relative youth, in our thirties and forties, we believed in fairness. And we didn't want to make ourselves victims. But you've got to let the bitterness go, or it will destroy you. You can't drink rat poison every day, hoping to kill a rat."

But it was a long, miserable road for the trio. There were times when Greg, emotionally exhausted, just had to walk away from it all for a month. "Many times I'd have to call John up and say, 'Man, I just can't handle this any more. It's your time to take over for a while.'"

John would fill in to cover those periods, and vice versa. The two leaned on each other. "It was probably the most galvanizing thing that happened in our partnership," said John. "After you've done that, you know what it's like to have a partner who will stand with you with swords drawn. I didn't have to worry about what was going on behind me. We hadn't done anything wrong, and neither he nor I were going to back down."

The federal jury trial finally began in 1997, in late October. On November 26, the jury went into deliberation.

After six years of investigation, with the final months filled with hearings and depositions, and two grueling weeks of trial, it was all over in a single day. The jury returned with a complete vindication of all three men on all counts. Greg remembers that after the verdict was read, the SEC's head litigator came up and whispered in Greg's ear how sorry he was that Greg and his family had to go through all this. Coming to a similar conclusion, the judge ruled that the case against Seahawk was so egregious that the SEC was ordered to pay the full legal costs of the trial.

Greg put out a press release with an olive leaf. "We hold no grudge against the SEC," he wrote. "They are just trying to protect shareholders. . . . It's an important job and I think they generally do a very good job of it. Unfortunately for us, the circumstances and issues surrounding our business were so complex and out of the ordinary for the SEC that they just couldn't get their arms around them."

Inside, he and John were seething. The defense of their personal and corporate honor had cut six years from their lives, forced them out of the company they had founded, and ridden hard on their marriages and sense of peace. They had spent nearly a million dollars to defend themselves. Through it all, the investors had stayed the course; in the six years, there were no shareholder lawsuits filed against Seahawk or its directors.

Greg believed that although the SEC never understood what their business was about, it had nonetheless decided to pursue the matter to its conclusion, perhaps to test its regulatory muscle in a field and with a company they didn't know what to do with.

When the two founders of Seahawk returned from the labyrinth and looked again at the company they had left behind, they saw that in their absence the new managers, Lawrence and Balch, had been unable to generate profitable new projects. They had nursed the firm through the crisis, but were less active in the field, and Greg and John felt that although the new managers were experienced offshore guys, somehow they had wandered from the goal. "They became guys selling stock for a living, not artifacts," said Greg. "They hired a team of guys to do the work; they never really got into the middle of it. They wouldn't go offshore. They'd say, 'You do the research, you do the searching; we'll stay back at the office.'"

After all the legal battles and inertia, John and Greg realized that Seahawk was no longer in a position to fulfill their grand dreams. Besides, they were prevented from going back to work there by Seahawk's settlement with the SEC, which stayed intact even though the underlying charges had been found without basis.

Dan Bagley had seen enough; he returned to his academic life at the University of South Florida. But the two original partners, as always equally stubborn and innovative, decided to strike off into new waters. In 1994, after leaving Seahawk, John and Greg had begun developing a new company they called Remarc International, Inc., the name derived from "remote marine archaeology." With Remarc, they were able to keep a hand in the shipwreck-recovery field, working for a while on a project off the coast of Brazil. For financing, they were supported by some of the same original investors who had funded Seahawk, investors who never lost their faith in the pair. Greg and Laurie actually moved with their two young sons down to Brazil for one summer in this period, living in a small village near Rio de Janeiro while Greg worked to develop local contacts and resources for South American shipwreck projects.

Once the trial was over, John and Greg reaffirmed the backing of key investors and merged Remarc into a fresh company they called Odyssey Marine Exploration, Inc. The name was intended to reflect their sense of the great mythic journey of Ulysses, who, like them, had almost arrived at his destination, only to be thwarted and thrown backward a distance that would have crushed others in despair. Ever persistent, the two partners reassembled a crew and returned to the journey.

Was there any doubt they would go on? If anything, they emerged stronger. The trial had taught them even more about preparedness and tenacity, two qualities absolutely necessary to keep a marine exploration business going in the face of dwindling resources and miles of bad luck. Odyssey went full bore; its first step was to hire a large team of researchers to build extensive files of potential targets — to identify the best possible shipwreck sites around the world for the new company.

"We have spent years gathering research," Greg said. "We've had researchers working for us around the globe, helping us create new portfolios of shipwreck projects, trying to winnow out which ones to chase. We spent a lot of money doing due diligence on these projects; we wanted to pursue only those that had a confirmed value."

During that period, Odyssey sponsored many expeditions, exploratory journeys that used the best new technology — sophisticated magnetometers, cutting-edge side-scans, increasingly capable submersibles. As more powerful tools emerged from the oil and cable industries, parity was growing among those who jockeyed for the most effective means of probing the ocean depths. John and Greg believed deeply that with the best research, equipment, and operational planning, there was no reason why a motivated, well-funded private company could not perform as well as governments and institutions. They were back in the exploration business.

The Odyssey partners resolved to work only in deep international waters, in part to avoid conflicts about ownership of the ship's hull, cargo, and artifacts. According to U.S. maritime laws, if shipwrecks and their cargo lie within twelve miles of the coast, jurisdiction over cultural artifacts, including coins, can be exercised by the state, such as the State of Georgia. But outside territorial waters, time-honored international maritime laws apply. Ownership can be claimed by a private company, with no license or official permit required.

John and Greg laid out a crucial set of four criteria for projects their new company would tackle. (1) The wreck must be in deep water. (2) The ship must have carried valuable cargo. (3) The research must provide a reasonable sinking location. (4) Ownership issues must be resolved through negotiation, not litigation; in other words, if Odyssey brings it up, can they keep it?

With the Seahawk experience behind them, Greg and John were developing a new model for shipwreck recovery projects. They were neither treasure-hunting adventurers nor ambitious scientists looking to score academic points. They were businessmen calculating potential profit, yet fascinated with the history and sheer human drama of shipwrecks. And their financial backing, once again fueled by many individual investors who shared deep interests in the subject matter, gave them time.

Odyssey had a vision; it would focus on those shipwrecks that would make money for the company. In making a profit, it could afford to document the archaeological knowledge and share that directly with the public. The plan was to sell a good number of artifacts recovered from a wreck to the public. This was rooted in a belief that this was a good thing, that individual ownership of some artifacts would create greater public support for shipwreck studies, rather than subscribing to the belief that each and every artifact, no matter how well studied or how common, belongs perpetually in a museum or research laboratory.

This direct and open business approach of Odyssey was liberating to some, anathema to others. Some in the oceanographic community still believed that shipwrecks should be examined only by academics or left alone; they compared important wrecks to the Pyramids and other historical remains, and their expression of this philosophy has sometimes been charged with emotion. Ann Giesecke, an attorney who helped draft the nation's 1987 Abandoned Shipwreck Act as a congressional staffer, has been one vocal critic of private initiatives in the deep ocean. She watched with concern the emergence of for-profit business models for shipwreck search and recovery. In particular, the salvage of the SS *Central America* in 1991 served as a warning flag for her.

At a conference in Rhode Island in 1998, she turned her guns directly on companies such as Odyssey. "Shipwrecks are part of a heritage that belongs to all of us and has to get special treatment," Giesecke said. "What it's really about for these salvors is protecting a lifestyle, and the government has no moral or legal responsibility to protect a lifestyle. . . ."

She approached Greg later during that conference to emphasize her point, couching it in patriotic terms: "In America, we don't sell our public resources, whether it's the Grand Canyon or the Indian ruins at Chaco Canyon."

Greg had already convinced many other archaeologists that shipwrecks should be treated no differently than antiques and old buildings that reside on land, that private ownership and profits could well be part of their study and protective management. But these arguments were largely lost on Giesecke and other traditionalists in the oceanic research community. Battle lines were drawn.

For Greg Stemm, there is a reason for his sense of urgency besides commercial interest. Odyssey's detractors talk about the benefits of leaving wrecks for posterity, but as Stemm has often pointed out, all shipwrecks do not last forever. Although in most cases the deepwater marine conditions are well suited to preservation, in other cases sunken ships are slowly being nibbled away by corrosion, currents, wood-boring mollusks, fishermen's trawl nets, and pollution. Eventually, nothing may be left on a given site but the sturdiest inorganic substances — metal, ceramics, stone. Of the oceans' hidden world of lost ships, surely thousands crumble into dust and oblivion each year.

Of the estimated three million shipwrecks that lie out there somewhere on the sea floor, perhaps each is not uniformly valuable as an archaeological site. But especially in the popular imagination, every wreck has a remarkable quality. It is a miniature Pompeii, a moment in time abruptly terminated yet amazingly preserved. In many ways, the typical shipwreck, lying at the bottom of the sea perhaps for centuries, offers a sharper insight into those last moments of human endeavor than does an archaeological land site covered by earth and rock.

There is a profound visual reality established by the underwater robotic vehicle, with its uncanny ability to float through the dark waters to bring a sunken ship slowly into its camera's light and focus. Within the cold, dark mausoleum of deep-sea pressure, the traveler's bag is still unpacked, still filled with extra socks and toothbrush. Cargoes of olive oil or shoes rest unmolested in their crates. The spars and lines that heaved and snapped apart in hurricane winds lie broken but in place, as if waiting to be reconstructed.

If Odyssey and other commercial companies don't participate in the effort to find and document more of those ships, Greg argues, will there be enough progress on both the preservation and the educational fronts? Will important historical wrecks with great intrinsic cultural value possibly be lost to the forces of nature — or to unscrupulous salvage operations? Will the public support for nautical archaeology grow quickly enough to keep pace with new frontiers in technology?

Traditional nautical archaeologists, pressed for time and money, have been excavating no more than a handful of ships each year, and few expeditions venture out into deep water due to the great cost involved. Moreover, academics by nature tend to work slowly, taking a long time to publish their research; even then, the information might reach only a handful of colleagues. At that rate, Greg Stemm believes, many sites and their potential to educate future generations will be lost. He knows the counter-argument that the longer one waits, the better the technological tools of exploration and interpretation will become. But he believes there is a balance to the question of whether to dig or wait, a middle ground that makes a commercial company with a lot of high-tech equipment and an interest in good archaeology a positive player in the field.

The Odyssey model proposed to find a wreck, determine its importance, excavate, create an extensive database of artifacts, publish accessible reports, and sell coins and redundant artifacts to raise money for the next project, all within a few years. Odyssey's explorers and archaeologists could manage this in part because they had the money to be able to work year-round, not solely in brief fieldwork outings squeezed in between university semesters. It was a new formula, admired by some, despised by others.

But the question remains: who should be allowed to explore, and how? And what should be done with the unique cultural and commercial materials recovered? The sheer potential of Odyssey and other private firms to use the newest technology to locate and recover shipwrecks in deep waters has stirred up international debate.

In 1995, the United Nations Educational, Scientific, and Cultural Organization (UNESCO) began to draft a "Convention for the Protection of Underwater Cultural Heritage." Greg Stemm was intimately involved in the process, serving four consecutive terms on the U.S. delegation. In meetings, he typically found himself the only private-sector person in the room amidst 300 archaeologists and lawyers.

From Greg's point of view, the eventual document adopted was neither positive nor likely to get much support. Although the final language was approved in November 2001 by the U.N. General Assembly, the convention has not been widely signed by key countries. Its emphasis is to encourage the preservation of wreck sites *in situ*. One provision, which would be a major barrier to private exploration of shipwrecks, states bluntly that underwater cultural heritage shall not be "commercially exploited."

And what exactly constitutes "underwater cultural heritage"? According to the language of the convention, it is "all traces of human existence having a cultural, historical, or archaeological character which have been partially or totally underwater, periodically or continually, for at least 100 years." This very broad definition has raised concern in an number of sectors and has caused both the United States and the United Kingdom to withhold their signatures. "This is a little like trying to create a comprehensive scheme to protect every building in every country that is over 100 years old," said Greg.

The language was praised, however, by representatives from academic institutions such as the Institute of Nautical Archaeology at Texas A&M, whose past president, Jerome Hall, said, "We are against private ownership. These things belong to the people."

On the other side, the more controversial provisions of the U.N. convention were damned as "global socialism" by experts such as David Bederman, professor of international and maritime law at Emory University in Atlanta, who famously speculated that a beer can tossed from a ship today might qualify as protected cultural heritage in a hundred years.

In a 1998 interview with *Preservation* magazine writer Adam Goodheart, Greg noted that the UNESCO proposal, if passed, would be "like putting $100 million worth of gold in a box by the side of the road and writing on it, 'Please do not disturb.' The artifacts are either going to be brought up legally, under the auspices of a government, in an archaeologically correct manner, or somebody's just going to come and do it at night. It's human nature."

Still, most professionals in the field agree that standards need to be set to protect significant wrecks and to create guidelines for research and recovery. Sensitive to the constant accusations of "treasure hunting," Greg formed the Professional Shipwreck Explorers Association in 1996 to set up voluntary standards of ethics in the deep sea for commercial companies. Its self-imposed code calls, for instance, for a Project Archaeologist to be along on any shipwreck excavation that may have historical or archaeological significance.

A key article in the Association's code states: "Members agree to hold out for sale only those artifacts that have been subjected to thorough study and investigation by the Project Archaeologist."

The code continues: "Those items that are deemed to be of irreplaceable archaeological value, and which cannot be documented, photographed, molded or replicated in a manner that allows reasonable future study and analysis, should be kept together in a collection which is available for study by legitimate researchers."

As the never-ending debates and discussions continued about how best to protect and manage the vast realm of underwater cultural heritage, Greg and John cut their ties with Seahawk. They returned to the sea with their new company, Odyssey, to follow their dreams and ambitions.

From years of research (and after a non-competition agreement with Seahawk lapsed), one potential project emerged to the forefront from among dozens of interesting options the Odyssey team believed to hold some promise. It had been promoted originally to Seahawk by "Dr." Lee Spence, one of the nautical world's favorite whipping boys. He was a man with a nose for shipwrecks, but also a treasure hunter who had been accused of faking his academic credentials, and thus had lost much credibility with the shipwreck community.

Spence had presented information gleaned from public records that he figured would provide a good payday. He had been poring one day through post–Civil War microfiche at the Museum of Maritime History in Norfolk, Virginia, and had come across a passage, dated 1865, mentioning a steamer that had "left New York October 18th for New Orleans, at 3:30 P.M., with crew and passengers numbering seventy-seven in all, a valuable cargo and $400,000 in specie."

The steamer was headed for New Orleans to help bail the city out of her misery.

CHAPTER 6

The Perfect Hurricane

IN THE SUMMER OF 1865 the nation was still in deep shock from the fraternal bloodletting of the Civil War. The fighting had left families split, businesses and properties untended, and friends separated. It had left veterans and prisoners stranded, sometimes thousands of miles from home. For many Southerners it was a time of disillusionment and rancor, a dark time in which they felt that everything they had held sacred had been violated. Starving and homeless families roamed the back roads along with wounded veterans limping home, bands of alienated highwaymen, and former slaves, many of them abandoned and bewildered.

In the North, vindication and a weary self-righteousness prevailed. But people were on the move. Some soldiers were mustering out and returning home; others were shipping out to newly created billets out West or in the post-war Reconstruction effort. Northern businessmen and speculators were trickling south, a few years later to be followed by a tide of "carpetbaggers" — politicians and meddlers looking to exploit the chaos of the South for their own ends.

In New York City, where the SS *Republic* lay at quayside, the city's spirited economy quickly began to regain traction. The nation's largest city and port, New York was already a roiling mix of rich and poor, of races and nationalities. It was a city of divided loyalties and complex economic interests, and had behaved with such ambivalence toward the Civil War that some had cynically called it the northernmost Southern city. During the war, even as the city's liberal activists spearheaded the anti-slavery movement, Wall Street financiers, commercial shippers, and merchants who had been heavily dependent on the cotton trade with the South had urged conciliation with the Confederacy.

On the other end of the economic spectrum, street-level agitations by sullen "Copperheads" — Confederate sympathizers — had openly protested the war and President Lincoln's Emancipation Proclamation. One out of every four New Yorkers was an Irishborn immigrant, and a vast majority of them labored in unskilled jobs as dock workers, ditch-diggers, cartmen, and coal heavers. Their fear ran deep that freed blacks would be content with lower wages and might take away their jobs.

But there was no lack of work. The deep-water merchant marine boom along the East Coast had seriously deteriorated during the war. Confederate raiders had seized or destroyed some 105,000 tons of Federal shipping, and another 800,000 tons had fled the Americas for foreign flags. And the cost advantage American builders once had with cheap lumber was vanishing with every acre of lost New England forest. After the war, wooden shipbuilding south of the Merrimack River in Massachusetts dwindled to nothing. New York built its last large wooden ship in 1869. Domination of many trade routes by American ships was over.

"Americans had firmly planted both feet on dry earth," wrote K. Jack Bauer in *A Maritime History of the United States*. "Never again, except under the pressures of wartime survival, would she challenge for commercial supremacy on the high seas."

In most other sectors of the economy, the Civil War didn't stop business; it just put a damper on much of it. The nation was again building momentum; too much opportunity awaited in the broad lands beyond the Mississippi and in the reconstruction of the South.

New steam technology had created an entire class of ships, and in the factories, steam power was driving the nation toward mass industrialization. For northern businessmen, the time after the Civil War was a time to recoup losses, to move on and seek out a new set of wealth-building risks.

To establish and run these enterprises, they needed reliable transportation. But travel by coach roads was still tedious and rough, and most railroads had been destroyed or severed during the war. The few railroads that worked were crammed with traffic and uncomfortable for passengers. Steamships, clean and fast, still offered the best ride. In the months after the conclusion of the war, dozens of steamship lines, their fortunes revived, resumed their regular routes along the eastern and Gulf shores, reconnecting the North and South. The nation's business and commercial establishments quickly turned, gratefully, back to making money.

In early October of 1865, the *New York Times* carried repeated ads for the fifth voyage of the SS *Republic,* the restored side-wheeler formerly known as the *Tennessee* (and for a short while, the *Mobile):* "For New-Orleans Direct, passage with unsurpassed accommodations." Among the passengers booked for that trip were Colonel William T. Nichols, recently retired from the army, and his younger brother, Major Henry Nichols. On October 18, the brothers each put down their $60 and stepped off Manhattan pier #9 onto the New Orleans–bound steamer. They found stateroom No. 13, stowed their baggage, and awaited the 3:30 P.M. cast-off. But the weather was heavy outside the harbor, so the steamship lay over until next morning at Staten Island, and embarked again at 9 A.M. on October 19. The voyage was scheduled to take eight or nine days.

At 36, William Nichols was a war-weary veteran, a man who had seen much and suffered for it. Born in Rutland, Vermont, on March 24, 1829, he was descended from 17th-century Welsh immigrants to Rhode Island. His brother, Henry, age 21, had also tasted too much killing. With a reputation for gallantry, young Henry had worked his way through the trenches of the Civil War to reach the rank of captain. He was among the officers present at Appomattox Court House when the Confederacy surrendered, and soon after he reached the rank of major. Both brothers, like countless numbers of young soldiers fortunate enough to survive the bloody War Between the States, had been shocked into early maturity.

Of the two, William Nichols became the greater over-achiever. As an admirer reflected later, William had "the advantage of starting poor," but he rose to work his way through preparatory school to become class valedictorian, then studied law and became an assistant clerk to the Vermont House of Representatives. But the legislative life didn't satisfy his ambitions; he had a hankering for the thrill of business pursuits.

A biographical article about Colonel Nichols published in 1895 in the *Maywood Herald*, a newspaper in a small Illinois town where Nichols later lived, described a man of action: "His genius was cast in a mechanical and business mold and naturally led him into different walks of social usefulness . . . his judicious investments in real estate brought large returns, and enabled him to execute many of the building improvements he had projected. . . ." In other words, the self-made William Nichols made his bundle early; he became wealthy from bold investments in real estate, initially in and around his hometown of Rutland.

In pre–Civil War America, Nichols and his generation saw a boundless unfolding of opportunities across the expanding nation for those ambitious and starry-eyed enough to cash in. Even as a young man, Nichols realized that railroads would quickly make inroads into the West. So he traveled to Chicago, perhaps reaching it by steamer up the Mississippi by way of New Orleans, and purchased a quarter section of government land in the new state of Illinois. For the next several years he bought and developed western lands, turning his New England real estate earnings into investments that would assure a lifetime of wealth for his descendents.

In December 1855, when William Nichols was 25, he became enmeshed in the struggle of anti-slavery agitators against the pro-slavery forces in Kansas Territory — a tumult that produced the fiery abolitionist John Brown and planted the seeds for the Civil War. In the Kansas conflict, Nichols had chanced upon the camp of pro-slavery "border ruffians" preparing for a raid on the town of Lawrence, and brazenly entered their camp at the ford of the Waukaruso River. He coolly assessed their numbers and resources, then left to carry his warning to the town of Lawrence.

But Nichols was at his most heroic at the Battle of Gettysburg in 1863. He had been elected colonel of the 14th Vermont Regiment, a post he had modestly declined, claiming "insufficient competency," but he was overruled by the unanimous affirmation of the other officers. In July 1863, with the Rebel army on the move in Pennsylvania, Nichols and his troops were attached to the Union's First Corps under General Reynolds when the armies met on that now hallowed field below Cemetery Hill.

When the Union line began to falter under the Rebel onslaught, relates the Maywood biography:

> . . . The Vermont Brigade was ordered up in haste. Advancing over a stone wall and past some bushes on the left at the creek, Nichols rode to and fro in front of his men to keep them in close and compact order. Neither he nor they comprehended the critical character of the situation. . . . Asking a brigade general how the battle was going, he received no direct reply. The officer only bit his lips and shook his head. An inspiration came to Nichols. Wheeling his horse he galloped to the front of the column and shouted: "Boys! Give the cheer! We are whipping them!"

Nichols' historian says that the rallying call spread throughout the entire Union ranks, which yelled so loudly that the Confederates thought heavy reinforcements had arrived and fell back. When General Robert E. Lee sent Pickett's troops into one last bloody sacrificial charge, Nichols was among those waiting.

> As the rebels came within easy range, the Vermonters sprang to their feet and poured into the rebels, who moved by the left flank, such a withering battalion and file fire that they were thrown into utter confusion. The 13th and 10th Vermont then swept around the dismayed force and captured the whole. A second attacking body met with a similar fate. Thrown into chaos by the destructive volleys of the 14th, it also threw down its arms and surrendered.

Since Gettysburg, though, fate had not been kind to William Nichols. He left the military in 1864, but the war's jarring disruption nearly ruined his business; in the waning days of the conflict he lost a fortune: some $100,000 in stock and wool investments. According to his obituary, "This calamity he met with heroic honor and fortitude, disposed of all his available assets, and eventually paid every dollar of his obligations. . . ."

But he had also been disabled for months with inflammatory rheumatism. Then, just before his and brother Henry's voyage on the *Republic,* William's daughter May died of typhoid fever.

So Nichols was going south not only to seek new investments, but also with hopes to recover his health and heal his mind. He took heart from the beginning stages of the voyage. "The weather is beautiful, and the ship bounds on her way like a thing of life," he later wrote to his grieving wife, Thyrza, who stayed home in Rutland, Vermont.

No pre-voyage manifest of the ship has been found, but later news accounts revealed that among the passengers on the *Republic* were families with children, army officers headed for new assignments, and a share of northern speculators. The first-class cabins were filled by the wealthier class of Americans; $60 was not a price the man on the street could easily produce. Dressed in top hats and silk, they breathed the warm salt air, played cards and dominoes, and drank wine, happy like the brothers Nichols to have survived the war. Porpoises gamboled in the ship's wake.

Newly refitted from a warship into a cruise liner, the SS *Republic* was a veteran as well. She was captained by Edward Young, whose son, Sarsfield, was also on board as first officer. Besides the paying passengers, the steamship carried 500 barrels of freight and a reported $400,000 — at least some of that money coming from the Bank of New York. Not surprisingly, the cash being shipped was all in the form of specie, or coins. In the mid-19th century, gold and silver coins, not bills, were the standards of exchange. When the Lincoln administration in 1862 and 1863 first authorized its famous "greenbacks," prototypes of our paper money today, to pay for the war effort, the public was skeptical. In everyday transactions, greenbacks were often discounted, sometimes commanding as little as half as much as their equivalents in gold coin.

Hard money was even more scarce in the former Confederate states. When the war ended, Northern bankers were eager to ship gold and silver coins by the keg-load on southbound ships such as the *Republic* to take advantage of the money's inflated purchasing power. They knew that in New Orleans, a $20 gold coin would buy twice as much as in New York. New Orleans was at this point the only large Southern city still able to function as an economic center, but she was largely broke — Union forces occupying the city for three years had paid for labor and supplies mostly in paper and I.O.U.s.

On the morning of Friday, October 20, the weather grew heavy. A gale was blowing in the morning, and it continued all day. "It caused considerable anxiety to the passengers," Nichols wrote in a letter to his wife, "and I think some to the captain of the ship. But she rode out the gale all day long, and at midnight the storm abated." The winds gradually subsided the next day, and by the Saturday afternoon "the sea became conspicuously smooth, and we were making good headway. Became quite well acquainted with several of the passengers this evening, and really the voyage began to assume a pleasant and agreeable aspect."

Also on board was a young army officer, Lt. Louis V. Caziarc, from Boston, who must have been good company for the Vermonters. On this October voyage of the steamship *Republic,* the lieutenant was returning to New Orleans to serve as Adjutant General for the Army Department of Louisiana. Caziarc had wheedled his way into the army at the age of 16. Three years later, in the spring of 1865, the young soldier had distinguished himself in the Union siege of Mobile, serving as aide-de-camp for a fellow officer from Massachusetts, Gen. George L. Andrews. Caziarc's assignments were with units of the U.S. Colored Troops, including the 73rd Infantry USCT.

The 73rd was one of the Civil War's first African-American units. First formed as the Louisiana Native Guards, and later known as the Corps d'Afrique, the several regiments from New Orleans included free-born "men of color," many of mixed ancestry, as well as some runaway slaves from surrounding plantations. Although many African-Americans rose in the ranks of the regiments, they served under white commanding officers and staff throughout the war.

But what distinguished the curious history of the Native Guards from that of other African-American regiments of the Civil War is that this remarkable unit served on both sides. The Louisiana Native Guards had first been a Confederate regiment, the only authorized black regiment raised by the South, but it was given little to do. After New Orleans was captured by the Union in April 1862, the unit was soon remustered as three regiments of Union troops. Given a chance to fight for the Union cause, they did, with great valor.

The Native Guards represented a varied mix of racial heritage and politics. "More than 80 percent of the free black population in New

Orleans in 1860 had European blood in their veins," writes James Hollandsworth in his book, *The Louisiana Native Guards: The Black Experience during the Civil War.* "The [Native Guards] were men of property and intelligence, representatives of a free black community in New Orleans that was both prosperous and well-educated. There were even slave-owners among its ranks." Still, it seemed their sympathies leaned more to the Union cause, and after they switched sides, they earned much respect in subsequent actions. At the Battle of Port Hudson in May 1863, 1,080 men of color fought on behalf of the Union. Of their performance, General Nathanial P. Banks had only praise. "Their conduct was heroic," Banks wrote. "No troops could be more determined or daring."

The Native Guards who served with such distinction in the war were also represented on the steamship *Republic* by one of their own officers. Traveling to New Orleans was Captain Charles S. Sauvinet, who in July had mustered out of the military as the longest-serving African-American officer in the Union army. Sauvinet, a court translator of German, Spanish, and French, had entered the war as a captain in the Confederate version of the unit; as he later testified, "If we had not volunteered, they would have forced us into the ranks." He later helped General Butler reorganize the new Union regiments of African-American troops, and was appointed a lieutenant in the 2nd Regiment (later, the 74th Infantry USCT). He was now heading home on the SS *Republic* to take a post as the cashier of the Freedman's Savings Bank of New Orleans, an institution that would play a role as one of the most important financiers of the coming reconstruction of the South.

Another army officer whose heroism was less certain was also on board the *Republic*. Captain Benjamin F. Ryer had commanded the 20th New York Light Artillery battery in Brooklyn. By his record, Ryer was a bit of a misfit in the army, a man who wrestled with alcohol addiction for most of his career. He had sought refuge from combat with an assignment in New York City. But the war caught up with him during the rowdy "Draft Riots" of 1863, when Union soldiers were forced to confront armed hoodlums protesting President Lincoln's call for 300,000 new soldiers through a draft lottery. Mobs of the city's mostly Irish underclass, men who feared economic competition from freed slaves, had been rampaging through the streets of New York for four days, lynching blacks and burning buildings. Capt. Ryer's battery at Fort Schuyler on the New York harbor was commanded to drop artillery shells into the mobs to quell the unrest. As many as 100 of the rioters were killed by the troops before the protests were silenced.

Two experienced steamship captains had booked on as passengers, perhaps returning home to civilian careers after the war. Captain George W. McNear, who had commanded the SS *Inspector,* was traveling to New Orleans with his brother Charles, as was a Captain Hawthorne, accompanied by his wife and two small children.

Below the main deck, the second-class passengers made do with less space and stale air. Perhaps they passed around a flask of whiskey or two as antidote to the constant movement of the ship as it churned against the Gulf Stream. Endlessly throughout the hours and days since leaving New York, the coal furnace below heated water into steam pressure, the massive single piston drove back and forth, the tall walking-beam on deck rocked up and down, and the two great paddlewheels revolved to bite into the sea and pull the ship through the waves.

Sunday, October 22, passed as another fine day at sea. "The passengers are all in first-rate spirits and dressed in their best attire. The porpoises are playing and sporting around the ship in the very exuberance of animal life," reported Col. Nichols. None on board had any inkling the ship was sailing straight into a great vortex of a storm, spinning its way northward to intercept their path.

Undoubtedly the conversations were brisk, often trenchant, buoyant with hopes of a peaceful, prosperous future. As the passengers mingled on the deck to enjoy the last warm days of autumn, the steamship chugged around Cape Hatteras and the Outer Banks of North Carolina, that necklace of barrier islands that forms the continent's easternmost bulge into the Atlantic. After Cape Hatteras, the *Republic*'s route would steam past the coast of South Carolina and Georgia to head doggedly into the stiff Florida Current. It was a long haul for the vessel, which had seen a recent cosmetic upgrade but whose hull was weakened by past years of work on the high seas and previous damage in storms.

Next morning, Monday, October 23, dawn broke as a calm day, but by 9 A.M. the wind began to blow from an east-by-northeast direction. The *Republic* was off the Carolina coast when the gale increased in ferocity. The storm now lashed furiously against the struggling, rocking side-wheeler. The cross chop waxed into towering swells that rushed violently across her white-pine decks. Passengers cowered in their cabins, gripping the furniture as the vessel lurched and pitched at the mercy of the seas. Those who escaped nausea, wrote William Nichols, tried to finish a late lunch at 2 P.M., but the ship sustained a roll that cleared the dinner table of its "pies, meats, vegetables, and condiments."

Steaming furiously south, Captain Edward Young could not outrun it. Before nightfall the wind shifted to the northeast, and the gale grew into what the ship's captain described in awe as the "perfect hurricane." A "cross sea" — choppy and running in contrary directions — roiled the Atlantic above 22 fathoms of water, and the winds howled at full strength. Now there was nothing to do but hang on and pray.

That night the soaked passengers huddled in their berths, sleepless, as the merciless storm grew even more intense. Finally Captain Young was obliged to abandon the course, turn the steamship's bow back into the fierce gale, and attempt to ride out the storm. New Orleans never seemed farther away.

Perhaps the first pangs of real fear arrived on Tuesday, October 24. "This morning we had no breakfast," wrote Nichols, "as the ship was rolling so heavily that it was impossible either to cook anything or set a table. It was as much as a man could do to walk from one side of the ship to the other, by hanging on to anything he could get hold of. Still the gales kept increasing. . . ."

Wrote Captain Young in a later report, "At 6 A.M. on Tuesday it was impossible to turn the engine over by hand; the ship fell off in the trough of the sea and became unmanageable, after trying for an hour and a half to work the engine by hand with 31 pounds of steam which was six pounds more than was allowed to be carried, consequently lost all use of steam pumps. The main spencer [a triangular sail] was blown to ribbons, paddle boxes, part of the house and everything on deck washed away. The gale was now at its height."

The ship's great piston had stopped operating, frozen at dead-center, halfway through its stroke of nine feet. The SS *Republic* was now without propulsion. With the 28-foot-tall paddlewheels stalled, she was utterly adrift, at the mercy of the waves and wind. Soon, the ship was rolling helplessly in the troughs created between the crests of the waves.

At 9 A.M. the ship sprung a leak from the fierce pounding of the waves, and water rose in the hold. By noon, the flooding had squelched the boiler fires, a disastrous occurrence for a large steamship in high waves. Without the main boiler, there was no hope of restarting the steam engine to get the paddlewheels going again, and the ship's pumps would not be able to keep pace with water leaking in through the weakened hull or splashing in from waves breaking across the deck. Captain Young fired up the donkey boiler, a small auxiliary source of steam, but it produced little pressure — just barely enough to keep the ship's pumps sucking at the water sloshing in the hold, giving hope that leaks might not overcome the *Republic*.

In desperate straits, passengers and crew divided into three work gangs at the fore and aft hatches, struggling for hours to dump as much of the cargo as they could bring up. If they could lighten the ship it might be able to ride out the storm, but the water continued to rise ominously. Rank and class had no more meaning. Colonels and waiters stood shoulder to shoulder and labored, all of them soaked, numbed by the cold, wind-lashed in the howl of the storm. The war veterans among them must have recalled the recent past, when men had closed ranks in battle and asked few questions. Into the sea went bolts of silk, ingots of tin, liquors, tobacco, varnish, foot lockers, and other heavy goods — "Every soul on board doing their utmost to save their lives," related Captain Young.

Their strenuous efforts were to little avail in the face of the perfect hurricane, which shrieked against the flow of the Gulf Stream with a relentless and mocking fury. The water was still rising in the hold. "When the cargo was put out," wrote Nichols, "we found that the water had gained on us."

They could not rest. "And all hands were set to work bailing the ship," continued Nichols. "I thought I could not stand, I was so tired from lifting out cargo, but I went into the hold of the ship and took my station to pass water in the buckets, and there I stood for twelve and one-half mortal hours, passing at the rate of from 25 to 50 pails of water per minute all that time."

Twelve and one-half hours of bailing! It was a fearful, endless time, as exhausted men toiled into the night and the storm raged. William Nichols, who had seen the wild swirl of struggle at Gettysburg, as desperate Confederate and Union troops clashed in mortal combat, was awestruck.

"I supposed I had seen something like confusion in battle," Nichols wrote, "but the scene at this time was sublime. The ship had 300 tons of coal, and as she lurched from side to side, the roar of the coal and water sounded like Niagara, and the water on the outside dashing against the ship was another distinct sound and horrid enough of itself. The wind was howling through the rigging like the demons of the sea, and to make it a perfect hell, the men, excited and yelling to each other, begrimed with black smut and engine grease, and their eyes glaring through the dim light of the raging lamps, made it a scene fit for a painter.

"I cannot describe in words the impression which it made upon my mind. It was desperation intensified. No man stopped to think what was the fate impending in a few hours, and yet but few hoped for anything but life, and none expected anything but death.

"At that time had the ship gone down, it would have been impossible to save a life, as the boats could not have been launched in that sea and in the dark."

The nearest port, Savannah, lay to the west across 100 miles of wicked, heaving seas. Unless the crew could lighten her load and restart her boilers, the SS *Republic* was finished. Passengers and crew spent a harrowing night clinging to their cots listening to the roar of coal and water.

They staggered to the deck Wednesday morning to find the wind still howling and the seas running heavy. But the ship was still afloat, and there was calm among the passengers. "Strange to say," wrote Nichols, "out of the chaos of the occasion, something like order has grown up. It was desperation, but men were just on the eve of exhaustion."

By 9 A.M. on Wednesday, though, all the pumps had failed, and Young could only hope for some miracle. As the hours passed and the ship continued to rock violently, Young knew he was about to lose his ship — anathema to a sea captain. Contemplating that dreaded event, he realized that the *Republic's* four lifeboats would not hold everyone, so at one o'clock Wednesday afternoon he ordered the crew to build a makeshift raft to carry the rest. A small detail of the crew quickly lashed three spars together in a triangle and worked to cover it with a thickness of three boards. Only a half hour later, the water rose above the engine room.

The captain had seen enough. "All hands to man the boats!" he bellowed above the roar of the storm.

The oaken hull of the *Republic* was groaning under the weight of the water sloshing in her hold, even as the hurricane winds raked her decks. Colonel Nichols, despite his exhaustion, marveled at the courage of his fellow passengers as they clambered down into the lifeboats:

> It was such a scene as I never expected to see under such circumstances. No confusion, no panic — people shaking hands and bidding each other adieu with all the calmness that they would exhibit if parting upon any ordinary occasion; no trying to get into the boats first, but one saying to another, "You go in this boat, and I will go in the next."

And in this courtly fashion, at least 80 brave but fearful individuals — ladies and children first, then the male passengers, followed by many of the crewmen — abandoned ship and clambered into the four lifeboats to be lowered onto the roiling seas.

An accurate count of the passengers and crew may never be known; researchers have not found a complete passenger list for the *Republic,* and numbers in historical accounts contradict one another. But the consensus holds fast that the evacuation of the failing steamer was a credit to the ship's officers.

Each lifeboat was assigned a leader. Captain Edward Young was to command Lifeboat No. 1. Lifeboat No. 2 was to be led by Captain Hawthorne, the steamship captain who was on the voyage as a passenger. Lifeboat No. 3 was under the leadership of the ship's first officer, Sarsfield E. Young, a young man in his twenties and the son of the captain. Lifeboat No. 4, actually a small captain's gig, was assigned to the second mate, Edward Ryan.

While the passengers and ship's officers were loaded onto the lifeboats, the remainder of the crew, mostly low-ranking sailors, were faced with a harrowing prospect of putting out to sea on the hastily built raft.

The lifeboats could barely hold their human cargo, so luggage and most of the belongings of the crew and passengers were left behind. The Nichols brothers, like everyone, had to abandon everything but the clothes on their backs and the contents of their pockets. Every article on board went down with the ship, noted Capt. Young, "save what the passengers and crew stood in."

Yet the evacuation was a case of grace under the most severe pressure, and perhaps the watchful eye of the Almighty. With death staring them down, the crew succeeded in launching all four boats, as well as the raft, from the heaving ship into the turmoil of wind and sea.

Nichols' overloaded lifeboat, the last to be lowered, was quickly swamped by the rushing waves. "Our boats got filled with water within 15 minutes after we started out," he wrote, "but we took off our hats and caps and soon bailed her out."

Hawthorne, on Lifeboat No. 2, a veteran seaman and disciplined observer, took a head count, and remembered that there were 21 men still clinging to the ship as it began to sink into the water. But wasn't that too many people? Where did they all come from? Indeed, like ship's rats, two stowaways had emerged from the hold of the sinking vessel and joined in the melee on the deck.

Captain Young oversaw the evacuation and stood on the deck of the *Republic* until the last. The turmoil in his mind must have been overwhelming. He was abandoning not only his ship but also his passengers and crew — including his own son, Sarsfield, serving as a ship's officer and now in change of a lifeboat bobbing on the high waves — to the fury of the storm.

For those left on the ship, death was a blink away. As the final, suffocating force of the sea bore down on the hull, the remaining sailors on board leapt from the *Republic*'s deck, floundering for their lives through the floating debris and breaking waves to get clear of the suction of the plummeting steamship. Behind them, 1,600 tons of wood, coal, and iron were sinking below the waves with a horrible low-pitched hiss. Captain Young, heroically staying aboard to shepherd his charges off the *Republic* to safety, actually went down with the ship, but miraculously fought his way back to the surface and struck out for his lifeboat.

The captain worked his way through the bone-chilling water, struggling to reach Lifeboat No. 1, and was hauled aboard, spitting seawater. He looked about him for the other 20 swimmers, and directed the oarsmen to back up through the flotsam that choked the pitching surfaces of the high waves. The Bostonian officer of the Louisiana Native Guards, Lt. Caziarc, who was fit and young, also repeatedly risked his life reaching out to pull flailing passengers into the boats.

"In a few minutes all but two were for the time safe in the boats," Young later remembered, "those two being in the thickest of the debris, and it was impossible for boats to reach them and night and darkness coming on, it is not known whether they were saved, though it is so hoped, being amply provided with floating material."

But neither of those last two spotted in the high seas — "an elderly sea captain" and "a German sailor," their names lost to history, not recalled or recorded in the accounts as everyone faced their own frenzied struggle to survive — ever reached the makeshift raft or any of the four small boats; neither was ever seen again.

At 4:00 in the afternoon of Wednesday, October 25, after two days of valiant struggle against her final great storm, the *Republic* gave herself to the deep and disappeared.

The seas were rolling 40 feet high, catapulting and pile-driving the lifeboats against each other. The last-minute plan had been for the four small boats to surround the raft, its unprotected platform awash from the breaking waves, with between 14 and 18 crew members, by various accounts, clinging to it desperately. The intention was that all would ride out the storm together. But it was an immense strain to keep the tiny vessels linked as they plunged up and down on the great swells. Desperate, and with sinking hearts, those trying to keep a slippery hold on the raft were forced to let go, to let it drift on its own. Without oars or sail, the raft soon floated out of sight, helpless in the fury of the hurricane. One by one, the lifeboats also drifted away from each other, into the darkness and their own purgatory.

The U.S. Weather Service at the time did not yet name hurricanes, but this storm needed little introduction for those unlucky enough to cross its path. From the newspapers of the day came the details of its wrath, stories of how it rent asunder trees on shore and masts at sea from Havana in the Caribbean to the storm-prone bulge of Cape Hatteras. The *Republic* had bulled head-first into one of the most powerful hurricanes of the decade.

"The steamship *Victor,* from New York 21st for New Orleans, was towed into Hampton Roads today by the steamship *Alabama,*" the *Charleston Courier* recounted on October 29. "She encountered a terrific gale from the 24th to the 27th, broke rudder chain and shifted cargo. Her boiler and engine were disabled, and she is leaking badly. The crew is exhausted."

Other reports told of the English brig, *C. W. Reaves,* sailing from Galveston for Liverpool with a load of cotton, dismasted while 100 miles south of Charleston, and of several ships that foundered off St. Augustine, Florida. On November 8, the *Courier* ran updates on the devastation discovered after the storm's onslaught struck Key West:

> Everything in the harbor went on shore, except the United States Steamer *Massachusetts,* and at daylight Monday morning twenty wrecks were visible from the island. The whole Florida reef is lined with vessels. Great damage was done to warehouses and wharves — every wharf was washed away. . . . Nearly every tree on the Island was torn up by the roots. It looks like a perfect picture of desolation.
>
> The Government schooner *Tortugas* lies pounded to

pieces alongside the Quartermaster's wharf. All of the vessels and Pilot Boats that remain in the harbor are blown high and dry on the shore, and are piled up about the wharf. . . . An American bark, from New Orleans, with 1,000 bales of cotton and 500 bales wool is on the reef, also a Spanish brig, loaded with flour, wine, etc. The gale blew from Northeast until 3 o'clock in the morning, then a lull, and then from Southwest.

For the survivors of the steamship *Republic*, the days following the wreck were torturous. They rolled in the maelstrom in their little boats, the winds of the hurricane not abating until the early hours of the next morning. At times the line between life and death seemed curiously blurred. As Thursday's light broke, the castaways could see only a vast, troubled sea stretching to infinity, monstrously indifferent to their fate.

But these men and women, who had already been stretched beyond their limits, somehow steeled themselves for more. Some of the men had recently suffered the horror of combat, had felt the debilitating internal fire of panic, and no doubt knew enough to keep their comrades calm. Together, mere specks in the ocean cosmos, they bailed and rowed for the chance to live.

Lifeboat No. 1 with its 17 passengers, including three children, led by Captain Young, fared best. After its first onerous night of bailing and pulling on the oars, heading directly into the wind and waves to keep the little vessel from capsizing, someone sighted a sail five or six miles to the east. Heartened, they leaned again on their oars and, tired as they were, made fast toward it. Bizarrely, as they stroked in that direction they came upon the scattered debris of their lost ship. The ripped-off deckhouse floated beside them like an apparition, with the steam pipe still standing from it.

Their savior was the brig *John W. Lovitt*, out of St. John's, New Brunswick, captained by Thomas E. Gillist of Yarmouth, Nova

Scotia, bound for Charleston with a load of Canadian lumber. The *Lovitt,* too, had been battered by the hurricane; she had lost most of her spars and canvas, as well as the superstructures of her deck. But she immediately pulled in the castaways, and two days later, on October 28, delivered them to Charleston port.

There, Captain Young offered his first statement on the events, revealing the fate of the *Republic* to the anxious public. In gratitude, his passengers took out a newspaper advertisement praising the Captain for bringing them through: "Your judgment and coolness saved many lives that would otherwise have been sacrificed. . . . Our prayer is that our Heavenly Father, who watched over us all in this our dire distress, may always watch over you and protect you wherever you may be, by land or sea."

Young returned the compliment, telling the *Courier,* "My crew worked admirably, no disorder or panic occurring. The passengers also behaved nobly, being cool and courageous, the ladies especially distinguishing themselves."

A few days later, the rescued inhabitants of Lifeboat No. 1 were steaming back to New York on the SS *Quaker City,* a mail-runner on the Charleston–New York route that had encountered the hurricane in the vicinity of Cape Hatteras. The storm had crushed the *Quaker City's* paddle boxes and shredded her sails, but surely those aboard her felt lucky to have come through the tumult with such relatively minor damage. All who experienced the storm were awed by the power of the winds and the size of the waves. The *New York Times* of November 2 gave ominous warning:

> The masters of all the various vessels which have arrived here, more or less damaged by the storm, assert that, within their experience, it was one of the severest gales known for many years along the coast. Tidings of other numerous disasters to the shipping interest will no doubt continue to reach us for days to come.

In Lifeboat No. 2, Captain Hawthorne, the man suddenly pulled into active duty from his passenger status, had rescued seven frantic crewmen, swimming in the treacherous waters after the *Republic*'s sinking, to add to his crowded little vessel. But his heart was mostly sick with fear for his wife and his two children, who huddled beneath a blanket in the tiny lifeboat. For the first night, and the next day, and the whole following night, the little craft plunged up and down on the great waves. To what avail was it to be a hero to others if he couldn't bring to safety his own family? Determined, Hawthorne kept the men at the oars and steered as best he could, running with the wind.

Their ordeal lasted two days. Hawthorne, in his clipped but comforting captain's log manner, reported their story to the *New York Times:*

> As we had no observations for a couple of days it was very uncertain where we were; according to the courses steered by me we must have been well to the Eastward, as I ran from 8 o'clock that night before the sea, and two oars pulling about a W by S course at the rate of three miles an hour, and left the Gulf at 6 P.M. on Thursday, abreast of Edisto Inlet.

At noon on Friday, October 27, Hawthorne's crew sighted a schooner, *Willie Dill,* on its way from New York to Port Royal, South Carolina. Weak but overjoyed, the shipwrecked crew of Lifeboat No. 2 managed to flag her down. The 23 survivors were duly delivered to Port Royal on Sunday, shaken, dehydrated, but alive. The *Savannah Daily Herald* reported, "Their small allowance of bread and water had given out when they were picked up. . . ."

From the band of survivors, which included three women and the two children of Captain Hawthorne, some grumblings were heard about the condition of the ship that been lost in the storm. "The passengers," the Savannah paper reported, "say that *Republic* was the old steamer *Tennessee*, and was totally unfit for a sea voyage."

In Lifeboat No. 4 (the small four-oared captain's gig), the second mate of the *Republic*, Edward Ryan, shepherded all eleven passengers to safety, but only after four days of deprivation on the open sea. One passenger, Army Captain Benjamin Ryer, the New Yorker who had faced the civilian protestors of the 1863 Draft Riots, was later interviewed by the *Charleston Courier*. Ryer's terse story touches on the deleterious effects of being on the water much longer than the first two lifeboats rescued.

> At times the boat would be half full of water. In this fearful situation they remained for four nights and three days, besides neither having food nor water for the whole of that time, as in their hurry to leave the sinking ship, they being the last ones, provisions or water never for a moment took possession of their mind. Consequently their sufferings were terrible.
>
> They were about giving up all hope of being rescued from a watery grave when a welcome sail hove into sight. It proved to be the schooner *Harper*, Captain Coombs from Bucksport, Maine. They were taken on board the schooner in an exhausted state. And much swollen, but in consequence of the careful attentions they received from Captain Coombs and the inhabitants of Hilton Head they are all doing well.

The *Charleston Courier* of November 2 noted that several women and children were among those rescued by the *Harper* on October 29. It added, in contradiction to Ryer's account, that the boat had managed to stock itself with "one shoulder of ham, a small quantity of bread and a few gallons of water." Perhaps Ryer's story demonstrates the confused state of some of the survivors after drifting for days on the high seas following a traumatic shipwreck.

The community in Hilton Head pooled their resources to help the castaways, who were penniless and helpless. They gave the two officers $32 each, while each civilian man was granted $20. The newspaper went on to note, in its genteel Southern fashion, "The women were also cared for pecuniarily." A few days later the recovering members of Lifeboat No. 4 were bundled off into the steamer *Guiding Star,* which had put to port in Hilton Head to escape the hurricane's tirade and which perhaps had been delayed there by the need to repair damages before once again setting out to sea.

On that afternoon of Wednesday, October 25, moments before the *Republic* lost its final duel with the sea, Colonel William and Major Henry Nichols had jumped with ten others into Lifeboat No. 3. The *Republic*'s first mate and son of the captain, Sarsfield Young, had been assigned to be in charge, but he lay prostrate in the bottom of the lifeboat, physically spent.

"By singular good fortune," the *New York Times* reported later, "Capt. George W. McNear, late of the ship *Inspector,* was on board the boat, and as [the] chief officer was exhausted by his efforts to save the steamship, Capt. McNear took the management of the boat, so as to give Mr. Young some time to rest; and the passengers kept rowing with a desperation which only the fate before them could inspire."

Through McNear's seamanship and the eventual revival of Sarsfield Young, this lifeboat, too, kept disaster at bay through the first black night by pulling oar directly into the onrushing waves, to keep the boat from taking on water abeam, and bailing constantly with shoes and caps. On Thursday morning the wind and current put up such an assault that no amount of rowing could make headway, so McNear devised a sail from a tablecloth that someone found in a bag. Harnessing the remains of the hurricane, they made progress, slipping steadily west toward the Georgia coastline.

They would not last long, however, without something to drink. A demijohn of water, a narrow-necked clay vessel sheathed in wicker, had broken before they could use a drop of it. The boat was otherwise stocked with only meager provisions: some thirst-provoking salt meat, and some hard ship's bread now soaked with saltwater.

Their salvation was found in three cans of preserved fruit, which McNear carefully husbanded until the very last. "Thirst," wrote Nichols, "more terrible than anything else I ever suffered, was added to our other calamities. We had not one drop of water, and with all the labor we had performed it seemed impossible to live without water. But we said little to each other in regard to it, and kept hard at work."

A correspondent for the *Charleston News* later wrote that the second night at sea, Thursday, October 26, was one "of intense suffering and insanity, and the invariable result of exposure, want of sleep and thirst, began to exhibit itself." But McNear guided the little lifeboat by the stars, working always to the west and the hope of an eventual shoreline.

Friday, October 27, dawned with little hope. "Our throats began to swell from thirst. . ." William Nichols wrote. To survive the ordeal, the retired colonel turned to the few sparse possessions that he had managed to carry from the sinking *Republic,* including a small locket, carried as a precious keepsake, holding a picture of his recently deceased daughter. He continued, ". . . and I took out May's gold chain and put it in my mouth, to keep it moist, and gave Henry a coin for the same purpose. His jaws began to set themselves, but the poor fellow worked without saying anything, and did his part like a man." The precious memento and a coin kept the two brothers on the edge of life through another long day adrift on the Atlantic waters.

With parched throats, the inhabitants of Lifeboat No. 3 felt their spirits flagging. When a sail came in sight, they summoned the will to give chase for hours, but it was a vain attempt that must have come close to crushing the remaining hopes of the bobbing little boat.

We began to pull for her, and pulled till we were exhausted, and had to give up in despair, as she had gained on us, instead of our gaining on her. At this point we were on the point of despair, and took off our clothing and jumped into the sea, to absorb moisture externally, which alleviated our suffering very much for the time being.

Hope had risen, then fallen again, as immutably as the waves they rode. How each must have felt — the twelve parched, weakened men on the lifeboat rowing for their lives — as they watched that distant ship's sail shrinking on the horizon.

But as hope fell, it rose again. Like a mirage, a miracle, a mirror image, another sail appeared on the opposite horizon. Though fatigued to the point of numbness, the oarsmen — William and Henry Nichols, Capt. George McNear, First Officer Sarsfield Young, Lt. Louis Caziarc, and seven others — reversed course and pulled for more than an hour in the other direction.

This time the tired rowers succeeded in gaining the attention of the passing ship, the *Horace Beals*, commanded by Captain Joseph Blankenship. As the twelve men were pulled on board, in a weakened state, Friday's daylight was coming to an end. They had been more than 50 hours at sea. They were nearly naked. But they had almost made it on their own; they were being picked up some 20 miles east of Hunting Island, South Carolina, about halfway between Savannah and Charleston.

"He treated us with all the civility and politeness which a true-born gentleman could bestow upon us," a thankful Nichols wrote of Capt. Blankenship. "We could not stand at first when we got on the deck, but water, coffee and something to eat, together with a night's sleep, restored us. . . . To a kind and over-ruling Providence, I return my sincere and profound thanks."

On Sunday, October 29, off Tybee Island, Georgia, the *Horace Beals* transferred the men of Lifeboat No. 3 to the SS *General Hooker*, which delivered them to Charleston the following day. When William and Henry Nichols felt firm ground beneath them, they found their way to a hotel. After buying some new clothes, the older brother took pen in hand.

No doubt Thyrza, his wife, had heard about the fate of the *Republic* by then. Given the couple's recent loss of their daughter May, William was anxious to write and reassure his spouse that he and Henry had survived.

Dear Thyrza,

    We were shipwrecked on the *Republic* somewhere in the Gulf Stream and something like 150 or 200 miles from the coast. We suffered everything but death but thanks to God, arrived here this morning safe. Lost all our clothes and baggage in fact everything except the clothes we happened to have on — we have our money — I cannot write you but a note as we are about to take the train for New Orleans — will give you full particulars as soon as I get where I can — I'll telegraph you just as soon as I get there. Henry and I are well — write father. With much love to all I am yours,

William

The four lifeboats were rescued, but there was no sign of the makeshift raft — until eight days after the wreck, when the two ragged castaways, Martin and Noolan, were pulled shivering onto the deck of the USS *Tioga* near the Cape Hatteras lighthouse. They were the only survivors of the 14 or more poor crewmen last seen clinging to that rickety triangle as it disappeared from the view of the lifeboats bobbing on the high waves, all trying to stay together as long as possible on that first terrible night at sea after the *Republic* had sunk beneath the waves.

CHAPTER 7

The Search for a Phantom

ITH THEIR FIRST COMPANY, Seahawk, Greg Stemm and John Morris had been aware of the lost steamship *Republic* and had followed her trail on and off since 1991. But after resigning in 1994 as directors and undergoing the SEC trial, the relationship with Seahawk pretty much soured for the two founders. The pair ended up suing Seahawk for monies due them for their personal defense of the SEC claims. After the trial, they turned their attention to their new company, Odyssey, researching and exploring other shipwrecks around the globe.

By the spring of 1998, though, Seahawk had abandoned the *Republic* project, and Greg and John's non-competition agreement with Seahawk had passed. Free to pursue the *Republic*, Odyssey added the ship to its target list and began to assemble its own files on the capsized side-wheeler.

As the story gradually unraveled for Odyssey researchers, it became increasingly clear that the Civil War–era steamer had been a star. Her history served up a delectable combination of high-seas adventure and human drama, a cinematic narrative itching to be told. The wreck had sunk in deep water south of Cape Hatteras, likely somewhere off the coast of Georgia. The wreck was certain to offer a time-capsule of a remarkable era right after the conclusion of the Civil War. Moreover, according to survivors, including the captain, the ship was reported to have carried a cargo of several hundred thousand dollars in specie, much of that sure to be in the form of gold coins, perhaps some silver. It was a great American story, and people would pay to have a piece of it.

Odyssey set out full bore to find the sunken side-wheeler, now code-named "*Bavaria*," after another known shipwreck in the general area. True to their new standards, the first phase was research, research, and more research. John and Greg would not commit physical resources until they had determined for themselves the most probable site of the wreck, which had proven elusive over the years.

Pinpointing the wreck site — or even the most likely search area — was like trying to solve a missing-person mystery: they would have to piece together many diverse strands of evidence to find the body. As the team of freelance researchers and Odyssey staff began to reconstruct the historical trail, they were stymied by an immediate oddity: the absence of all records of the *Republic's* departure from New York. There was no passenger list, no cargo manifest to be found. The information was inexplicably missing from the usually fastidious commercial maritime records. After Odyssey's researchers had scoured all possible places without success, one theory emerged, reflecting Sherlock Holmes' dictum that if all other possibilities are ruled out, the remaining one is likely true, no matter how improbable. They began to suspect that the Customs office in New York had been manned by a corrupt official, who for some reason had destroyed the paperwork of the ship's embarkation. There may have been a scandal of some sort, for indeed the facts showed that this official later committed suicide.

For the Odyssey team, though, the far more important question was where the *Republic* might have ended up. Where had it capsized in its final moments fighting the storm? And what forces of nature had then come into play as the lifeboats and raft scattered and the ship sank to the bottom?

At the Tampa office, Greg, John, John's brother, David Morris, who had been engaged as a financial manager, and researcher Lange Winckler considered the possibilities. Using every scrap of information available, they reconstructed the voyage of the steamship.

Besides tracking the ship's theoretical path after she passed Cape Hatteras and was hit by the hurricane and tossed about for several days, they also tried to account for the probable routes of the survivors in four lifeboats and a raft to each of the five rescue sites. Poring over the newspaper reports of the day, they sifted through every mention of the *Republic*, every sighting by another ship. Using complex computer models, they fed in an amalgam of the reported wind speeds, currents, bearings from ships' logs, survivor accounts, and known coordinates of lifeboats when found by passing ships.

It was neither an easy task nor an exact science. In 1865, most news about ships in transit came from vessels as they passed each other. There were no ship-to-shore radios with which to convey positions in between sightings — or to call for help. If two ships passed close enough to each other, the ships' officers would often exchange signals, sometimes hailing each other with bullhorns. In their logbooks, they would record each vessel sighted and its position, and pass the information along to local newspapers when they reached their own destinations. Steamship executives, merchants, and families of passengers would glean the shipping columns for reassurance that all was well and on time. Investors sitting in their men's clubs, smoking cigars, would pore over these maritime reports, speculating and spinning every piece of news, much like the modern-day "day traders" who followed Odyssey's movements on the stock exchange.

For instance, printed in a section of the *New York Times* called "Marine Intelligence" were bulletins from 1865 such as these:

Steamship *Zodiac,* Bukley, Savannah 72 hours, with mdse [merchandise], and passengers to Murray & Nephew. Oct. 21, passed ship *Virginia,* of Bath, bound in. 23rd, 7 A.M. 30 miles S.W. of Hatteras, passed steamships *Leo* and *Quaker City*: same day, 8 A.M. saw steamships *Victor* and *Raleigh,* bound S; 2 P.M. 25 miles N of Hatteras, saw side-wheel steamer showing a white signal with star in the center, bound S. Has had heavy head winds during the entire passage. . . .

The SS *Zodiac* would appear again in subsequent bulletins. She had similarly been forced to battle the great north-by-northeast gale that tore apart ships and shorelines up and down the East Coast. She arrived in New York on October 26, the day after the *Republic* sank, and dutifully passed along all the information she had.

She did not report seeing that vessel of the Cromwell line, the *Republic,* which she should have passed en route. But perhaps at first that was not considered unusual, given the wild storm, which would have made sightings at sea more difficult. The fate of the SS *Republic* would trickle in later as the first lifeboats of the missing steamer were brought to safety.

In the waning days of October 1865, after the sad news filtered in of the wreck, there was little interest in determining the exact spot of the sinking. In the mid-1800s, a ship lost in deep water was gone forever. It was pointless to speculate where a shipwreck might lie on the bottom, after being swept one way by a hurricane, pulled the other by the Gulf Stream, because the technology to reach the wreck site did not exist. No one could hope to recover anything from it.

Even 135 years later, with modern ROVs and computers in the arsenal, to narrow the possible location of a wreck site on the sea floor — even to a very large search area — remained a formidable challenge. The complex factors of hurricane and current could have blown a helpless vessel, adrift once her boilers failed, very, very far from her intended course.

It was left, then, for Odyssey Marine to tackle the puzzle of the *Republic's* current location on the sea floor. The team began with a rough starting point: the first news accounts of the 1865 sinking. "Off the coast of Georgia" was the general position given in early bulletins. A subsequent report came a few days later from the *Charleston Daily Courier:* "She was about 70 miles east of Savannah in the Gulf Stream."

Other tantalizing details had emerged within days of the wreck in the marine shipping reports. The SS *Morning Star*, arriving in New York on October 29, had "passed two ships partially wrecked in spars, at Latitude 32.35 and Longitude 77.25." On the 27th, it had passed "a quantity of wreck matter." Either might have been debris from the *Republic.*

In addition to the wreckage sightings, the locations where survivors were rescued furnished other clues. Captain Edward Young's lifeboat, first to be picked up, was found on October 26 by the *John W. Lovitt* 100 miles southeast of Savannah, Georgia.

The other three lifeboats, two rescued on October 27 and the last on October 29, were found scattered like ripples in the storm at various points off the 100-mile stretch of coastline stretching from Savannah northeast to Charleston.

And the raft, the flimsy platform that started with 14 or more sailors on board and ended up with only two, had drifted over eight days almost 300 miles farther north. Riding the Gulf Stream, the raft had traveled back nearly to the Cape Hatteras lighthouse before quartermaster Oliver Martin and waiter James Noolan were rescued by the USS *Tioga.*

Subsequent shipping news published after the first early reports offered additional leads. A report in the "Marine Intelligence" column in the *New York Times* of November 9, 1865, told of a sighting dated October 26 (the day after the *Republic* sank) of a ship's small boat in some wreckage: "October 26 lat 31 05 lon 79 45 passed a vessel's yawl fast to a sunken wreck."

Was this a description of the remains of a severely battered steamship?

Odyssey's research team, studying each bit of information closely, found the reports often seemed to contradict each other, a common aspect of the shipwreck-research winnowing process. "One piece of data says it's got to be here; another says it has to be there," Greg said. "But you keep comparing, always looking for the area where the data overlaps. This is the area of greatest interest; it becomes your primary search area."

David Morris teased state-of-the-art software to produce likely target areas, running complex algorithms to factor in every scrap of available data. With more thorough research, a new search area was already developing beyond the earlier Seahawk operations.

But for Greg, the free-thinker, using computer models seemed sketchy. "It's too easy to rely on some historical person's latitude-longitude fix, found in a log somewhere," he said, "and use it as a linchpin of your search. But who knows how precisely that person figured or recorded his position? What if he made a little mistake in his calculations? What if he wrote the numbers down wrong? To him, it might not have mattered much."

One thing was clear: there were no confirmed positions for the steamship after the time she got swept into the hurricane. So the lifeboat coordinates would likely be the key to solving the puzzle. Odyssey would have to run the film in reverse — sending the lifeboats backward to the ship and unsinking the *Republic* — to find that elusive spot at the very last moment of the aging steamship's seafaring life. But could that be done?

"Because they moved at different rates, were handled by different people, and were picked up on different dates," explained researcher Lange Winckler, "these lifeboat locations were spread hundreds of miles apart. The hurricane wind and waves had taken them on an eddy current, a circular motion. And the lifeboats were spread out over this vast curve."

Somehow, that pattern contained the answer. The quest was like that of a Zen archer, needing to sense without knowing, to seek some deep, invisible association of arrow and target, wind and time, action and patience.

In May 2002, Odyssey began what all hoped would be the final phase of the search. They defined a large search area off the coast of Georgia. From a company called Aquatica they chartered a 115-foot supply vessel, the *Polo Pony*. The plan was to cruise a grid, mapping what they felt was the most likely part of the Gulf Stream.

The *Polo Pony* would begin to "mow the lawn" — the painstaking process of steering careful lines back and forth across the enormous search area. The surface vessel towed a side-scan sonar at the end of a two-mile-long coaxial cable. The sonar device, gliding just 80 feet above the bottom and more than a quarter mile beneath the waves, pinged out its steady signals, charting the sea bottom along a half-mile-wide path of ocean floor.

The sonar created a visual image, transmitted via its towing and communications cable to a monitor in the ship's operations center. There, a printer recorded the images for later review. The images were also watched in real time, round the clock, for any suggestion of sea-bottom anomalies, things that shouldn't be there — including man-made objects such as wrecked ships.

Three sonar technicians alternated in eight-hour shifts, studying the monitors as the side-scan sonar skimmed over endless miles of mostly dull, sandy sea bottom. They drank dark coffee to stay awake, fighting the impulse to take their weary eyes away from the screens, knowing that the shadow of their target — the outline of a sunken steamship — might drift past at any moment.

The initial search area was a narrow trapezoidal shape covering 600 square nautical miles — a vast, intimidating expanse of open water. Sometimes the sonar fish, more than a mile away in the darkness, seemed like a bait minnow on the end of a long, long cast of line. And the little *Polo Pony*, rolling in the Gulf Stream, seemed like a toy boat, vulnerable to the forces of heat and wind that often coalesced into rampaging storms that struck North America's eastern coastline. But the team persevered, crossing out the squares of the charted search area one by one.

Secrets are tough to keep in the cozy world of undersea exploration, and by the time Odyssey's search operation got underway, there was competition to find the *Republic*. Odyssey got wind of another entrant into the field: entrepreneur Herbert Humphreys Jr., known as "Herbo," whose company, Marine Archaeological Research (MAR), was based on Grand Cayman Island. He had a track record of some success; in 1986, he had worked the Spanish treasure ship *Maravilla*, a shipwreck previously found by Marx but abandoned. Other companies were also reported to have been out on the ocean with sonar equipment; some appeared to be monitoring Odyssey's trips on the "Bavaria" project, a common tactic for rival firms. This was serious competition.

Herbo Humphreys had already covered a good piece of ocean in the same search area, and in 2002 he came to Greg to discuss a joint venture. He offered to share his data for a slice of Odyssey's potential profits. Greg declined; he wasn't sure he could trust Herbo's information. There was just no way to know how diligent the side-scan operators had been on someone else's ship.

Odyssey would go it alone and search the enormous area itself. That was the only way, Greg and John calculated, to be absolutely sure everything was covered. But the specter of a race was looming, and they knew it could make the project more expensive and risky.

The survey manager of the *Polo Pony* was John Astley, a talented if headstrong deep-ocean engineer from England. Astley had personally supervised the operations of the ROV *Merlin* and devised the data-logging system used in the Dry Tortugas excavation in the early 1990s. Of all the research on the *Republic*, Astley had latched on to the report from the November 9, 1865, issue of the *New York Times*, in which a passing ship described "a vessel's yawl fast to a sunken wreck," at a point located about 90 miles out to sea, level with Brunswick, Georgia, and the Sea Islands, well south of Savannah. Astley made these coordinates his point of departure.

Finding a ship-sized deposit of wood and metal on the vast Atlantic floor was a daunting mission that demanded high levels of performance and equipment. Astley was technologically brilliant, but he tended to alienate many of his colleagues, and bickering had created a palpable tension among shipmates. As the *Polo Pony* cruised back and forth in the Gulf Stream through the summer months, some fundamental weaknesses of the project became apparent: the sonar gear was capable of searching only a 500-meter swath, the procedures were inconsistent, and morale on the ship at times was depressingly low. In spite of these challenges, the expedition completed its extensive search — but without finding even a hint of the *Republic*.

The *Polo Pony* returned empty-handed at the end of August, but her voyage nevertheless proved a valuable period of trial and error. Even before the mission was finished, the Odyssey partners realized they had to upgrade their search equipment. Many of the problems resulted from trying to integrate Odyssey's gear onto a leased vessel not designed for the project. They decided to look for a better ship as a platform for next year's operations — and to expand their crew.

"Most deep-ocean engineers who work for the big companies think in terms of day rates," said Greg, "not in terms of results. The technical guys would tend to just go and run the lines, and at the end of it, they'd say, 'Where's our money? We ran our lines.'" Greg felt they needed to handpick individuals with more of a results-oriented mentality.

Odyssey would eventually, it hoped, need academics as well: archaeologists and conservators. But not yet. For now, this was a straight deep-sea search operation, and the company was relying on talented people from commercial oil, cable, and engineering firms. Others came straight from the business world. One of these was a 35-year-old Cuban-born Canadian engineer and entrepreneur, Ernie Tapanes, who joined Odyssey in the fall of 2002.

"Ernie was a relative newcomer to the world of ocean exploration," Greg remembered, "but he was so passionate about it, he was one of the best hires the company ever made." Greg had met Tapanes earlier that year, when Ernie was running a complicated deep-ocean shipwreck search off Cuba, in partnership with the Cuban government, and was looking for someone to help analyze some difficult side-scan images. Greg and John had accumulated about as much experience in the highly subjective art of side-scan interpretation as any deep-ocean engineers in the world, and Greg shared his knowledge freely with Ernie as they reviewed the acoustic anomalies. A friendship formed, and when Ernie took a break from his Cuban operation, Greg offered him a slot at Odyssey. In September 2002, after the *Polo Pony* had exhausted her mission, Ernie inherited the primary responsibility for locating the *Republic*.

Ernie's first task was to find the perfect search vessel. The trail led him to the Harbor Branch Oceanographic Institution, where Tapanes ended up purchasing the *Edwin Link,* one of the world's most renowned research vessels. She had been custom built in the 1960s by the late aviation and underwater pioneer Edwin S. Link. Ernie contributed the vessel to Odyssey in return for a good chunk of stock, becoming a major shareholder and tying his fortune to Odyssey's success. Greg and John would rename their latest acquisition the RV *Odyssey*.

The 113-foot craft had history. She had played a role in the early exploration of the seas as a platform for the U.S. Navy's first deep-saturation dive experiments. She had also been involved in the "Man in the Sea" program of the 1980s. Besides Link himself, many of the 20th century's eminent figures in research and exploration — Jacques Cousteau, Werner von Braun, and the original Apollo astronauts — had been on board. Three decades earlier, Link had used the vessel to launch the world's first ROV, called CORD (Cabled Observation and Rescue Device), a remotely controlled vehicle equipped with television cameras, lights, and hydraulic-powered claws and cutters.

Sadly, that breakthrough piece of technology had been inspired by an earlier disaster in which Link's own son, Edwin Clayton Link, having launched from the same research vessel on a routine dive in the Florida Keys, died in a submersible accident. Clay Link's underwater vessel got trapped in the wreckage of an old destroyer, and the oxygen had run out. Haunted by that tragedy, the bereaved father had put his brilliant engineering skills to work and developed a rescue device, the unmanned CORD.

The ship's history seemed to hang on it like an obligation. Greg and John knew they had to assemble a special team. They wanted people who not only had impeccable technical credentials but also were willing to immerse themselves in the coming project. The two partners wanted a team to appreciate the sweep of the historical narrative, a team that would make it a personal challenge to find their target, the Civil War wreck.

Ernie was the right man to step in after the unsuccessful search of the summer of 2002 to tackle the question of what to do next. A meticulous manager, he left little to chance. When Tapanes analyzed the voyages of the *Polo Pony*, he felt there was a chance that critical gaps might exist in the sonar record. If so, it meant sections of the sea would have to be re-examined. He'd have to return to cover those gaps and do it with steadier, more efficient equipment. Odyssey had been taking a journey of two steps forward, one step backward, shaking out mistaken notions and cantankerous gear as it went.

"Out of all those years of searching, on and off, for the *Republic,* much of the time was spent getting over a learning curve," Ernie said later. Now, with the company's new vessel, he set out to prove the learning had not been in vain.

Under Ernie's guidance, the team would return with higher-resolution, longer-range side-scan sonar to inspect the inconclusive targets that the *Polo Pony* had identified. Was there a chance that one of them was the sunken steamship? A couple of months after the purchase of the *Edwin Link*, and an exhaustive refit allowed by a three-million-dollar investment in the company by St. Petersburg entrepreneur James MacDougald, the newly christened RV *Odyssey* steamed out into the sea to continue the hunt for the steamship *Republic.*

But trouble quickly erupted. The ship, with space for a working crew of 14, proved too small for the additional supervisory talent, and the voyage quickly turned into a battle of wills between the original survey manager, Astley, and the new leader, Ernie Tapanes, who had a fresh approach and different equipment.

"John was a brilliant, brilliant guy," said Greg. "But his old system didn't talk to the new equipment. We had to take his basic frame-work and completely rewire the software in the middle of operations. And John was not much of a diplomat. The crew was upset and unhappy. When you have dedicated people putting in sixteen-hour days, and they're left feeling that they haven't done a good job, it's just too tough on the *esprit de corps.*"

After their years of history with Astley, John and Greg faced a tough decision, but decided to go with Ernie. They placed the search in his hands, and Astley returned to shore. Astley's new role was to help develop the software needed for archaeological excavation work — if they located the *Republic.*

But the learning curve was arcing even higher for Ernie, whose own credibility (and personal investment) was now on the line. As the RV *Odyssey* steamed back and forth along the parallel lines of the search pattern, the mighty Gulf Stream was proving as much of an adversary for the bigger ship as it had been for the leased *Polo Pony.* For one thing, the technicians discovered that even their new sonar gear operated only when towed directly with or against the strong current — in other words, when traveling north-south lines. If they tried to tow the sonar on an east-west course, they got distorted images. *Everything* began to look man-made.

The search was also plagued by immense sand formations called mega-ripples, ridges on the sea floor sculpted by the current into hydrodynamic shapes. "You're looking for something hard and high," explained Ernie. "Metal objects abeam of the sand ripples. Something that says, 'Hey, I'm different around here.' But the mega-ripples can hide entire ships behind them."

The strength of the Gulf Stream caused constant underwater instability, often forcing the operation to balk and lose valuable time.

"With a lightweight sonar fish, it's like towing a toothpick in a river," said Ernie. "And so much cable is out there, flopping around, that if the sonar operator sees a hill on the bottom and says, 'Winch in,' the fish might not get the signal soon enough. If it didn't react in time, it could slam into the bottom, with catastrophic results."

Ernie would stand on the heaving deck, light another cigar, and worry if they had missed parts of the seabed. Their new rig still seemed outmanned, overwhelmed by the turbulent conditions and the vast size of the search area.

Three times during the 2002 survey the sonar teased them with images that might have been the side-wheel steamer. But on closer examination, with higher-resolution sonar, the anomalies proved to be fruitless dry holes. The *Republic* was in hiding; she was not willing to stick her head up from behind a mega-ripple and announce herself. This was going to be grueling, steady work, and Ernie had to stretch to come up with a positive take on their lack of success.

"The Gulf Stream keeps the average Joe away. It protects the wreck," he said. "Out of one hundred people who could even do this kind of work, only a handful could do it in the Gulf Stream.

"It would just eat the others up."

Winter passed and the RV *Odyssey* churned on, scouring the ocean floor with her new sonar, darting in and out between harsh cold fronts that battered the *Odyssey* and her crew. But none of the targets yielded anything remotely resembling a steamship.

In the spring of 2003 the team was back at the drawing board. A researcher at NOAA had just finished reconstructing a chart of the historic 1865 hurricane; it now suggested that the eye of the storm had passed to the east of the ship's last known position. The fresh data meant that strong winds, coming down along the western side of the counter-clockwise swirl of the storm, must have blown constantly from the northeast.

"There was a contest going on," said Ernie. "A pretty tough contest between the winds and the current."

Which force had been more powerful in those days of October 1865 — the Gulf Stream pulling the ship north or the opposing hurricane winds pushing it southwest? This was the crux of the matter.

Project historian Lange Winckler was busy plotting all the information on a large nautical chart of the Georgia seacoast. His push-pins and little flags made it look like the mockup of a naval battle. However, even with the new weather data, the research team had to admit that, despite all their sophisticated computer modeling, the last position of the *Republic* was impossible to calculate by trying to track the ship's course after passing Cape Hatteras. After losing power, she had drifted for two days as the hurricane pushed her one way and the current pulled her the other.

It was time for Greg, John, and Ernie to come up with a new creative approach. The discussion returned, as it often had before, to the spot where Captain Young's lifeboat had been picked up by the *Lovitt*.

Young's was the first survivor vessel to be saved. That rescue had occurred in the shortest time after the sinking, and in a specified location recorded in the *Lovitt*'s log. But just how far had the lifeboat traveled from the site of the *Republic*'s capsizing the night before? In which direction? Furthermore, how accurate was that documented position of the rescue?

From the accounts, the desperate passengers of Lifeboat No. 1 had been pulling through that first night for their lives *against* the oncoming waves, likely making little headway, just trying to keep from sinking. At eight o'clock next morning, they saw a sail five or six miles away, then pulled with renewed vigor toward the sail and reached the *Lovitt*.

Captain Young's report also noted curiously that the lifeboat, on its final push toward the rescue ship, rowed through the floating debris of the *Republic*'s deckhouse.

Previous researchers had latched onto that fact, but concluded that the deckhouse would have ended up far north from the site of the sinking, riding the powerful Gulf Stream current through the entire night and into the next day. Therefore, the earlier assumption was that the shipwreck site was well to the south of the lifeboat's pickup point. That's primarily why John Astley, leading the first Odyssey search on the *Polo Pony*, had been searching to the south.

The new historic data from NOAA began to offer another intriguing scenario. "The early searches didn't take into account the power of the hurricane winds that fought against the Gulf Stream," said Ernie. "We started to get another picture when we were able to check the old weather chart as well as meteorological data gathered during the 1865 storm. And anecdotal information was gathered from fishermen knowledgeable about the Gulf Stream.

"We began to suspect that the force of the wind was probably about *equal* to the current at the time of the *Republic*'s sinking — essentially stopping the progress of the floating remains of the deckhouse in its tracks."

The three other lifeboats were adrift for days before being rescued. Subject to varying winds, and powered by oars and makeshift sail, they had wound up far from the wreck near Charleston and the South Carolina coast. The raft had also drifted for many days after the storm winds abated, ending up far to the north. But Lifeboat No. 1, after a single night of rowing against the wind and waves, had ended up in almost the same spot as the floating deckhouse.

A new theory was emerging: if stronger winds than first calculated had pushed harder than expected against the Gulf Stream, cancelling each other out, was it possible that the floating deckhouse had not traveled far at all from the wreck site?

Was it possible that the lifeboat, much lighter than the remains of the deckhouse, would have been pushed by the winds even farther south . . . but had rowed valiantly through the night . . . to end up in virtually the same spot as the wreck debris?

If the Odyssey team was right, the spot where the *Republic* sank should be much nearer than earlier calculated to that point where Lifeboat No. 1 had spotted the *Lovitt*, then rowed to meet the rescue ship, ending up at the recorded location, roughly 100 miles off the coast of Georgia.

It was an intriguing, complex reconsideration.

At a meeting of Odyssey's executive committee in April, the team thrashed out the new reasoning. Using the push-pin chart, they penciled a box to define a new search area. Though connected to the old area, the new box reached farther north to include the key area where the floating deckhouse had been seen and Captain Young's lifeboat had been picked up.

The area searched by the *Polo Pony* had not come close to that pickup point. The new search area shifted to the north and east, with the lifeboat pickup point roughly in its center. The actual plan for 2003 was in the shape of four trapezoidal boxes. With some overlap of the area already covered by the *Polo Pony*, the entire grid covered some 1,000 square nautical miles.

Ernie outlined the three scenarios: if the greatest influence on the lifeboat and deckhouse debris had been the wind, the shipwreck would be found north of the pickup point. If the Gulf Stream had been the stronger factor, then the shipwreck would be found south of it.

And if the wind, waves, and current cancelled each other out, the shipwreck would be right in the vicinity of the pickup point.

The summer of 2003 off the coast of Georgia was torrid. The sea was often uneasy with a mix of thunderstorms, sweltering heat, and six-foot swells. The RV *Odyssey* rolled heavily in medium chop; in heavy weather it was bearable only by the saltiest sailors.

Odyssey's gear was again upgraded. An advanced Edgetech Chirp side-scan sonar and a fully integrated new Cesium magnetometer gave the explorers new capabilities. Without needing to deploy an ROV system, they could quickly determine whether an anomaly was an odd bit of underwater geology or a potential shipwreck. The magnetometer would spike if a target had the great mass of iron known to be part of a vessel like the *Republic*.

Ernie was a true believer in the mission, but the monotony of the search operation was wearing him down. After weeks at sea, the sonar had "mowed" only one of the four new search areas — the one to the extreme northeast, which included the lifeboat pickup spot. Nothing had been found.

Now he was pushing the ship into the adjoining box to the west. The sea seemed unreasonably vast and empty. "With all the endless days, sticking to your guns, rolling out of bed every morning," he said, "you start questioning — do we have our information wrong? Is the ship findable?"

By then, the various crews engaged in the hunt for the wreck, first by Seahawk, then by Odyssey, had combed a total of 1,500 square miles of ocean. Odyssey had already closely examined 24 promising sonar targets with high-resolution sonar and ROVs. In the past two years alone, Odyssey had found a fighter jet, a custom sailboat, and an 18th-century merchant vessel filled with blue-and-white porcelain and Chinese-export ginger jars. The "Blue China" wreck held promise for a future excavation. But the *Republic* had evaded them.

They had examined their primary research area, then the secondary area. Now they were picking along the edges of the improbable.

Odyssey badly needed a score — a quick infusion of success. The drought between significant shipwreck finds had been deep and long. Since forming their new enterprise, Greg and John had been forced, year after empty year, to dilute their ownership in the company. They sold shares, then sold more, until they became only minority holders.

Worst of all, they grew worried, checking and rechecking their information for clues to help narrow their search. Greg would sit for hours and just stare at the nautical chart, with all their notes and estimates written on it. "I know the shipwreck's out there," he'd say. "Somewhere on this chart . . . I know it's there. We just have to stick it out."

The real stress looming in Greg's mind was that Odyssey was stretching its credibility with key investors and backers, people who had been with them since the earliest days of Seahawk. He knew their concerns, recalled the dreaded conversations. "One particular investor calls me every month: 'Are we rich yet, Greg?' He's been calling for fifteen years, and he'd say, 'What's the problem this month?' It's just painful. I think it's easier for *us* to deal with failure than it is to pass on that lack of success to the other true believers."

Adding to the stress was that the company was trying to decide how to juggle another promising new project that was developing that summer. Two years earlier, another Odyssey expedition had found a wreck near Gibraltar they thought could be HMS *Sussex*. The *Sussex* was a British warship lost in deep waters in the Mediterranean Sea in 1694, reportedly carrying a large cargo of gold bound for Italian mercenaries who were harassing the French from the Piedmont region. It had been another long-term project simmering on the edge of possibility for years.

Now Greg and John had made progress in negotiating the complex legal rights needed to permit Odyssey's exploration and excavation of the British warship site off the coast of Gibraltar. Operations were planned for the summer of 2003, but bureaucratic challenges in negotiating a complex agreement with the British seemed never-ending. The *Sussex* was potentially a huge prize, yet again was likely to bleed big money for operations before yielding a payoff, if any, in recovered gold. It was an intersection of hope and hard reality. What should the partners do?

The *Sussex* offered a golden gleam of potential wealth. Was it a greater gleam? At least at the Gibraltar site, they had located an actual vessel, although it was not yet clearly identified. Should they abandon their unsuccessful search of the open sea for the *Republic* and concentrate on *Sussex*?

No. John and Greg needed to be patient and work through all the roadblocks of the British deal. Their future plans depended on building the faith of governments and partnering with the navies of the world. So they had to maintain their composure while the legendary British bureaucracy ground them down with demand after demand.

But funds were tight. In some ways, the company was crossing an icy ledge without a rope, clinging with fingers and toes and strength of will. It wouldn't go broke as long as loyal investors hung on, but the boys from Tampa were stretching their credibility. They would have to find the *Republic* first, and soon. If so, and if the reported $400,000 in specie was intact, they could use that to finance the European expedition.

Hope was still alive for John and Greg, but waning fast with each square crossed off the huge search grid. Each square was now less probable than the last. Yet once again the two partners found a positive glimmer in those Atlantic waters off the coast of Georgia. Compared to the legal and cultural snares in a project involving a British warship sunk in Spanish waters, the *Republic* project was much simpler. If they could find the ship, excavation could be started soon after; it required no permits for the recovery phase. And John and Greg were confident that the Civil War–era ship would contain what they needed to fund the next big project.

Despite its missing manifest records, the *Republic* was known to have been carrying an immense quantity of what was the most profitable and marketable type of artifact possible: 19th-century American gold coins. If Odyssey could find the SS *Republic* before all funds ran out, they could recapitalize the company and raise the money to fund the expensive *Sussex* recovery.

Greg and John decided to hold off announcing a public stock offering, their backup plan to raise *Sussex* financing, as long as possible. They were still hoping that Ernie Tapanes, chewing on the end of his Cuban cigar, had the magic touch — that he would find the elusive American side-wheeler.

But in mid-July 2003, with no sign of success off the coast of Georgia, Greg flew to Gibraltar to start warm-up activities for the *Sussex* project. John meanwhile prepared to negotiate the purchase of a second complete ROV system, which meant also buying a ship capable of handling the large crew and needed equipment. They drew up the documents for the new stock offering, hoping the next round of financing would be successful. Time, they realized, had run out. They had stopped counting on the *Republic*.

On July 25, with supplies dwindling and attention wandering, a blocky shape formed on the sonar screen of the RV *Odyssey*, operating about 100 miles off the coast of Georgia. The jaded technicians stared at the object with pessimism.

"It might be just a sailboat," said J.J. Jackson, an experienced

Odyssey technician who had started his career in deep-sea sonar for Alaskan fisheries. He had seen a lot of ocean floor. Terry Snyder, another sonar man with many expedition notches in his belt, wasn't sure. "Let's go back, let's go back," he urged Ernie.

Sailboats are narrower, thought Ernie, unless it's a catamaran. But he marked the spot and left the anomaly in his wake. The RV *Odyssey* moved on to finish covering the entire search block. That took some discipline, because, as Ernie headed the ship back to Jacksonville for fuel and supplies, the square-shaped sonar image was rattling around in his mind. The target was intriguing but he wanted no more false alarms. He preferred to come back later and take high-resolution sonar images to pin it down.

Ten days later, Ernie and the *Odyssey* crew returned to sea for a better look at the blocky shape that lay in 1,700 feet of water. They spent two arduous days taking nine sonar runs past the object, at different angles, zeroing in on its shape, incrementally creating a three-dimensional form. "At 300 meters range, it looked really good," said Ernie. "Nicely square. I knew the only structures that might be left down there from a steamship would be the boiler and the engine room, so we could expect to see a square object with something high in the middle."

As the sonar images came in, taken at a distance of 50 meters from various angles, they could suddenly see everything, as if they had taken a photograph. Ernie looked over at Terry Snyder for some sort of confirmation.

"You know," Snyder said in his trademark laconic manner, "this looks a lot like an engine compartment of a paddlewheel steamship."

They could even make out that the port side of the boiler was beat up, but its starboard was intact. A large field of debris lay scattered south of the wreck. The bow had no structure, but the stern sat up like a shelf. With an electronic measuring device, they calculated the dimensions of the wreck.

The length matched published dimensions of the *Republic* within a foot. The diameter of the side-wheels also matched within a foot. Double boilers sat in a wooden hull, not the steel hull of a false positive target. And from the middle of the wreck emerged the soaring A-frame profile of a walking beam.

"As soon as I saw the measurements, I knew we'd nailed it," said a surprised J.J. Jackson. "I'm not an easy person to convince, but I've never had an image like this. You could really see it — just like the power plant was standing there, ready to go — the double boilers and the wheels. It measured perfectly to what we knew of the *Republic*.

"It's very rare that happens. Nothing ever comes together this well — most of the time you have to do sonar runs over and over. So after nine passages, when you get that kind of redundancy . . . it's incredibly nice, really sweet."

By now, Jackson's preliminary profiling of the site had turned into a small joke on board the *Odyssey*. They decided to call the sonar image "Sailboat No. 1."

Ernie took an image of the scan, climbed to the bridge, and e-mailed it via a satellite link to John Morris in Tampa. It was late in the evening, but Ernie knew John would get the message with little delay. "He's always on his computer," said Ernie. "He's a guy who gets by on four hours of sleep a night."

John examined the image. It was eleven o'clock at night in Tampa. His partner, Greg, was in Spain, where it was five o'clock the next morning. John reached for the phone and dialed. He listened to the phone ring a few times, then the receiver was picked up on the other end.

"Why don't you check your e-mail?" said John laconically. "And tell me what you think."

Greg asked what this was about.

"Turn on your computer," John insisted, "and download this sonar image I just got from Ernie." Within minutes of Ernie's sending his message, both partners — one on each side of the Atlantic — were staring at the same ghostly outline on their screens. For these two steeped in the history of the ship, the image was clear. The wreck, they were convinced, could only be the steamship *Republic.* Here she was at last. Odyssey's string of bad luck had ended.

"We didn't find any of our target shipwrecks for years," Greg said later. "It was like flipping pennies; you'd figure that it would come up heads after three or four tries. Well, in searching for the *Republic,* we flipped a coin for ten years before it came up heads. There was just a string of tails."

He added, "We weren't searching for an abstract. We knew that the ship was out there. I can't tell you how many times I sat there staring at the chart. Somewhere on that chart, it's there! You're just scratching your head!"

The blocky shipwreck lay just several miles to the northwest of where the *Republic's* Lifeboat No. 1 had been rescued. It looked like the trailing winds of the October 1865 storm had held their own against the exhausted oarsmen pulling through the night and the pervasive might of the Gulf Stream.

"When we finally found it, I marked it on the chart in my cabin," recalled Greg. "And I just sat there, looking at it. I was so amused by the idea that it had been there all along. But once again, it all came down to the Gulf Stream. That was the thing you couldn't ignore. It was a huge problem. I felt completely confident about everything in the operation — except whether we were going to be able to work in the Gulf Stream."

The game was not over; in some ways, it was just beginning. Greg and John were sure they had the SS *Republic.* Now they had to prove it. On August 2 the RV *Odyssey* team returned with a small ROV, one already outfitted with a manipulator claw and a video camera. The camera was needed to document what had been only outlined by the sonar. And they had to recover at least one artifact to legally claim the right to work on the wreck.

But to make it work in the formidable current, they had to strip the little ROV down as much as they could to take all excess weight off. "It could barely hold its position," said Ernie. "We practically killed the thing."

At 1,500 feet deep, the thruster end-caps were cracking. The ROV was forced to operate on half-thrusters, with no sonar, and there was a broken tilt on the camera.

"We're working on borrowed time," Ernie told his team, "but we've got to go to the end with it." They pushed the small ROV on to a depth of 1,700 feet.

The first views of the broken ship sitting on the sandy floor of the deep ocean were breathtaking. They could see that the ship's bow was stubbed out, as if she had piled into the bottom front first. Coal was spread like inkblots around the corroding metal. And there was the massive, copper-sheathed rudder. Carefully, they photographed the rudder, then slowly, with the ROV's manipulator claws, they picked up a brown beer bottle and a hunk of wood.

"Let's pull it in," said Andrew "Irish" Craig, one of the ROV technicians. "We're pushing our luck."

"No, no, we need to have a shot of the paddlewheel," Ernie insisted.

"You're crazy, this ROV will never last."

They "flew" the ROV out to find the paddlewheels, but the pilot took a wrong turn at one of the cross beams. They squandered precious time as they reversed direction and made their way back. Gradually, the bent and corroded iron boilers and the eerie skeletons of upright paddlewheels materialized in front of the camera.

"Nobody died on the ship," J.J. Jackson said later, "but there was a ghostliness about it. You could almost feel that moment when the heat of the boiler went cold."

As the ROV hovered above one of the paddlewheels, the video

camera captured the scene. For Ernie, the compelling footage would unequivocally identify the wreck as a 19th-century steamship. "All the skeptics say they need more proof," said Ernie. "Now they'll come around. Some people need to have a colorful video, brilliant and clean, before they'll believe anything."

Several days later, on August 6, John Morris delivered the bottle and the piece of wood in a bucket of saltwater to the federal court in Tampa to "arrest" the site — to keep anyone else from legally tampering with it. Located 100 miles offshore, the wreck lay beyond the 12-mile limit of authority that the federal government had over cultural artifacts, and far beyond the State of Georgia's jurisdiction. Legal sanction was nevertheless needed to proceed. "We had to walk the court through some pretty unusual admiralty rights issues," Greg said. "They're not used to dealing with them."

On August 12, the court named Odyssey as "Salvor in Possession," the first step to gaining exclusive rights. The court action provided notice to other parties to file any claims they might have against the ship or its cargo.

The 19th-century steamship was now Odyssey's prime project; the HMS *Sussex* would have to sit on the shelf for the time being. As news of the discovery of the shipwreck was released, Odyssey stock began to soar. The next step would be to convince serious investors and backers that the wreck was clearly the coin-laden *Republic*. But the preliminary evidence looked solid.

Within days of finding the ship, with a new five-million-dollar financial offering in place, the company had completed purchase of the support vessel for which John Morris had begun negotiating in anticipation of turning to the *Sussex* project. She was a 251-foot former fishing trawler turned into a deep-ocean survey vessel known as the *Northern Prince*. She was outfitted with dynamically positioned thrusters; these allowed her to remain stationary over a site deep in the water below. They renamed her *Odyssey Explorer*.

To pair up with their new vessel, the team had located a huge and idle cable-industry ROV. With its considerable size, it would be ideal for working in the stormy underweather of the Gulf Stream.

Odyssey decided to refit its new ship in Baltimore, the port that in 1853 had launched the SS *Tennessee*. They sent an overhaul team under the supervision of Roy Truman, an Englishman and 30-year veteran of commercial ROV and deep-ocean exploration work. For Truman, this was a boyhood dream come true. "I quit my job to do this," he said. "I always said that if I had the money, I'd go buy a ship and an ROV and go looking at the bottom of the ocean."

Truman, who lived in Annapolis, Maryland, but kept a home in northern England, got into ROVs after a harrowing incident. "I was in the cable-laying business," he said, "and we were off the coast of Ireland with the U.S. Navy, trying to recover a manned submersible trapped on the bottom. We got them up with only hours to spare, and the cable company decided that they would never use manned vehicles again. They wanted a commercial ROV designed. I was sent by my company to help in the design work in San Diego at the Bell Laboratories, in 1976."

Roy Truman's new challenge, the ROV that Odyssey renamed *Zeus*, was originally a seven-ton, van-sized robot built to bury trans-oceanic fiber optic cable. It ran along the sea floor on treads like a tank. Already outfitted with precise acoustic positioning capabilities, it was rated for depths to 8,200 feet. It featured two titanium manipulator arms, hydraulically driven, that were sensitive enough to handle fragile glass artifacts, yet powerful enough to toss wood and rock aside.

"It was a system designed to travel over a cable route on the sea floor and bury the cables as it went," explained Jim Starr, one of Odyssey's ROV supervisors, also a veteran deep-ocean recovery engineer. "It simply blew a trench into the sea floor, emulsified the bottom material so the cable buried itself by its own weight, and was safe from fish nets or sabotage."

To repurpose the ROV for salvage and science, Odyssey had to build virtually a new vehicle. They took off the treads and replaced them with skids. They also had to replace the powerful bottom-scouring equipment with a water-evacuation system, which could operate as either a giant suction device or a blower, but was delicate enough to work around sensitive areas without damaging them. In the ROV's original set-up, most power had gone into the hydraulic system that operated the trench-blower. Now, that power was redirected to its manipulator arms and to the thrusters that enabled it to "fly" — to maneuver deftly around a wreck site.

"Those old motors were huge," said Starr. "I could barely pull one off the deck. All that metal — and strictly for cable burial."

Zeus was a beast. It ran at 200 horsepower, one of the most powerful ROV's ever built, and needed a large frame to support that kind of stress. "A smaller vehicle wouldn't work in the Gulf Stream with its continuous current," noted Starr. "It couldn't do the multi-tasking. This is a work-class ROV, the largest size. But you would never know, from a driver's standpoint, that it's so big. It has the response of a smaller ROV. Only if you needed to work in a tight space would you consider a smaller one."

Few companies or institutions had attempted to fabricate an ROV with specific archaeological capabilities for the deep sea. Ocean celebrity Robert Ballard, a geologist who has been the public face of ocean exploration for decades, had recently unveiled his new deep-ocean ROV for archaeology, *Hercules II.* Ballard's machine was designed for lighter, more delicate scientific work, and was intentionally much smaller so it could be moved from one ship to another. But with a dedicated research vessel, Odyssey could afford to permanently mount its huge ROV system and not have to worry about moving it.

"This is now a new class of vehicle — there's nothing else in the world like it," said Starr with obvious pride. "The navy has similar ROVs, but they are made only for certain functions. This is a search, salvage, photo, and lighting sled, with 200 horsepower, able to handle high-definition cameras, 35mm film cameras, and a variety of lights. It can be a video-mosaic sled to document the site. Then it turns seamlessly into a sled to retrieve objects, load a fourplex gently with glass artifacts, and bring it up. I see no end in sight for this vehicle." The ROV was seriously complex, yet deliciously simple, just a frame on which to hang the needed ornaments such as lights and cameras.

In September, after three intense weeks of refitting the ROV and welding its crane to the ship, a mission team of 43 men embarked on the *Odyssey Explorer* from Baltimore harbor, led by Greg as head of operations, and Roy Truman as his right hand.

Compared to the part-timers who fill many academic expeditions, these men were pros. Both of the deck ROV supervisors, Robert Leedy and Jim Starr, were veterans of the oil and gas industries and deep-ocean U.S. Navy projects. They and their crews were used to working around heaving ships and submersibles under offshore conditions, day in and day out.

Both the master of the ship, Mike Paterson, and his chief officer, George Renardson, were Englishmen whose utterances in a heavy Yorkshire brogue were so undecipherable that they might as well have been speaking Polish — which would have been preferred by the rest of the crew, mostly from Poland, who came with the ship. The meals served good-naturedly from the galley of Polish cook Janusz Rutkowski were heavy on carbohydrates and starches, with an old socialist flair for the dull, but no one suffered from malnutrition. It was a working ship. The only frill was a television lounge that pulled in satellite signals for important football games and news. But there was something new, too.

This time there were scientists. On board were archaeologist Neil Cunningham Dobson, a 47-year-old Scot who had spent time in the British Merchant Marine, and conservator Herb Bump, 73, former head of marine conservation for the State of Florida. Dobson had excavated a 17th-century galleon off the east coast of England with SCUBA. When he signed on to work with Odyssey, Dobson came under fire from his colleagues in academia, who questioned the value and potential of this endeavor. But Dobson knew where he stood on the matter. "The archaeology on the *Republic* is made possible by the search for money," he said, "but while we're down there, for whatever reason, let's take advantage."

Dobson considered himself a new realist in the profession. "Let's face it," he said, "only the commercial side has the money and the toys and technology to carry it out. It's time that archaeologists learned that by working with the commercial side they'll be able to do so much more.

"I like the astronaut analogy. It's the closest to what we're trying to do in deep water. The archaeologist can't be in charge of the whole thing. He needs the engineers and computer programmers to get him there. Only then does the archaeology start. We can't dictate, as we might on land, exactly what goes on. The 'astronauts' and engineers operate the equipment to get me there, for my own work.

"And at the end of the day, I don't care whether a university or a commercial company pays me to do archaeology. I perform to the same standard regardless, as I am a professional. For underwater archaeology to succeed in this century, you have got to live with your neighbors — technology and business."

Also aboard the *Odyssey Explorer* was a three-man film crew from National Geographic television, as well as Jonathan Blair, a veteran photographer for *National Geographic* magazine. The *Republic,* after all, was a hell of a good story. But the launching in mid-September was delayed. Ready to set off into the Atlantic for a test run, the *Odyssey Explorer* faced the same conditions that the steamship *Republic* had over a century earlier. Hurricane Isabel was brewing in the Atlantic.

Always the optimist, Greg had hoped to get in some test maneuvers and dives before she hit, but the plan was quickly scuttled as the hurricane bore down on the coastline with sustained winds of 100 miles per hour, throwing up 20-foot seas. The storm made landfall at North Carolina's Outer Banks, tearing past Cape Hatteras to strike near Kitty Hawk on September 19. Millions were left without power in North Carolina and Maryland, and more than a dozen lives were lost. In the protection of Baltimore harbor, the *Odyssey Explorer*'s staff and crew moved the ship to a safer berth, hunkered down, and rode the storm out. Some took it as an omen: what the Gulf Stream claimed could not so easily be recovered.

One of the most damaging tropical storms of the decade, Isabel tore a vicious path through much of the northeast coast of the United States. Just two days later, on September 21, *Odyssey Explorer* ventured forth from Baltimore for trials, now in a quieter sea. The winds seemed back in their bottle. After a week, it returned to port for supplies and prepared to steam south. On October 7, a hundred miles off Savannah, the ship settled into position over the site of the wreck and cranked up its new system.

The first mission was simple but crucial: to find something akin to a name tag on the wreck lying at the bottom to confirm without a doubt that they were on the site of the SS *Republic*. The operation began as most deep-water search and recovery projects do. To hover over the site, the *Odyssey Explorer*, the mother ship, heads directly into the Gulf Stream, matching the current, so she effectively stays in one place. Additional side-thrusters help to keep the ship positioned accurately.

To launch the ROV, a crane lifts and pivots the multi-ton device from the starboard deck into the water, a four-man team loosening the ratchet straps and guiding it down. The giant ROV floats near the surface like a shining jellyfish, twisting and bobbing in the waves. Then it sinks, dragging a line of floats behind it, and reels off steel cable from a winch on the ship's stern. In the cable's core are glass fiber-optic lines; these transmit operational signals from the *Odyssey Explorer*'s control room to the underwater ROV.

The pilot and co-pilot "fly" the ROV from their seats at a console, something like the cockpit of an airplane contained within a metal "control van" welded to the aft deck. The pilot moves the immense ROV with a joystick that approximates the controls of a sophisticated computer game. He holds the set of three black levers on his knees, so he can virtually feel the movement of the 7-ton robot operating as much as a mile and a half deep in the sea below. His eyes are fixed on the monitor's screen, which displays video streaming from a camera mounted on the front of the ROV. It's a master-slave relationship; whatever the pilot does with his stick, the ROV repeats below.

The deep-ocean video scene also plays on another set of monitors in the data documentation and navigation room. There, four technicians record important data, such as each artifact's time of recovery and coordinates.

There is also a third control room. On the bulkhead of a large archaeological "offline" room in the lower deck, a 42-inch color plasma monitor displays the movements of the ROV — like an endless *National Geographic* special. Here is where the managing team of Greg, Ernie Tapanes, archaeologist Dobson, and conservator Bump watched the movements of the ROV in high definition, ready to relay any instructions by radio to the pilots and the deck supervisor.

As the ROV works on the bottom, it is stabilized by a heavy clumpweight that hangs suspended from the cable some 30 meters above the ROV. The clumpweight stabilizes the cable against the strain of the current that blows like wind at the nearly half mile of cable above. The ROV can then ramble more freely, like a dog at the end of a leash, without having to fight the drag of the entire rig.

Zeus's electric motor drives a pump that hydraulically feeds oil pressure to the thrusters — propellers that move the machine up, down, and sideways. This hydraulic pressure also works the manipulator arms and the jaws at the end of the arms.

The ROV as originally designed was capable of great force. Now its two major excavation tools were much more delicate. One is called a venturi hose; six inches in diameter, it can act as either a blower or a vacuum to remove sand from a spot of particular interest. The other device is a soft suction cup, called a limpet, that can pick up individual artifacts gently without leaving a mark on them.

As *Zeus* roamed the cold darkness around the sunken ship's skeleton on those early October days of 2003, its video unambiguously revealed the remains of an old steamer, sitting upright but at a tilt, half-buried in an overlay of sand and coral hardpan. The bow was shattered but the stern seemed intact. Whatever vessel it was, the wreck formed a hillock on the plain of the ocean floor, a mound of debris in the middle. Under the weight of the cargo, the hull had collapsed like a cooked onion, leaving cave-like spaces underneath the shattered decking.

Two men were reported to have died flailing in the open waters as the *Republic* sank. Those two, described only as an elderly sea captain and a German sailor, never reached any lifeboat or the raft. Their bodies undoubtedly drifted off to far lonelier parts of the sea floor and were not likely to be found near this wreck. This was not a gravesite.

As the ROV floated silently over the site, the team saw an amazing variety of artifacts. Across the wreck lay piles of patent-medicine bottles, cases of inkwells, bolts of silk cloth for dresses, elegant decanters, glass buttons, porcelain dishes, and metal bedpans. Stacked window panes glinted back at the camera. Bottles filled with fruit appeared ready for pies. Leather shoes clung together spoon-fashion in a non-existent crate — soles lost at sea. Ceramic and milk-glass religious items lay strewn about — praying angels on their knees, a sculpted Madonna and child. Candleholders lay like cordwood, their packaging dissolved.

If this were the SS *Republic*, everything that the city of New Orleans had needed in the months after the Civil War rested here in a compact pile beneath 1,700 feet of water — a time capsule of aid, relief, and reconstruction. Many unopened boxes, crates, and pieces of luggage lay scattered among the spars and remnants of pine decking. Each bag surely held an intimate subplot: someone had once leaned over it, packing it with socks and shirts and underwear, perhaps adding a present for Aunt May in Baton Rouge.

In the stern lay the immense rudder, the size of a station wagon. Only its copper sheathing, with its brass gudgeons and pintles, held the decayed wood together. The boiler was encrusted with green and yellow algae and coral, and fish filled the engine room, their eyes reflecting the lights of the ROV like so many stars.

As the ghostly high-tech *Zeus* floated silently by, red crabs pirouetted among the scrap metal. In the bow lay the intact windlass, with its chain still holding onto the anchor, flukes erect, waiting for something to cling to. Magenta fish darted among the eerie spokes of the paddlewheel skeletons, and the 30-foot-tall walking beam, shaggy with marine growth, towered above the site like a Druid deity.

"Standing in defiance," breathed Neil Dobson, eyes fixed on the panorama unfolding on the huge screen. "It seems like a memorial to the place — the old lady, battered over the years, but still standing, saying, 'I'm not done yet.'"

Neil and Herb Bump had predicted there would be little original archaeology involved with a wreck from 1865, that all variations of the artifacts were probably already well known and catalogued. But there was power in the tumbled composition of the shipwreck; it was a collage of the familiar that had become a work of art, an evocative still-life, except that the constant wash of the current bathed and scoured everything in a stream of plankton, sand, and debris. Once a locus of disaster for humans, cast from their cabins to drift for days at the mercy of wind and wave, the shipwreck had now become a shelter from the endless flow of the Gulf Stream for fish and shrimp.

"You could spend years there excavating the wreck," said Neil, wistfully.

On the second day out, October 9, the pilot of the ROV spied something metallic between a ruin of spars. He panned the camera to zoom in on the object: a ship's bell. The recovery team was delighted, yet apprehensive. Recovery of this crucial object could be a moment to confirm years of persistence — or send them all back to the monotony of scanning an endless sea floor.

The next day, *Zeus* returned to the spot. Carefully, it clamped its viselike claws around the bottom of the cracked, 14-inch-tall hunk of brass and slid it into a large plastic container on the front of the ROV. Then, so slowly, it lifted the bell to the surface.

Corrosion blurred much of the engraved name, but four letters were clearly etched within a stylized ribbon: *SSEE*.

Was it indeed the right ship? After a brief moment of concern, the answer became obvious. The original bell of the *Tennessee* had never been changed when the ship was renamed.

Now it was beyond doubt: Odyssey had its prize, after years of seeking.

CHAPTER 8

Plantation Bitters
& Greenback Speculators

WILLIAM NICHOLS AND HIS brother, Henry, survivors of the lost *Republic,* were happy to be delivered by the steamship *General Hooker* to Charleston. There, for the first time in days, they could sleep in a nice hotel on dry land. If they were shaken by their recent ordeal, they nonetheless decided to proceed on to New Orleans.

They caught a train to the shattered city of Atlanta, where William posted a long letter to his wife, Thyrza, detailing the adventures of his interrupted journey. Somewhere, William may have also managed to replenish his substantial funds; he was not intending to abandon his search for attractive investments around the New Orleans area. When and how he was able to tap into his considerable financial resources is a small mystery. Certainly when the *Republic* had been abandoned, no one was allowed to carry anything onto the lifeboats but what they had on their backs and in their pockets. Perhaps he was influential enough to know somebody in Charleston or Atlanta who helped him draw money from a local bank.

From Atlanta the two brothers continued southwest to Mobile, Alabama. On Mobile Bay, they boarded a local steamer; as they left the bay, they passed the site where Farragut had led his fleet through deadly minefields just a few years earlier. The local packet headed out to the Gulf of Mexico and followed the coast west and into Lake Pontchartrain.

There, it docked on the north shore of a narrow isthmus between the lake and the nearby Mississippi where the French had built New Orleans at the mouth of the great river. Amid the Pontchartrain docks and working-class eating houses, the Nichols brothers boarded a local train that took them into the heart of the city.

Arriving in late autumn, they had missed the worst of the debilitating heat of a New Orleans summer. But the squalor of life in that once-great cosmopolitan city must have been a shock to the brothers, who were used to the disciplined life of New England. To be fair, the despised Union occupation had cleaned up the worst of the sewage and standing water that had bred disease. New Orleans in November 1865, as the Nichols brothers strode down its streets, was a healthier place in many ways than it had been before the war. But the city was still a hotbed of bitterness and unfulfilled dreams, and just starting to find traction for its economic recovery.

Writes historian Henry Clay Warmoth of those times, "New Orleans was a dirty, impoverished, and hopeless city, with a mixed, ignorant, corrupt, and bloodthirsty gang in control. It was flooded with lotteries, gambling dens, and licensed brothels. Many of the city's officials, as well as the police force, were thugs and murderers."

The Nichols brothers found a porter to carry their bags along the granite-brick of Canal Street to a hotel in the American Quarter, where the desk clerk was sure to speak English. Later they may have strolled down to the edge of the muddy Mississippi, the lifeline of New Orleans. There, they would have seen that a gritty commerce had already emerged from the chaos, that the wide wooden wharves had come back to life.

Indeed, on October 25, the day the *Republic* sank, 15 steamships had left from New Orleans, most en route to Mobile, Memphis, and other regional ports. And among the arrivals that day, according to the *New Orleans Picayune,* was "the *Alabama,* direct from Liverpool. It is the first arrival of a steamer from a regular line, and is consequently quite an event in our annals." The *Alabama* had chugged through the swells of the Atlantic, making the crossing successfully in milder weather before the late October hurricane had struck.

New Orleans had survived the war. The city was never burned or razed, as were Atlanta and Richmond. Its inhabitants were never fired upon, or evicted. But New Orleans was short of everything from paper to gold. As the fall of 1865 progressed, the city was in desperate need of the cargo carried by the steamship *Republic,* like a wounded man needing a blood transfusion. The Civil War, with the Union naval blockade of Southern ports since 1861, had stifled commerce and throttled enterprise. Great fortunes accumulated by the "Bourbons" had been lost, and the plantation economy of cotton and sugar that surrounded the Mississippi Delta had collapsed along with the slavery that allowed it to thrive. Many planters simply deserted their homes. Some turned to trades. And those who stayed could no longer afford to keep their estates up to antebellum standards. The New Orleans banks were in a state of ruin, stuck with worthless Confederate money and credits that would never be redeemed. More than half the wealth of Louisiana had been swept away by the war.

At war's end, the federal government had hoped to pull paper money out of circulation and return the nation to a gold and silver standard. But not enough hard coinage existed anywhere to soak up the virtually worthless stacks of paper money. Especially in the South, gold and silver had nearly vanished, and people yearned to feel the jingle of coins in their pockets.

"There is so little silver here that it affords no scope for operations of any magnitude," the *Picayune* noted on November 1, 1865 — a sad report already well known to the newspaper's impoverished readers. Paper bills sold at a fraction of their face value, and, compounding the chaos, in that month a rash of counterfeit U.S. currency bills, in $50 denominations, hit the streets of New Orleans. With his Yankee gold, earned in investments in Vermont and land deals out west, now replenished, Col. William Nichols was loaded to deal.

The old aristocracy of the city must have looked on the Northerners, flaunting their gold double eagles, with scorn tinged with envy and a bit of fear. So many things had changed for the worse in their upper-class eyes. Throughout the city, this was a painful time of social flux as new classes of people moved into prominence. On the rise were the sons and daughters of German and Italian immigrants. They held considerable amounts of urban real estate and had begun moving into channels of power, a new white class replacing the Bourbon aristocracy.

The cultural flavor of the city was under attack on all fronts. The multiracial Creoles, who spoke mostly Spanish and French, were protesting the introduction of English and complained of the large number of "Americans" being appointed to new courts and offices. These same Americans were interfering with their beloved public parades and balls for Mardi Gras, events long central to their distinctive heritage.

Even more provocative for many old New Orleanians, African-Americans were pressing forward in the opening acts of their liberation. July 1865 saw the establishment of public schools for blacks, opened by the Bureau of Refugees, Freedmen, and Abandoned Lands, commonly known as the Freedmen's Bureau, a federal program to create opportunities for former slaves. Whites with nostalgia for a past when no such thing would ever have been considered put up a furious protest. The *Picayune* published parts of a speech by one Mr. Austin at the Ninth Street Market:

> This is the white man's government. God never intended that the Negro should be equal to the white man. (Here the great crowd gave a tremendous cheer). The Negro is at present a drug in the country. Even the Freedman's bureau, which has

pampered him in his sloth and idleness, has declared he must work or leave the country.

Racial resentment that went to the core of Southern identity seethed on the streets. Not only was the black population free, but some African-Americans had been put into positions of authority. And nothing enraged some Southerners as much as black policemen taking weapons away from white men who brandished them in public.

In his book *Race and Reunion*, Civil War scholar David Blight analyzed their anger: "The bulk of white Southerners had experienced the psychological trauma of defeat; their world had been turned upside down, and they simply could not abide the presence of assertive blacks wearing uniforms and carrying guns, organizing union leagues, or voting and serving in the legislature and on the judicial bench."

Yet of all major Southern cities, New Orleans was the only one that was functional. That's why the city drew in not only Northern opportunists, but also Southerners eager to get on with civilian life. Did William Nichols know that one of his adversaries at the Battle of Gettysburg, former Confederate General James "Ole Pete" Longstreet, had set up shop in New Orleans as the head of a lucrative new insurance company? Longstreet, however, was among the few Confederate leaders who chose to deal with defeat by moving on to a new reality. He even joined the Republican Party, which was anathema to old-guard New Orleanians as a bi-racial party that allowed African Americans to belong. In the heated rhetoric of the times, Longstreet was socially ostracized and branded a traitor to the Southern cause.

In this social and economic maelstrom, at a time when New Orleans was running on dregs, the cargo of the *Republic* would have been an important infusion of goods and cash. Some of the merchandise cast overboard at the height of the storm, such as boxes of shoes, may have been headed upriver for plantations and other towns, since New Orleans was still the supply point for much of the Mississippi Valley.

More likely, most of the lost items were headed for the city itself. The new schools, for example, needed the slates and inkwells that were lost at sea. Dress-making shops on Canal Street had to restock their shelves with bolts of material. And sorely missed by men and women alike were the contents of the many clear and colored bottles of patent-medicine elixirs, which promised to conquer all woes and cure all malaise. Instead, thousands of those bottles lay spilled across the bottom of the deep ocean somewhere off the coast of Georgia.

These were concoctions mixed and marketed by Northern opportunists, although with names like Drake's Plantation Bitters, a number of the products seemed targeted for a disenchanted Southern populace, who surely needed a stiff shot of something to cure the uneasy feeling that things weren't going to get better any time soon. On the day of the *Republic's* sinking, the *New Orleans Picayune* had advertised that very product with the claim: "Certainly Plantation Bitters will do it when nothing else will. Melancholy, depression, hypochondria, insanity, all spring, more or less, from a diseased stomach, and this Plantation Bitters is a sure cure for."

"More or less" was at least a token gesture of a 19th-century version of truth in advertising. In 1865 an understanding of medical principles was still unclear. Illnesses were thought to be derived from the four "primary humors" — blood, phlegm, yellow bile (choler), and black bile (melancholy); this theory of substances that ruled human physiology was first proposed in the late Middle Ages. In a city where diseases such as cholera and yellow fever ran rampant, patent elixirs of all types were common, especially among the working classes, who couldn't afford doctors.

Another reason, though, for the broad popularity of these medicines of uncertain benefit was their high alcohol content. In an age of creeping temperance, a slug of bitters was an acceptable way for a lady to get a little buzz on.

Even the occupying Union army relied on patent medicines, recommending one particular concoction, "Dr. Hostetter's Stomach Bitters," to its soldiers as a means to ward off New Orleans' slew of evil diseases. An indication of its main active ingredient, Hostetter's was also sold by the shot in saloons. Without dwelling on the alcoholic content of 45 percent by volume, ads for the product claimed it offered "a positive protection against the fatal maladies of the Southern swamps, and the poisonous tendency of the impure rivers and bayous." Sadly for the thirsty men and women of New Orleans, hundreds of Hostetter's bottles now lay at the bottom of the Gulf Stream.

But the greatest setback for New Orleans from the loss of the side-wheel steamer was noted only in passing in the paper: "We see it stated that there was not less than $400,000 in gold coin on the ill-fated 'Republic,' from New York for this port." It was a shrug of the shoulders from a city becoming used to loss and defeat.

That fall, the *Republic* was only one of several steamships due to arrive in New Orleans with hard money from northern ports, so perhaps her loss was not an event of tragic proportions. True, each arriving ship was anxiously awaited by the investors, banks, and merchants who depended on the goods and currencies she carried. And $400,000 in sorely needed specie would have made a real impact on the city's economy. Still, the voyage of the *Republic* was not an orchestrated public relief effort or act of charity; it was business.

The basis of the game was that the purchasing power of hard currency in the South was nearly double that in the North. So sharp-eyed northern bankers were looking for quick profits in arbitrage — trading on the relatively higher value of hard money against bills and notes. A man carrying gold and silver coins might well trade them on New Orleans' Canal Street for ten times their value in greenbacks, then take the paper money back to New York or to a U.S. mint, where he got full value in return. Under the laws of the day, there was nothing illegal in that. So speculators who had the gold or silver coinage and the means to travel beat a trail to the South's beleaguered cities after the end of the war.

The real loser was the federal government, forced to cash in the flow of greenbacks bought up on the cheap. By and large, the Southerners found scarce benefit from this game; they had little choice but to sit on the sidelines and try to get what they could from the paper money in trade. The Northerners and their local allies with cash had the upper hand, and they were not generally loved for it.

The money carried on the *Republic* came from private sources, not government, and its intended destination in New Orleans has not been found in any shipping records. But the distribution may have been similar to the coinage from another steamer reported by the *Picayune* on October 25:

> . . . the *Evening Star* brought $376,412, embracing 100,000 to Messrs. Brown, Bro. and company, $84,000 for the Citizens' Bank, $50,000 to the Canal Bank, a like amount to another party, $47,456 to Mssrs. Wm. Edwards and company, and $10,000 to Mr. J. Barker. The *Evening Star* also brought $525,000 in National Currency on freight, but how much more came by mail and through other channels we can hardly conjecture, the aggregate amount being variously estimated at from $1,500,000 to 2 million dollars.

This was a huge river of cash. While the profits flowed elsewhere, at least the hard coinage could be expected to soothe a bit of the pent-up demand for it. But even though coin arrived by the millions of dollars, it did not seem enough to satisfy the needs of an immense area whose economy had been shattered. On November 10 the newspaper reported, "The *General Washington* has come in with 1,000,000 in specie plus greenbacks worth $319,483." Then came a polite lament: "The supply of domestic Exchange is still unequal to the demand."

For profit or not, the parade of coin-laden steamships was the city's lifeline. But with the heavy coastal traffic through the Atlantic's mercurial waters, shipwrecks were fairly common. The *Picayune* reported on October 25 of another potential tragedy: "Considerable uneasiness was felt here on account of a report, extensively circulated, that the steamship *North Star*, of the New York and New Orleans Star line, had been lost. It was, however, subsequently learned that she sprung a leak at sea, and put into Norfolk before taking much water."

The Nichols brothers, gold-rich and with the glow of survivors rescued from near death, must have been bemused by the colorful confusion of New Orleans, a tropical port where all the earthly pleasures paraded in the streets. But they were practical New Englanders, and their mission was business. William had to regain the family capital and pay back a debt he owed to his father.

The term "carpetbaggers" had not yet come into use and does not apply to speculators or investors like the Nichols brothers or the Northern bankers who had sent money on the ill-fated *Republic* hoping to turn a profit in the New Orleans area. The term, later applied mostly to political opportunists, was derived from the cheap luggage used by those who swept into the lingering chaos of Southern communities to reap the benefits of others' ruin, men eager to make personal gain and then disappear as quickly.

William Nichols was not a carpetbagger, but a serious investor who would risk his money and, as it turned out from his steamship journey, his life, to seek opportunities in the South after the war, and his conduct was never known to be unethical. Certainly the Colonel had a lot of money at his beck and call, despite his recent misadventures in speculations near the end of the war, reported to involve staggering losses of $100,000. Undaunted, William and Henry wasted no time after arriving in New Orleans in 1865 to venture out from the Crescent City to Marshall, Texas, in Harrison County across the state line from Shreveport, Louisiana, to try their luck.

In a series of bold moves, William Nichols rapidly bought up two bankrupt plantations, complete with livestock, tools, and $30,000 worth of cotton, which he promptly sold, gaining the profits to pay for yet more land. He also purchased a three-quarter interest in a large Texas tannery, complete with 2,800 acres of land and 8,000 hides in process.

The *Republic's* other 49 survivors moved on with their lives as well, although few were as richly documented as that of William Nichols. Records show that William's younger brother, Maj. Henry J. Nichols, stayed in the Texas area. In 1867, he was married in Marshall to a woman named Lillie Fassitt Purnell, daughter of Maj. Thomas F. Purnell of the 54th Indiana. Together they had six children. Census data shows Henry listed in 1870 as a lawyer, then in the 1880s he finds work as a traveling salesman for a Dallas dry-goods company. For his Civil War service with the 11th Vermont Infantry and 1st Vermont Heavy Artillery, he drew a pension, which noted he had been wounded in the left arm. He died in 1910, in his mid-60s, and was buried in the Officers' Lot at Arlington National Cemetery in Washington, less heralded but perhaps no less a war hero than his wealthier sibling.

Through military records, we know that the valiant Lt. Louis V. Caziarc of Boston went on to a distinguished career in the army. After the shipwreck, he reached New Orleans to serve as aide-de-camp to General Edward R.S. Canby, who in 1864 had been appointed military commander of the West Mississippi Division.

Canby had succeeded Benjamin "Beast" Butler and General Nathanial Banks as commander of the division headquartered in New Orleans. Canby had been charged with restoring not only military but also economic order. The general had arrived in New Orleans while the war was still raging to discover that commerce between the North and the Gulf Coast region, legal and illegal, was flourishing in the city — and that Union troops, both navy and army, were thick in the middle of the contraband trade. General Canby had set about to weed out corruption and restore discipline to the Union forces under his new command.

Showing up in New Orleans after war's end, Lt. Caziarc must have taken to his role serving as Canby's aide, as the young officer repeatedly requested service with the commander. Caziarc went on to serve with General Canby in Charleston in the reconstruction efforts of the entire Southeast. Although he suffered bouts of malaria in 1869, he recovered sufficiently to join Canby again at Fort Klamath, Oregon, during the insurrection of the Modoc Indians.

The Modoc War in the Tule Lake area of northern California was a treacherous and heartbreaking affair in which Canby was killed by a Modoc chief named Captain Jack, who had accepted peace but needed to save face in front of his people. As Captain Jack sat with a delegation of Modocs to hear Canby's speech, he suddenly drew out his pistol and shot the general in the face. He proceeded to pull out a knife and stab Canby several times, then stripped the general of his uniform and put it on himself. Caziarc was in the middle of the melee, trying to protect his general, and later joined the expedition to hunt down the assassins. Captain Jack and five of his men were later hanged for the crime.

Promoted to captain and transferred to the U.S. Army Signal Corps, Caziarc became part of the lore of the disastrous Greely Arctic Expedition of 1882. The bumptious Lt. A. W. Greely had commanded 24 men in a vain attempt to reach the North Pole, sponsored by the Signal Corps, but his expedition bogged down. The nation anxiously read confident dispatches sent back as winter closed in. An article in the *Saturday Evening Post* of September 14, 1883, quoted Caziarc as saying: "There is no reason to believe that the Greely party will suffer for want of food even though relief fails to reach them this year; as there are several stations at which provisions are stored that are known to Lieutenant Greely." But only seven of the 25 explorers survived the ill-fated adventure, including Greely himself, barely lasting through a starvation-plagued, harrowing winter until saved. Greely eventually became one of the founders of the National Geographic Society.

In his vivid and varied career, Caziarc went on to teach military history at Bowdoin College in Maine. In 1901, promoted to the rank of major in the Artillery Corps, he accepted duties as the supervisor of police, provost marshal, and head of the Secret Service Police of Havana, Cuba. He retired in 1906 with the rank of brigadier general.

Capt. Charles Sauvinet, the African-American Union officer, served five years as the cashier for the Freedmen's Bureau in New Orleans. The bureau was established to help emancipated slaves integrate into American society as freed laborers, but its policies enraged the city's white blue-collar workers, who could see only their own downfall in the rise of the blacks.

Sauvinet, as a prominent member of the African-American community in New Orleans, must have been a target of the white laborers' spite and anger, but he managed to survive the infamous "Mechanics' Institute Massacre" and later offered testimony in Congressional hearings into the cause of the tragedy. The riot occurred in the summer of 1866, less than a year after the sinking of the *Republic.* Sauvinet narrowly escaped harm when a mob of white Confederate veterans, aided by New Orleans police and firemen, attacked a delegation of white "radical" Republicans and their African-American supporters, including a good number of veterans of the Louisiana Native Guards.

The delegates had come to the city, despite threats, to agitate for civil rights. They were meeting in the Mechanics' Institute building at the time of the vicious attack. At least 37 people were killed and nearly 150 wounded in the mayhem, mostly African-Americans, but also crusading whites such as Anthony P. Dostie, a dentist, whose advocacy of rights for black citizens provoked rage among the rioters. Dostie was shot in the spine and stabbed in the stomach with a sword.

Charles Sauvinet must have had the mark of authority on him, for he soon parleyed his bank job into one of the city's most influential positions. In 1870, only four years after the massacre, Sauvinet became sheriff of Orleans Parish, the first African-American sheriff in the South. He sent his son to Howard University in Washington, D.C., and was active in the early struggle for American civil rights, winning a case in the New Orleans district court in 1871 against a drinking establishment that refused to serve him because he was a "colored" person. Sauvinet cited the Civil Rights Act of 1869 and was awarded $1,000.

The fate of Captain Benjamin F. Ryer, who had helped lead one of the *Republic's* lifeboats to safety, was less noble. His service record shows a descending spiral of unexplained absences, disorderly conduct, arrests, and confinements in army prisons. Although alcohol was never mentioned in his record, he was said to "lose consciousness" at awkward times. After being given chance after chance to straighten out, on April 13, 1870, he was "cashiered and dismissed from the service by sentence of General Court Martial," as the record states.

The *Republic's* captain, Edward Young, died in Brooklyn, New York, in February 1891. His obituary, published in the *Brooklyn Daily Eagle,* noted that the American sea captain, born in England in 1813, had served with distinction as commander of a number of clipper ships but that the steamship *Republic* was his last charge, that he had lived a quiet life in New York thereafter until his death.

Captain Hawthorne (whose first name is yet to be discovered) died while commanding a ship in a Florida hurricane, only ten years after the wreck of the *Republic.*

For all the other passengers on the steamship, New Orleans had been their destination on that interrupted journey in October 1865. After the shipwreck, some of them probably continued on, as the Nichols brothers had, to the city on the crescent of the Mississippi River. But if they had known New Orleans before the war, they would have discovered it a changed city from the one they remembered. As summarized in a 1900 history:

> [New Orleans] narrowly missed its destiny, which would have made it the greatest commercial city in the world. When the Civil War erupted New Orleans was at the height of prosperity. But the Jeffersonian dream that it would become the port and emporium of the entire Mississippi Valley (for which the Louisiana Purchase was made) failed. Instead, steam allowed ships to go upstream on the Mississippi, railroads connected the east coast to St. Louis and Chicago, and the way West went through land instead of steamships.

If economic greatness was lost, the city's party mood proved unquenchable. After the Union occupation, the first ship that arrived in port carried fine wines and silks from France — staples for all the dandies and ladies of the town. City newspapers were already running with gossip and gaiety, after long years of grim wartime news. A newspaper column called "Town Talk" devoted itself to the praise of fair ladies: "Saturday and Monday were perfect gala days for le grande Canal," crowed the *New Orleans Times* of October 25.

> Such an array of youth and beauty it seldom witnessed, even in our city of beautiful women . . . (but don't let it reach the little beauties' ears. It won't do to let them know how pretty we think them; it might — remember we only say it might — make them a leetle vain).

SS *Tennessee* depicted as passenger ship for the Morgan Line (oil painting by Charles Drew, 1860). The ship was later was renamed the USS *Mobile* in 1864, then in 1865 became the SS *Republic*. *Image: Peabody Essex Museum, Salem, Massachusetts.*

View of busy Baltimore Harbor in the 1850s. View is from Federal Hill, looking across inner bay toward Fort McHenry. Fells Point (where *Tennessee* was built by John A. Robb) is seen at upper right of far shoreline across bay. The machine works (Charles Reeder and Sons) where her engine and boilers were built were on the near shore, approximately in center of this view. *Image: Enoch Pratt Free Library/ State Library Resource Center, Baltimore, Maryland.*

Only 5'2" and weighing 120 pounds, William Walker was a forceful speaker and a fearless fighter who raised a private army of men called "filibusters." Many of his irregular troops were transported to Nicaragua aboard the SS *Tennessee*, which later carried some of the survivors home to the U.S. after his defeat. *Image: © Corbis*.

Below: "Immigrants" for the army raised by William Walker for his Nicaraguan adventure. From boys aged 14 to men in their 60s, Americans flocked to the call for mercenary troops to support Walker when he headed to Central America. *Image: Library of Congress*.

NICARAGUA.—FILLIBUSTERS REPOSING AFTER THE BATTLE IN THEIR QUARTERS AT THE CONVENT.

Port of New Orleans from Mandeville Street, circa 1858–1859. New Orleans was America's hub in the Gulf of Mexico for ships from around the world. Here, cargoes were unloaded and dispersed to points up the Mississippi, with cotton and other goods reloaded for export. During her colorful history, the SS *Tennessee*, later SS *Republic*, made many stops at this port with passengers and cargo. Painting by Marie Adrien Persac. *Image: Williams Research Center, The Historic New Orleans Collection.*

New Orleans Mint. Many of the coins that eventually ended up in the shipwreck of the SS *Republic* were minted here. *Image: Library of Congress.*

Flag Officer David G. Farragut, later Rear Admiral, was one of the Union's great heroes of the Civil War. In a bold attack, he captured New Orleans in 1862, then led the naval forces that eventually were victorious on the Mississippi River and at the Battle of Mobile Bay. At several points during the war, he adopted the USS *Tennessee* as his flagship, and was aboard her when word of the surrender of Vicksburg arrived, a moment considered one of the turning points in the war. *Photo: Library of Congress.*

As depicted in *Harper's Weekly,* Farragut's squadron enters the Mississippi River to attack New Orleans in April 1862. *Image: Naval Historical Foundation.*

Massachusetts officer Lt. Louis V. Caziarc, a passenger on the final voyage of the SS *Republic*, distinguished himself in the war at the land siege of Mobile as aide-de-camp to Gen. George L. Andrews. Caziarc's appointments were with units of the U.S. Colored Troops, including one assignment as lieutenant for the 73rd USCT, originally known as the 1st Regiment of the Louisiana Native Guards from New Orleans. The African-American regiments had white officers like Caziarc in command roles but had their own line officers at lower ranks. *Photo: courtesy Steven and Janice Caziarc.*

The Louisiana Native Guards (later known as Corps d'Afrique and eventually as regiments of U.S. Colored Troops), served — curiously, as did the steamship *Tennessee* — on both sides of the War Between the States. The Native Guards were first mustered in 1861 as a token Confederate regiment. Mostly, however, the men were kept unarmed and inactive, and eventually the unit was disbanded. After Farragut took New Orleans in 1862, the Native Guards were reorganized as three Union regiments, after which they served with great valor at the Battle of Port Hudson and elsewhere. One of the African-American officers of the Native Guards, Capt. Charles S. Sauvinet, was on board the SS *Republic* when it sank in 1865; this image shows his unit, the 74th Infantry USCT, circa 1864. *Photo: Albin O. Kuhn Library and Gallery, University of Maryland, Baltimore County.*

William T. Nichols served as colonel of the 14th Vermont Regiment and fought heroically in the battle of Gettysburg.

Henry Nichols, younger brother of William Nichols, rose to the rank of major in the Union army and was among the officers present at the Confederate surrender at Appomattox. Both William and Henry were survivors of the SS *Republic* shipwreck.

A richly detailed letter from William to his wife, Thyrza Nichols (below), described the sinking of the ship and his eventual rescue, but may never have reached her. Thyrza died of typhoid fever shortly after receiving an initial telegram stating William and Henry had survived the shipwreck. *Nichols family photos: courtesy Thyrza Nichols Goodeve.*

Greg Stemm as a toddler with his grandfather Clifford "Papa Shell" Shelkofsky, who lost his life in a boating accident when a larger ship passed too close to their small boat while the pair were shark fishing in the Gulf of Mexico.

Greg with his uncle, Cliff Jr., in Papa Shell's fishing boat. This is the same vessel that capsized when Greg was eight years old, leaving the youngster stranded in the Gulf, clinging to the overturned boat. *Photos: courtesy Cliff Shelkofsky Jr.*

Above: A young John Morris (in water, at left), with brother David and father Bob on Indian Lake in Michigan.

Just back from his tour of duty in Vietnam, John Morris prepares to board his father's Piper Aztec. *Photos: courtesy John Morris.*

The crew of the yacht trip that resulted in Greg and John's entry into the ROV business. Back row from left: John Morris, Candy Cressor, Laurie Stemm, Graham Hawkes, Debbie Christen, Greg Stemm, Capt. John Heese. Front row: Ann Bagley, Dan Bagley, Sylvia Earle, Patty Guarino, John Christen, and Bubba Guarino (holding child). Inset (at left) is the original phone message from Bubba that started it all. *Images: courtesy Greg Stemm.*

The Research Vessel (RV) *Seahawk* purchased by Greg Stemm and John Morris at auction from the University of North Carolina in 1986. It would become the platform for their first ROV and side-scan systems.

Photo: Odyssey Marine Exploration.

Dan Bagley and Greg Stemm with some of the nearly 17,000 artifacts recovered from the Dry Tortugas shipwreck.

Gold bars (below left) and chains, silver coins, rare astrolabes, and many olive jars were brought to the surface, along with items as small as seeds and pearls. A fork and a plate bearing the papal seal (below right) were also recovered from this deep-water wreck of a Spanish colonial ship believed to be part of a famous 1622 fleet hit by a hurricane. *Photos: Odyssey Marine Exploration.*

The Dry Tortugas operation was carried out from the 210-foot *Seahawk Retriever* (top). A custom-designed remotely operated vehicle (ROV) named *Merlin* (middle) was the first of its kind developed for deep-ocean archaeological excavation. *Merlin* could record the exact position of artifacts, then pick up delicate items like astrolabes (right), pottery, or organic materials without damage using its manipulator arms. *Photos: Odyssey Marine Exploration.*

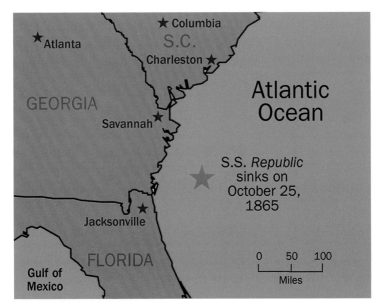

THE STORM ON THE COAST.

Particulars of the Loss of the Steamship Republic.

Safety of the Majority of Her Passengers and Crew.

One Boat-Load from the Ship Still Unheard Of.

The Captain's Version of the Disaster.

NAMES OF THE PASSENGERS.

It will be remembered that the steamer *Republic*, running on Cromwell's New-Orleans line, between that city and New-York, was wrecked off the coast of Georgia, on the 18th of October, in a heavy gale of wind, proving a total loss. When the ship was on the point of going down, four boats and a raft put off from her. So far as learned, only three of the boats have been heard from. The first was in charge of Capt. YOUNG, of the *Republic*, who was picked up by the brig *J. W. Loville*, of Nova Scotia, and carried into Charleston, S. C., arriving there on the 28th of October. It contained fourteen persons. The second boat was in charge of the first officer, with twelve persons, and after terrible sufferings it arrived in Charleston on Monday last, the 30th of October, having been at sea for six days. The third boat was commanded by Capt. HAWTHORNE, an experienced sailor, who was passenger on board the ill-fated vessel. He succeeded in arriving safely at Hilton Head, with twenty-four passengers, all in good health. The remaining boat and the raft have not, as yet, been heard from, and fears are entertained of their saf---

NAMES OF ---- ------------

The Captain's bo-- ------------

sons :

Capt. E. Young, ------------
H. Morehead, S ------------
C. Whitney and ------------
and two childr- ------------
---; John Hu- ------------
- Leary, sea ------------
--- ----- ---

An article from the *New York Times* in 1865 details the loss of the SS *Republic* at sea. It was one of many pieces of information used in the search for the ship, which sank approximately 100 miles off the coast of Georgia in deep water.

To read more of this and other contemporary newspaper articles, including the letter of appreciation to Capt. Edward Young from passengers saved by his gallant efforts, visit www.lostgold.net.

Map: Rebecca Hagen/Odyssey Marine Exploration. Article: New York Times.

The RV *Odyssey*, the ship that conducted the search for the SS *Republic* wreck, was originally custom built by deep-ocean pioneer Edwin Link in the 1960s. *Photo: Jacques de Rham/Odyssey Marine Exploration.*

Ernie Tapanes, Search Project Manager, on the RV *Odyssey*. Behind him is the small Phantom ROV that acquired the first imges of the SS *Republic*. *Photo: Laura Lionetti Barton/Odyssey Marine Exploration.*

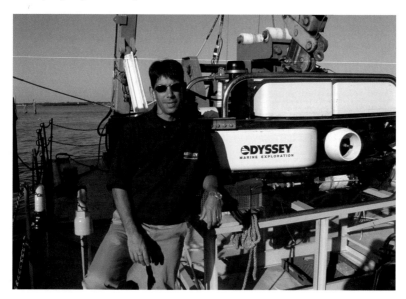

Odyssey's deep-tow Edgetech side-scan sonar "fish" is lowered into the water. This device is towed behind the research vessel, traveling close to the ocean floor to search for anomalies on the sea bed. *Photo: Ernie Tapanes/Odyssey Marine Exploration.*

A sonar "fish" sends data back to shipboard computers. Transducers on each side of the sonar device send out pulses of sound or "pings." For each ping, the fish listens for an echo. Objects on the sea floor reflect the sound; metal is best, but rock, pottery, and other relatively hard objects also reflect well. Acoustic "shadows" help researchers determine the height of an anomaly. *Illustration: Laura Lionetti Barton/Odyssey Marine Exploration.*

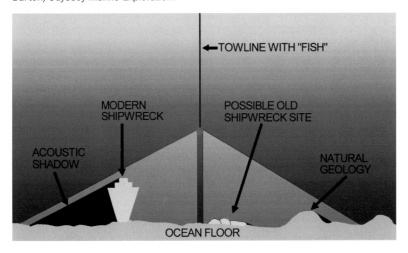

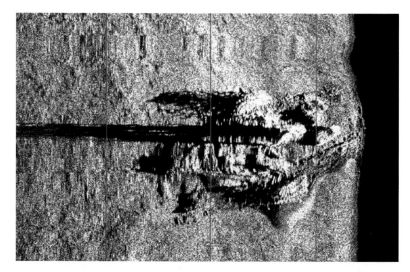

One of the first high-resolution sonar images of the wreck believed to be the SS *Republic*. This was the image e-mailed to John Morris and Greg Stemm by Ernie Tapanes. The paddlewheels and long acoustic shadow cast by the walking-beam engine are evident. *Image: Odyssey Marine Exploration.*

The crew of RV *Odyssey* in port soon after the first visual inspection (with an ROV) of the steamship site. They are displaying a bottle recovered from the wreck which would be used to file Odyssey's admiralty "arrest" of the site. *Photo: Laura Lionetti Barton/Odyssey Marine Exploration.*

Yes, that certain *joie de vivre* was creeping back into New Orleans. The citizens of America's most vibrant, theatrical city would simply have a good time with what they had left. On that same October day as the *Republic* was foundering, her crew desperately hammering together a makeshift raft and lowering lifeboats into a raging sea, a *Picayune* article chimed in, that for better or for worse: "Our city is full of people. . . . We are credibly informed that thousands of people from the north are coming hitherward. The South is supposed to be the El Dorado that was the dream of early adventurers to America."

But even in that new El Dorado, tragedy would again chase down William Nichols. He soon learned that his wife, Thyrza, had fallen sick from typhoid fever, the deadly illness that had so recently claimed their daughter May. On November 15, Thyrza had died, just days after her husband had arrived in New Orleans. Perhaps, as she lay stricken with grief and fever, her death had been hastened by the shock of hearing that her husband's ship had sunk in the Atlantic. The family rector, Roger S. Howard, wrote to console the Colonel:

> She was as well as usual and as cheerful as could be expected considering the scene of affliction. She had so recently pressed through until she heard of the wreck of the steamer in which you and your brother had taken passage. This was Monday, the 30th of October. . . . She was in a state of painful suspense and anxiety until she received your telegram that you and your brother were safe. The excitement seemed to have kept her up. For when she heard from you, a reaction seemed to take place, and she was seriously ill. And took her bed that night.

It's not known if Nichols returned to Rutland for the funeral, but a man of honor would have done no less. Yet he was soon back in Texas to finish business. When the Colonel later returned to Vermont, partly to secure a National Bank loan from the government, he was greeted by a fawning article in the local newspaper: ". . . he makes his appearance among his friends here, apparently as young, active, and free from care, as if nothing particularly troublesome had happened, such are his fortitude, and the elasticity of his nature."

The article went on to list some of the Colonel's adventures, and concluded proudly, "Colonel Nichols is no drone, no laggard — but a genuine, live, true-hearted Yankee. And here, we would ask, when will Vermont awaken to her true interest, and her people go into manufacturing, no matter what, so that such of her enterprising sons as Col. Nichols may find inducements to stay at home?"

No inducements worked. Nichols was a resilient man, one who survived and pressed on where others would have faltered. He promptly married his widow's sister, Louise, praised in the Rutland paper as "a woman of high culture and character." In February 1869, with his new bride and his surviving daughter, Lucy — whose sister May had died of typhoid fever shortly before William's trip on the *Republic* — Nichols moved west to Chicago, still lured by the western horizons and their opportunities. In the prairie of Illinois, west of the Des Plaines River, he founded his own town, and named it Maywood after his dead daughter.

Nichols had foreseen how railroads would soon tie the continent together, and he constructed a train station in Maywood to attract the passing line. He laid out the town in neat squares and became the town patriarch. As the Midwest blossomed, the Colonel was known as a shrewd Chicago businessman. He invented agricultural tools such as the "Maywood scraper and ditcher," and the screw-harrow, later known as the "pulverizer." He and Louise had two sons, Edward and Harry.

A biographical sketch of the town's founding father, published by the *Maywood Herald* in 1895, tells of Nichols' death in 1882: "Genial, kindly, and honorable, Colonel Nichols was remarkable for unswerving integrity. Military service in the patriot army gave finer edge to his genius, and greater toughness to his nature. . . . His career was magnificently successful. . . . his life was one that impressively teaches others how to clothe themselves with honor and nobility."

The Nichols family has survived and thrived. The great-great-granddaughter of William Nichols is also named Thyrza — Thyrza Nichols Goodeve — a Manhattan-based writer and university lecturer, a slim woman with doleful eyes and a gentle way. She found letters from her family's past in a musty old family trunk left by a late uncle. "It was like an archaeological dig, layer by layer," she observed. Toward the bottom of the trunk she found a letter with a pale pink ribbon around it, written from Gettysburg.

My dear wife, I write you from the battle field. We have been engaged for 2 days and momentarily expect the renewal of the battle. The losses in my regiment are 17 killed and 68 wounded. They have fought well. I am uninjured. God bless you and the children. I am trying to do my duty. If I fail, I wish you to feel that I fell in a noble cause and that it is as much your sacrifice as my own. Much love to all my friends and to the dear ones and you.

Yours as ever,
William

"It moved me greatly to hold it in my hand," Thyrza Goodeve said. "That letter is so precious, a piece of life. I thought of it like a treasure. Just by coincidence, I read the letter on July 4, the same day that he wrote it, 140 years before."

Ms. Goodeve owns an heirloom gold chain and locket containing a miniature tintype of her great-great-grandmother. The first Thyrza stares unswervingly from the metal image, her eyes seeming to glint above her stiff, black New England habit.

Thyrza Goodeve also has a photograph of Colonel William Nichols, standing in his uniform with black boots shining, posing with a long beard and stern face, hat in hand, sword at his side. William Nichols was much more than a survivor of a shipwreck. He was a man who also had lost and regained fortunes, who had faced down Pickett's charge at Gettysburg and suffered the unquenchable sorrow of losing both a wife and child within a few months. The shipwreck was perhaps merely a passing inconvenience to the Colonel.

Amazingly, the Nichols family had not even passed along the story of the shipwreck in their oral history. "We didn't even know about it," said Goodeve. "That was never talked about. And I think it was only a small detail of his life. The rest of his life nearly shoves it out. You know, people were used to death — children dying, soldiers dying, mothers dying from disease — that a shipwreck just didn't seem to have the same impact.

"William seems very American," noted Thyrza Goodeve. "Very practical, decent. No self-pity to him, he was always moving on."

CHAPTER 9

The Excavation Begins

THE GULF STREAM IN autumn is like a Wagnerian opera stage — charming with softness that moves the heart, then full of bluster and grandiose themes. The *Odyssey Explorer* sat on target through the month of October 2003, its crew and staff learning how to perform deep-water archaeology, figuring out how to harvest the riches of their El Dorado. On calm days the ship hovered over the site like a helicopter, buffeted invisibly by the majestic sweep of the Coriolis force, fighting the natural order by staying in one place, and struggling to extract things that the sea was loath to give up.

On those days the clouds were puffy cumulous, with dark flat bottoms chiseled by the rising updraft of heat, and the water was a wholesome Clorox blue. Flying fish skimmed across the surface. Herons landed on deck, blown off their migration course.

Hurricane season was waning, but the sky erupted now and then with a squallish nor'easter that set the ocean roiling. These storms sent the ship bouncing through the choppy waters back to Jacksonville, Florida, the Atlantic port of operations for the *Odyssey Explorer*, to take shelter. There, the ship's crew waited, idle, until the seas calmed enough to permit work to resume on site.

The team was doing "pre-disturbance" work, mapping and documenting the wreck before excavation or recovery could begin. A company solely interested in recovering underwater treasure might have simply dredged the site and sorted out the artifacts on deck, but Odyssey had made a commitment to do good archaeology — and also knew that damaged artifacts, especially coins, lose their value alarmingly fast.

The team's first step was to lower five acoustic transponders to the sea floor and plant them around the perimeter of the site. Because signals from satellite-based global positioning systems (GPS) cannot penetrate 1,700 feet below the surface, the recovery team needed an underwater positioning system of its own. Signals from the sea-floor transponders would enable the technical staff to create an exact electronic grid to pinpoint where each artifact was found. It was an underwater version of the pegs and strings that archaeologists use to make physical grids on land-based sites.

The next step was to create a photo-mosaic of the entire site, using a still camera mounted on the ROV. Over 4,600 digital stills were taken in 23 dives during October. From those, the shipboard data manager would select the best shots of each area, then stitch an amalgam of some 1,200 separate photographs together, like a quilt, using specialized software to make a seamless portrait. The resulting photo-mosaic took the darkness from the site and turned it into a well-lit visual image. The team would be able to see every piece of the grid, and its relationship to neighboring sections, as if they were flying over a Friday-night football field in a helicopter.

The man tasked with creating the mosaic was Gerhard Seiffert, Ph.D., a geologist from Germany. Earlier in the summer, Seiffert had joined the Odyssey team ready for a challenging adventure. He had read about Odyssey on the Internet and impulsively e-mailed Greg, saying he'd be in Malaga, Spain, where Greg was conducting *Sussex* business, and would remain there until Greg could see him.

"I stayed there for three weeks," Seiffert said, "taking a Spanish-language course. And finally I met Greg at the airport just as he was leaving to begin the recovery work on the *Republic*. I told him I was used to working in twelve-hour shifts, and could do everything he wanted. We made the deal, and I was in Baltimore a week later."

Seiffert was only one of a team of technological craftsmen operating — and often jury-rigging — the equipment. While the ship was supplied from Jacksonville, other sonar and navigation specialists moved in and out of the lineup, fine-tuning the process. Maintaining the *Odyssey Explorer* with its crew and equipment on site cost $20,000 a day, so time was not to be wasted.

But the early dives were consumed by shakeout test runs for the massive, finely tuned ROV system. The complex suite of tools took time to coordinate. Every detail and connection had to click, and at first those moments were rare. A hose connection would snap, cables would tangle, oil would leak from hydraulic lines. Real operational time in the water at first was frustratingly short.

"For the first three weeks," said Greg, "every dive was a nightmare during recoveries. But you have to keep an even keel, or else you die of the stress overload."

Operations weren't the only challenge. Odyssey seemed to be a burr beneath the saddle of several government agencies. To avoid run-ins with naval vessels, Greg had alerted the Pentagon that they would be working on the site. But the base in Jacksonville apparently did not get the memo; officials demanded that Odyssey move its ship to make way for aircraft carrier and submarine maneuvers planned for the same area. Greg stood his ground despite threats to board and impound the vessel. When the local commander got the word that Greg had cleared the research ship's presence with the Pentagon, though, the attitude changed. As the exercises commenced, the *Odyssey Explorer* bridge crew maintained a friendly relationship with the nearby naval vessels. In fact, they had no doubt that once the games were in full swing, the subs took advantage of the underwater noise from *Zeus's* loud motor and other acoustic noise to play hide and seek from the surface vessels trying to track them down.

The Coast Guard and the U.S. Customs Office were equally perplexed by the ship's movements. When the *Odyssey Explorer* steamed back to Jacksonville on October 1 without observing proper protocol, in the opinion of those tracking her activities, she was forcibly boarded by the Coast Guard. It seemed that Odyssey had been late in requesting anchorage — according to recently enacted Homeland Security rules, which were being interpreted differently from one government agency to the next. The Coast Guard boarding party stationed guards throughout the ship and herded everyone into the galley and TV lounge, where the guardsmen kept them for three hours of questioning: Who are you? How long have you been here? What has the ship been doing?

No one was allowed back in his cabin, and if someone had to use the toilet, a Coast Guard officer stood beside him with the door open. When the Guardsmen concluded there was nothing illegal to be found, they slipped away. The staff and crew returned to their cabins to find a mess. "They had tossed personal belongings, notebooks, and scientific manuscripts on the floor," said the disgusted chief officer of the *Odyssey Explorer,* George Renardson.

The whole thing left archaeologist Neil Dobson, an active British Coast Guard officer, upset and miffed. "I was shocked," he said, "that they searched the crew's cabins without the crew members being present. They were totally unprofessional, aggressive, and badly led."

The actions of the Coast Guard were part of the new law enforcement mandate of the Patriot Act that followed the tragedy of September 11, 2001. The incident was doubly onerous for members of the Polish crew, who were singled out for special interrogation. For them, the tactics were chillingly reminiscent of the police state they thought they had left behind. "This is taking me back to the old days," one of them said, with sadness.

Sea conditions were as murky as the politics. On Monday, October 20, *Zeus* was on Dive No. 16 when the surface current in the Gulf

Stream increased to six and a half knots. So much debris was drifting past the video camera that the monitors were showing a sub-marine version of a snowstorm. "At times like this," said Roy Truman, the operations manager, "I'd say it's impossible to do any work."

But work went on. As the night shift stayed up late trying to finish calibrating the precise electronic data lines across the wreck site, one of the transponders died. Then the connection between the venturi hose and the manipulator arm broke on the ROV. That night, the 25-knot winds of a nor'easter hit, sending the *Odyssey Explorer* catapulting from trench to wave trench. Deployment would have been madness. Everyone caught up on their paperwork as the ship retreated to Jacksonville on Thursday.

A day later the ship ventured out for more pre-disturbance work. Although the ROV was transmitting a tantalizing video stream of artifacts, Greg would allow no artifacts to be brought up before the photography was finished. And the photography was taking a griev-ous amount of time.

"Every day is a struggle," said Neil Dobson. "One step forward, two steps back." But he agreed with Greg. "It's crucial for the archae-ology to get really good pictures of the artifacts in place. Like a col-lection of religious items we found lying exposed on the sea floor. These are things that reflect the society as it was. It's quite poignant to see these images of the icons, just sitting there, unbroken."

Herb Bump, the conservator, twiddled his thumbs and shook his head. He needed artifacts to conserve. "We've been out here for thirty days," he muttered, "and accomplished nothing."

Greg was unmoved; he intended to stick to the plan. "We're just hammering out the details," he said stoically. Greg did his best to be the group cheerleader as he bounced between control center and pilot room, writing out the daily operations schedule, incrementally, one detail at a time. But it was clear to all that pre-disturbance work was costing a bundle as the ship hovered over the site into the fifth week.

Even the archaeologist Dobson was showing signs of impatience; unlike a land-based dig, on a deep-sea project a marine archaeologist on a ship has little physical work to do. Working with remote-controlled robots, Dobson had nothing to touch, no surface to scratch with a shovel blade or trowel, no dirt to smell.

"There's no real archaeology here," Neil stated one night in a moment of frustration. "There's little we really need to know about a Civil War–era steamship that hasn't already been found."

Dobson, a man of action whose earlier career had included work as a survival instructor, was bristling for something to engage his considerable energy. The image on his computer screen-saver was emblematic. It was a cartoon of a Scottish warrior in a kilt charging into battle, and the motto, "The Oatmeal Savage." Neil was a tall, personable man in his forties with a terse Scottish brogue and a restless zeal. He had already deflected many of the barbs tossed by his colleagues in academia. He knew why he was there: for the real archaeology. Although he said it didn't exist, his instinct told him otherwise.

He often shared with the others on the ship his philosophy about the project: the treasure was incidental. "For me, gold is just a yellow metal," he liked to say. "It just causes trouble. When gold's involved, you need security. And everybody's suddenly interested."

To be sure, the academic community was watching the expedition with a stern eye, tinted with pessimism. On board the research vessel hovering off the coast of Georgia, Neil was worried; was the heavy-duty ROV too big, too intrusive for delicate work?

Mostly, he wanted Odyssey to be honest. "The worst they can do is do salvage, while hiding behind archaeology," he said, carefully parsing the word "they" to preclude himself.

"I've seen enough academic fancies, and I've been involved in treasure hunts. I've listened a lot to both viewpoints. On one side there's a sort of withdrawal symptom that pure academicians go into — it's mine, how dare you criticize my methods?

"Then on the other side, there are pure salvagers who just want to go down, get it, and sell it. Why don't they just be honest and say, 'We won't do pure archaeology. The goal is the recovery of gold'?"

Greg sighed as he sat down to dinner on Friday night, October 24. He was sure Odyssey could do both archaeology and salvage. But things were not going well. Earlier in the day a solar flare had occurred that had thrown off data transmissions from navigation satellites around the world.

"In deep-ocean work, there are one thousand things that can go wrong," he observed. "Five hundred of them you can predict. Three or four hundred, you can handle reasonably well — depending on your expertise and ability to figure things out.

"But there will be a hundred that you can't predict, and that you have to accept. No one sitting down to plan a deep-water project would have thought of solar flares being a problem."

Neither the photo-mosaic nor the electronic grid were finalized by Saturday, October 25. But the weather was too rough to send the ROV down. The sky was a woolly gray, with some gunmetal darkness loitering on the horizon, hinting of gales. Most of the afternoon had been spent on repairs to the damage caused by the 23 survey dives: a bent forward-thruster mount, a torn cable, damaged lights.

"There's a break in the hydraulic line; we're leaking oil," said Ernie Tapanes at the afternoon briefing. Ernie was a quiet man, so people listened when he spoke. He was concerned. "Things are bent up. If we keep handling the manipulators like that, we'll spend all our time on deck, fixing the damage."

If there was disgruntlement among the crew, most kept it to themselves. The rest of October 25, the anniversary day of the sinking of the *Republic* 138 years before, passed without ceremony.

Back in Odyssey offices in Tampa, the company's financial wizards — David Morris, Mike Barton, and the new company attorney, Guy Zajonc — were watching their resources dwindle as the ship hovered in the Gulf Stream. "The company has six million dollars of warrants sitting out there at $2.50, and they're going to expire on November 21," Zajonc noted glumly.

Warrants are financial instruments issued by a corporation to its stockholders giving the holders the right to buy new stock at a fixed price ($2.50 in this case) at any time before a stated date. The problem was that Odyssey stock was then selling for only a bit higher on the open market. Instead of exercising their warrants, investors were sitting on the sidelines, waiting to see how the street price fared. The millions that the company had been hoping for as additional investment from the warrant holders was on hold for the time being.

Being tight on cash was nothing new for Odyssey. But how long could they dawdle out at sea, painstakingly making a virtual site map, to the tune of $20,000 a day?

Odyssey had little debt, but an enormous burn rate of money. As November approached, the balance of one million dollars in the bank would last about six weeks.

"We're out of money," David Morris said finally.

"Well," said John, his brother, "we'd better find some gold."

John was considering calling off the operation until they could figure out new financing. Greg, on the other hand, wanted to keep "feeding the neighborhood," as John put it with typical bluntness — that is, keep everyone on the payroll — until the money ran out.

The financial conundrum ratcheted up the pressure on everybody. Why not just go for the gold as quickly as possible and forget about the mapping? It might save the company.

But holding steady was part of a calculated equilibrium that Greg cultivated. He admired the philosophy of Ram Dass; he had even befriended the philosopher, had once spent a day sailing with the guru. "He wants to bring you back further and further into the center," Greg explained about Dass. "You get rid of the highs and you get rid of the lows, and you find that Zen state. . . ."

For Greg that meant, "We've got to stick to our plan." He was not willing to let the money affect the commitment to do things properly. "We don't start serious excavation until we get everything — the procedures and equipment — working right. And we've got to get the pre-disturbance work done.

"So I can sit across from George Bass, and hold my head up and say, 'This is what we did.'"

Bass was the noted underwater archaeologist from the Institute of Nautical Archaeology at Texas A&M whom Greg had debated on the *Today Show* during the Seahawk years — the man to whom Greg had argued that commercial archaeology could be viable in the future of the field.

The ship had been on site for nearly a month now. All Odyssey had to show for it was the old corroded bell of the *Tennessee*, a few portholes, and some pretty bottles. The gold could be anywhere on the wreck. It was not known where the coins had been stored on the ship for the journey. Had they been kept in the captain's quarters, where only ships' officers had access? Or lower in the hold, where their weight would help stabilize the ship?

If the gold was in the spaces below the deck, no one knew if the ROV was even capable of digging through the hardpan limestone crust of the sea floor to reach it. Could the sheer weight of the strongboxes or kegs, or whatever containers the money was in, have caused them to crash to the bottom when the ship first struck the sea floor — or later, as the ship's timbers slowly rotted?

Neither the ship's archaeologist nor the conservator seemed convinced that the site offered much in the way of original archaeology. The pressure was growing: why not just try to dig straight into the pile and find the gold?

Yet, Odyssey had made a promise to the public that it was capable of following archaeological procedures, even in deep water. And to the keen observers in the United Kingdom, looking ahead to future projects, the excavation of the *Republic* would be a litmus test to see if Odyssey could handle more historically sensitive wrecks such as the *Sussex*. After all, an archaeological excavation had never been satisfactorily finished at the depth of the wreck of the *Republic,* at 1,700 feet. A host of critics waited for Greg and John to stumble; some expected that when the archaeology turned difficult, Odyssey would give up and turn to outright treasure hunting. The credibility of the company was on the line. Odyssey had to do the best science possible and hope that time would not run out.

Problems continued to eat at the schedule. On Monday, October 27, short circuits and flooding plagued the still-camera system. The underwater strobe light supplied by the National Geographic Society to flash and illuminate the darkness kept shorting out. Photographer Jonathan Blair of *National Geographic* magazine roamed the ship in despair of getting decent shots. As the ROV technical guys helped him get the bugs out of the system, Jonathan lamented that Odyssey's camera was inadequate. He feared it didn't have enough resolution to produce good magazine photographs.

But the camera from *National Geographic* was not functioning right either, and Odyssey's camera was busy working on the photomosaic. Jonathan was growing frustrated.

Greg kept his cool. "It's like trying to push a bulldozer. We're driving this big machine, but it doesn't help to get behind it and try to push it along faster," he said. "It will go at its own pace. You can only sit in the seat and steer it.

"This operation will take time. We have a lot of young men here, working hard, who've been on the ship nearly two months since mobilizing in Baltimore — that's a lot of time. We can't put more pressure on them or it won't work."

By Tuesday evening, October 28, Jonathan and the Odyssey techs had patched up the strobe system one more time, and *Zeus* was on its way to finishing the still photography of the wreck's perimeter. Then, at a depth of 600 feet, not even halfway down, the strobe broke down again. Jonathan wanted to hide behind a rock. The lights had worked just fine on deck and, to his chagrin, fired again just fine when they came back onboard later. The problem seemed to have something to do with pressure.

Okay, said a steady but tight-lipped Greg, forget the strobe. Let's just use the lights we have — the four continuously shining lights set beneath the ROV. However, without the stronger flashes of the strobe, the ROV had to fly closer to the wreck and shoot more photographs. That meant more computer work to stitch the pictures together, and more time. The mounted ROV lights were barely adequate to photograph the large paddlewheels and the walking beam. *National Geographic* magazine needed more than that. Then one of the ROV lights went bust as well. Jonathan despaired.

The next day the connections on the starboard light were fixed by Bob Leedy. In doing so, he found a good-sized hole in one of the wires; the battery had shorted to the frame, drawing off most of its juice. He designed a solution. Leedy was from Baltimore — a confident man with the tough talk and analytical skill needed on the high seas. He had lived all over the world, and took everything in stride.

Greg paced the deck with his thermos cup of green tea, running options through his head.

On Wednesday night, October 29, a cold front pushed through and bludgeoned the ship with winds of 70 to 80 knots. It arrived in the dead of night, offering a taste of what the passengers of the *Republic* had put up with for several days before their ship sank. Waves crested over the bow of the *Odyssey Explorer*, and lightning lit up the sky with a cold fluorescence. Sleep came only in snatches, as bunks flopped up and down with each stroke of the waves, accompanied by the banging of pieces of weighty equipment on the deck above, twitching against each other. Water sloshed over the side and doused the ROV, but several attempts to cover it were futile. The cover kept catching the wind like a sail. Mike Paterson, the master of the ship, called all hands off deck, except for emergencies. It was too easy to imagine a crew member being washed overboard.

The *Odyssey Explorer* struggled back that night to Jacksonville to wait out the gale. The crew had already been at sea for more than a month without a port call, but few on the Polish crew had proper visas to go ashore, and the U.S. Customs Office was not in an accommodating mood. Even Neil Dobson, whose visa ostensibly allowed him to move in and out, was accosted by Customs officials waiting at the dock. Neil was incensed, muttering Scottish oaths about American incompetence.

To the Customs office, something didn't look right about this Odyssey setup: a ship with foreign registry (the company had maintained the original Bahamas registry for the vessel), with an alien crew, that kept going 100 miles out to sea and sitting there, never visiting another port. Those were the habits of drug runners. So each time the ship came back to Jacksonville, rubber-gloved inspectors moved in to rummage through baggage and personal belongings.

Things weren't much better when *Odyssey Explorer* returned to the site the next day, Thursday, October 30. The crane began to balk, the photo strobes were still misfiring, and a strange red border mysteriously appeared to outline each individual mosaic photograph. Fitted together, the photos looked as if they were nested in spaces in an egg carton. And a nagging short circuit still existed in the ROV light that Leedy ostensibly had fixed.

Jonathan Blair ran up and down the ladders in a state of agitation; he wrote memos to Greg about needing a complete overhaul of gear. More critically, six of the eight bolts from the plate that attached the crane to the ROV were broken or missing. They had apparently been breaking from stress and falling out of their holes.

Jim Starr saw the empty holes just in time. *Zeus,* hanging on by only two slim steel rods, might have come loose anytime during the launch operation. Seven tons of machinery crashing around the deck could do a lot of damage.

On Halloween Friday, October 31, Jonathan and crewman Jim Gibeaut worked all morning to make sure that the fittings on the strobe light were tight. Gibeaut had previously created a gadget to separate the wires from the metal, which may have been what was shorting things out. Once more, they fixed the problem.

The ROV went back to work in the early afternoon, ready for the photo-mosaic on the main shipwreck site. Finally, the still-camera units were firing off their shots as specified, every eight seconds, at an altitude of 21 feet above the sea floor. At long last, the pre-disturbance work was going to be finished. A set of photographs should be in before the night shift came on. Back in Tampa, the Odyssey executives were tapping their pencils against their desks and anxiously awaiting the next update.

Zeus glided silently as a blimp across the site that afternoon, flashing its potent system of lights on every detail of each corner of the wreck. Occasionally a scarlet crab or chartreuse fish would wander into the frame, adding spots of random color to the mosaic frames. On the deck of the *Odyssey Explorer,* enjoying the full October sun, two stowaway goldfinches flitted about, and a peregrine falcon rested on a winch box in the bow, using the ship as its resting place before resuming some wayward flight.

The ROV crew clearly needed a break from the frustrating pre-disturbance learning sessions. As Gerhard Seiffert and others pieced the mosaic together, Greg had the pilots practice their recovery skills by picking up bottles from the thousands that lay in the debris field. There were beer bottles, wine bottles, bitters bottles, snuff bottles, medicine bottles, gin bottles, pickle bottles, sauce bottles, and pill bottles with stoppers still in them. The scene was, as Neil put it, "as if someone had tossed a bag of rice on a football pitch. And then asked you to pick up all the pieces."

To bring artifacts to the surface, Odyssey had constructed a large steel-and-wire mesh basket with 16 chambers, a contraption they called a fourplex. In each chamber they put a white plastic laundry hamper, weighted down from underneath and outfitted with bungee cords so it could be easily lifted in and out of the frame. But the first time they lowered the device off the stern, the baskets were dislodged by heavy wave action. And the tension on the guide wire was so taut that the wire broke, whipping backward, luckily missing everyone's head.

"If this job was easy," Greg said defensively, "everybody would be doing it. We're trying new procedures here, doing some things for the first time. We're adapting industrial machinery for scientific purposes."

The fourplex was more a case of the ROV industry meets Wal-Mart. The men kept tinkering with the unit until they got the discount-store plastic hampers to stay in the mesh structure.

The pilots got pretty good at picking up bottles. They would bring *Zeus*'s limpet into position above a bottle and turn on the reverse pressure in the venturi hose. *Plip!* The soft suction cup would attach itself to the broad glass surface, and the manipulator arm could lift up each bottle and gently deposit it into one of the white laundry baskets sitting in the metal fourplex.

Gathering bottles could be considered pre-disturbance work rather than the beginning of the excavation proper, since many bottles were fanned out in the debris field of the wreck, instead of between the gunwales of the ship. But it wasn't just a practice exercise: there was a nice market for Civil War–era bottles. Collectors' catalogues showed prices ranging up to several thousand dollars for choice specimens. Greg knew that after Odyssey researched and documented the bottle types, many of them could be sold to the public, with historical information and a certificate of authenticity to show they came from the *Republic* wreck. It was their first hint of income from the site.

If there were gold coins in the debris, however, no one had found them. Continuous ROV flights over the site gave no clues to the location of any such treasure. Most likely, excavating the entire site, much of it buried in sand, would take many expensive months. Nobody was talking about treasure until the preliminary work was done.

By the end of the practice session, the ROV had picked up nearly 300 bottles, surfacing only when the manipulator arm lost its limpet cup. The arm had rooted around for it in the sand, to no avail. "I've beaten the machine," said Neil Dobson, elated in his exhaustion. The archaeologist had been up for 21 hours straight, logging in bottles.

"This is archaeology in a hostile environment — underwater bungee archaeology," said Neil with his usual irreverence. "You bounce down and do some archaeology, then bounce again and do some more. Up and down." He grinned, one of those grins that seemed to have a secondary meaning tucked into the curl of his lip. He enjoyed being the maverick.

After a brief hiatus for resupply at the beginning of November 2003, the *Odyssey Explorer* returned to the target. The learning process was painfully time-consuming, but Greg considered it worthwhile training time. "That's the real difference between us and the institutions and academics," he said. "We've had fifty to sixty days to figure out how to do this. Nobody gets two months of deep-ocean technology time to map and practice like we have! It's an expensive luxury in this field."

November 5 was another day of waiting and practicing; no surprise to the oil- and cable-industry professionals who made up much of the team. They were used to being out at sea for long periods without a payoff. But the specter of finding gold rode in the back of everyone's mind, like the thoughts of a bunch of kids awaiting Christmas. Two more weeks of this, Greg knew, and the company would have to consider pulling the plug, at least for the time being. Most of the team on the water had no idea how tenuous the project had become.

Ship's watches were twelve hours on, twelve hours off. The time was shortly after 1 P.M. and deck supervisor Jim Starr's crew had just come on. The men were drowsy from their morning's sleep. The previous watch had left the artifact-recovery device waiting for the new shift on the sea floor, a few slots still unfilled in the baskets of the fourplex.

So the first task for the new shift was to fill the remaining spaces with bottles and whatever other artifacts could be found on the debris field, then retrieve the unit. The electronic mapping grid had not been finalized, so excavation of the hull itself had to wait. At least the last watch had gotten a chance to fly the ROV around the site looking for promising locations to probe; everyone was tired of the endless photography and its esoteric demands.

As Roy Truman exited the control van to start winching up the fourplex, he left Jim Starr with pilot Gary Peterson, a young, towheaded Ohio farm boy with sharp eyes and reflexes. Peterson's deftness in fabricating tools was legendary among his shipmates. "The Gary Peterson Show," they called the suite of tools that Gary created to solve varied problems: handles to grip venturi hoses, snaphooks to close fourplexes. When a specific implement could be improved, Gary would disappear into the ship's shop, and after hours of whirring tools and buzzing welders, emerge holding a beautifully designed tool.

Peterson also had a knack for piloting the ROV. "It's like a video game in a lot of ways," he said. "When I sit in front of the screen, I see the ship symbol on one corner and the ROV in another place. And I never think of myself as being here on the ship. I'm there, on the ROV."

Jim Starr agreed. "It's 'telepresence' — the ability to transport yourself to another place. It's what all good airline pilots and other skilled people have."

That afternoon, the operations van was loaded with talent. Co-pilot Alan Smith was an ROV specialist from England. Smith also had a nickname: the Oracle of Zeus. "Alan knows every aspect of the system," said Starr. "He's been re-wiring and creating new software. We had to reprogram the computer, no easy task. The technical staff here could handle the job, in its pieces, but only Alan Smith could do it in his sleep."

Jim Starr, the deck supervisor, was a solidly built man with a gray beard and receding hair, and a calm, comforting presence. In 25 years in ocean engineering, he had taken part in many historical retrievals, including the salvage of the lost *Challenger* capsule. "That was an awful job," he said.

On this afternoon, some unscheduled time was available for the ROV, so Starr got on the intercom with Neil Dobson, who was managing from the project headquarters room inside the ship. "What do you want to do now?"

"I dunno," said Dobson, cheerily. "What do *you* want to do now?"

"We just made some repairs to the venturi system," said Starr. "Let's go test it out."

"Where do you want to go?" said Neil.

"I dunno, where do *you* want to go?'

In truth, Starr had already picked a place to test the venturi — in the stern. While the ship had last been in port in Jacksonville, Greg had invited a researcher from the SS *Central America* project to visit the team and speculate on where the gold coins could have been stored on the *Republic*. "Here," the man had said, pointing to a schematic of the *Central America*. "In the stern area. That's where we found it." That matched Odyssey's own research — that valuables might likely be stored in the stern, in a limited access point controlled by the officers of the ship.

"There's that big sand berm just forward of the rudder," Starr told Neil. "The ROV's gonna fit right in there, and it's in the high-probability area."

Pilot Gary Peterson deftly flew *Zeus* to the stern, forward of the rudder, as Starr peered into the monitor. "Just kind of wedge yourself in there, carefully," he told Peterson. They could see an expanse of sand beside a thick beam. Peterson landed *Zeus* so the front of the ROV's platform rested on the beam. Co-pilot Alan Smith turned on the venturi tube and started sucking up sand.

"It's doing well," said Starr, as the hose was digging a good-sized hole. Then, through the cloud of grit, Jim Starr saw the rounded edges of a metal object.

He blinked, and moved closer to the monitor. "Stop!" he shouted. "Turn the system off. I see a coin!"

"Yeah, right," was the immediate reaction of everyone gathered around the monitors. For more than a month, the crew had been flying over the wreck, photographing and probing, dispensing black humor about finding gold in every little niche. They had already leapt in response to several false leads that turned out to be seashells or pieces of copper, and they weren't ready to be fooled again.

"No, no, I'm serious," Starr blurted. The sand berm was starting to slide back down on itself, burying the object, so Smith turned the vacuum back on. Starr reached over and grabbed the pan-and-tilt control for the video camera and zoomed in on the spot.

Well, it sure looked like a coin. On the monitors, they could even see the characteristic ridges on the side.

No one said anything for several pregnant minutes. Starr looked over at the intercom, expecting to see the light coming on, followed by Dobson's excited voice. Nothing. After a pause, Starr pressed the intercom button and hailed the archaeologist.

"Is there any interest in this?" he deadpanned.

"Yes," Neil said, slowly. "I can make out some lettering on it."

In the project room, the Scottish archaeologist wasn't jumping up and down. It's just yellow metal, he thought, as he studied the screen. Messes everything up. He knew that from this point on, for quite a while to come, the primary mission would become the retrieval of the treasure.

In the control van on deck, co-pilot Smith turned the venturi back on, and five more coins quickly emerged from the billowing sand. It was a pirate's dream. Searching for the coins was expected to require an arduous, time-consuming excavation. But in a flash, the team had chanced on the treasure in a brief blink of unscheduled ROV time. In one moment of richly earned luck, Odyssey Marine Exploration had found the end of the rainbow. The accounts had been true, the research accurate. The SS *Republic* had carried a load of gold specie. And here it was, in a patch of sand.

Ironically, Greg, whose passion for every detail had marked the persistent search for the *Republic's* hidden wealth, had gotten off the ship at the previous port visit in Jacksonville; he was not on board to witness this historic event. Greg would not learn of this dramatic change in fortune until the next morning.

Deck supervisor Jim Starr took his cue from Dobson and kept calm. A long-time professional, he was thrilled to be the one directing the shift that found the prize. On the other hand, none of the gold was his to keep.

"This wreck is loaded with fascinating items," he said. "A gold coin is just one of them. For those of us who are contractors, it's just another artifact off the wreck. I was certainly pleased, and I almost felt, okay, my job's done. But it's all the other problems that come up on a day-to-day basis that keep this job so interesting."

Choosing to probe that particular patch of sand had not been a random act or a fluke. Anticipating the search for the coins, Ernie and the data-log technicians had plotted the stern of the ship into six sections, designated A to F. The place that Jim Starr took the ROV to test the venturi pump was square #1 in section A — literally square one of a planned investigation of the entire wreck-site, which consisted of some 2,000 such squares.

It seemed that the *Central America* and the *Republic* had indeed followed similar security precautions, keeping valuables in an out-of-the-way place: the stern of the ship. But this early unscheduled ROV flight was also a piece of tremendous luck. The find was sorely needed for the company's survival, just as the last trickling sands of available funding ran through the hourglass neck.

All night the venturi hose sucked sand from the site, and an improbable scene emerged. In the glow of the ROV's lights, casting the undersea gold-field in brilliant clarity, the manipulator arm moved in slow motion. Gold coins cascaded from the curved rim of a buried wooden keg in a scene from the story of King Midas. The barrel staves had deteriorated; their worn edges looked like eroded sedimentary rock. Many coins inside were still in stacks, like poker chips; others were loose and scattered in the sand. Coins lay tumbled between the decayed wood in flowing lines like the tresses of the $20 Lady Liberty herself.

Gathered around the big monitor screen in the project room, Ernie, Roy, and Neil stood star-struck. As the video camera zoomed in on the gold hoard, they leaned forward in a kind of collective gasp. It was a lot to take in. They didn't have a container ready to bring up any coins, so they instructed the pilot to fly *Zeus* around the wreck site, looking for some substitute. Thus it was that the first gold coins recovered from SS *Republic* were placed in a white ceramic chamberpot.

When *Zeus* returned from the site in the morning of November 6, the white chamberpot held 86 coins; some were shiny like jewelry, some were covered with a light gray-green film. Most were "double eagles," $20 gold pieces from the 1850s and early 1860s.

The call to shore reached John Morris first. He happened to be fishing that day with friends, a respite from the intense pressure that had been building in the Odyssey offices.

It started as an unusual day on the water with calm seas and clear skies. When the owner of the fishing boat, Captain Mistretta, asked John what he would like to catch that day, John said that he'd like to catch the biggest grouper of his life. Several hours later, while trolling over some promising rock structures, John's rod bent double — almost down to the level of the water.

At first everyone thought the lure had snagged the rocks, but as the boat moved on, it became obvious that he had hooked a very large fish. Sure enough, John had caught the largest grouper of his life.

When the captain asked the fishermen what they would like to do next, Ben Norbom, an old friend and original investor in the earliest days of Seahawk, said he'd like to catch a large kingfish. John piped in that he, too, would love to catch a big kingfish — but he was chastised by George Knutsson, one of Odyssey's directors, who suggested that after catching the grouper of his dreams, John's next wish should be for success for the *Republic* expedition.

Captain Mistretta positioned the boat for kingfish, and Ben began fishing with a large ladyfish as bait. Sure enough, within minutes, the drag on Ben's reel began to sing as a forty-pound king took the bait and stripped line off the reel. John was attempting to help Ben move around the boat when John's mobile phone began to ring.

"George, please answer that for me," John shouted, caught up in the action.

After a few seconds of listening to the voice on the other end of the line, George looked over at John and called out, "It's Ernie Tapanes. I can't really understand what he is talking about, but I think you better take the call."

John abandoned the fight to land the kingfish and grabbed the phone. In a cryptic language that had been previously agreed upon, Ernie told John that they had "found several of the objects that they were looking for." As the enormity of Ernie's message sank in, John told his fishing partners that they needed to head back to the dock.

There was a lot of work to be done, but all things considered, he had to admit he couldn't have asked for a better day of fishing.

When Greg got the call from John, he was at lunch in Tampa at an Outback Steak House with some folks that he could not let know about this sudden change in fortune. He had to react to the stunning news from John as if it were nothing. He hurried through the lunch and raced back to the Odyssey office, where a small group was gathered in the conference room. Greg told them of the message from the ship, but conscious of the considerable effort that still lay ahead, Greg kept his emotions under wraps, at least in front of the team.

"For me," he recalled, "it was more a sense of relief than exuberance. After so much time and work." In typical fashion, Greg quickly had the group discussing the next dive, talking about how to improve collection procedures.

"If we were treasure hunters, we'd be done now," said Greg — in other words, it would be time to scoop up the rest of the coins with a dredge. But Odyssey planned to finish the archaeology, surrounding the coins with historical context, a sense of what life was like 138 years ago. This, Greg knew, would help pay off the bills, too. "It's enlightened self-interest," he said. "People will pay to own a piece of history, to feel that they're a part of the story, to enjoy the romance of it."

But the rest of the team, crowded together in the late afternoon of November 6 in the Odyssey conference room, with its walnut paneled walls and classic ship paintings, was more celebratory. How many hours had they all sat together around the big work table, asking question after question to try to find the hidden key to the *Republic*'s location? A bottle of champagne was popped open, and congratulatory toasts passed back and forth around the room. John Morris was there with his wife, Ellie, and his brother Dave, as was Laurie Stemm, several members of the board, the research staff, the communications personnel, and others.

As the impact of the moment sunk in, with so much having hung in the balance, tears flowed for a few of those present. But in all the photos snapped, John especially had an unquenchable smile across his face. For him and Greg, the discovery of the first coins of the *Republic* was a tremendous victory, a confirmation of long persistence and belief in each other and the team they had assembled. While it was not just about the golden gleam of a few disks of precious metal, they all knew what this meant: the operation now had a real likelihood of financial success.

The *Odyssey Explorer* hustled the coins to shore. Greg and John flew to Jacksonville to meet the team and picked up the coins to return to Tampa. When the small batch of gold coins was taken to a local numismatic company for assessment, the report was stunning.

Most of the coins fell into the "uncirculated" category; some specimens were worth between $30,000 and $50,000 each. Their brilliance was intact. The curly hair and crown of Lady Liberty, who decorates the $20 gold piece, were sharply defined. One of the 86 coins was so rare that it was not even listed in any of the extensive numismatic catalogs.

Early speculation about the potential total value of the find, inevitable and understandably optimistic, was based on the math involved. If the original cargo indeed was $400,000 in specie, as reported by the captain — and if all happened to be in the form of $20 gold pieces — this meant perhaps 20,000 coins were strewn across the sea floor at 1,700 feet deep in the Atlantic.

And if each coin was as valuable as those first pulled to the surface in the chamberpot, and averaged even a modest $10,000 apiece in today's value to collectors, the treasure of the *Republic* could exceed a staggering $200 million.

The potential was not lost on the financial world, which quickly accepted Odyssey into the American Stock Exchange. No more penny-stock stuff; from now on, anybody could buy the stock without filling out extra forms acknowledging the considerable risk. The company was suddenly in the driver's seat.

The *National Geographic* film team met Greg in Jacksonville, eager to head out and film the coin recovery work. This was the payoff that the filmmakers had hoped for.

But the work was only beginning on the *Republic* site, which was quickly looking to be one of the most valuable wrecks in U.S. history. The collection system needed to be refined. A few of the first coins had suffered small scratches during their recovery. One of the conservators had accused Odyssey of trying to clean them with a toothbrush, a mortal numismatic sin. Greg knew they needed a far more delicate approach to handling such valuable items. Ever the tinkerer, he went down to the ship's galley and found a big kettle, like a lobster pot. He glued some patches of carpet to the bottom and covered the top with a plastic funnel. Voila! An instant coin pot that could be attached to the front of *Zeus*.

Next they experimented with filling the pot with Agrasil, a type of glycerine-based material — an idea suggested by Greg's mother, who had a penchant for coming up with creative solutions. However, after several trials, it didn't hold together well. The substitute they ended up using was an oil concocted by another of John Morris's brothers, Marty, who happened to be in the business of developing specialty lubricants. The thick stuff that went into the pot looked like chicken broth, minus the onions and carrots. The viscous fluid cushioned the coins as they came down through the funnel tube and lubricated them so they didn't scratch each other. The lobster-pot method was typical of the whole learning process on the *Odyssey Explorer* — a constant jury-rigging, often combining high- and low-tech approaches and plenty of outside-the-box creative thinking, with everyone pitching in to offer ideas.

The gold recovery was clearly going to push aside other archaeological work for the time being. Archaeologist Neil Dobson, the

Oatmeal Savage, was testy. The coin recovery part of the operation was clearly not his cup of tea. He wanted to dig his teeth into the other cultural artifacts scattered about the site, temptingly visible on the underwater video footage shot as *Zeus* flew from one cluster of coins to the next.

But for all his bluster, he recognized that the coins were going to pay for the complete examination of the wreck site. He knew that the other objects lying on the sea floor would be studied later, more slowly, as pieces of an educational treasure with great interpretive potential — the black-and-white domino pieces, the nested shoes, the schoolchildren's slates. With its fascinating background story, the Civil War–era shipwreck and its artifacts, a snapshot in time frozen by disaster, would be a remarkable archaeological opportunity.

The dominoes suggested a vision of two passengers sitting on the deck of the *Republic,* wrapped in blankets, playing games on a small table. The boxes of shoes might otherwise have ended up on display at a haberdashery on Canal Street, New Orleans; perhaps a freed slave who had never owned good shoes in his life would have come in to buy them. The scattered school slates might have been carried by boys and girls who would live in an entirely different United States following the bloody fratricidal war. There were stories to be told.

Despite the skepticism of some colleagues, Dobson realized that he was working on a cutting edge of underwater procedures, developing new techniques usable by others in the field as well as on future Odyssey projects. "There's no requirement for Odyssey to do archaeology," he said. "But we have adapted a commercial ROV to serve as a research platform. We're developing new methods of acoustic positioning, coin retrieval, developing new tools to find and recover artifacts like bottles. The fourplex bucket system allows us to stabilize and protect artifacts until we're ready to bring them up. Everything is logged in; for any dive, we have video to cover everything from discovery to recovery.

"In a period of a few months, working in the Gulf Stream — one of the earth's most hostile environments — we've been able to hold station and safely recover artifacts as small as coins.

"It's incredible. It's never been done before at this depth."

On Wednesday, November 12, the ROV came dripping up into the warm night, its lobster pot filled with a new batch of 80 coins. Bob Leedy wrenched it off the submersible and hauled it into a narrow deck room, where Neil and Greg had set up an assembly line for processing coins. Neil would lift the coins from the salt-water bucket, and Greg would spray them with fresh water and place them in individual dishes.

This time, the coins were all silver — U.S. half dollars. It was an unexpected bonanza. The more variety there was in the haul of coins, the more attractive the overall historical context might be to collectors. These silver coins were listed in coin books valued up to $2,000 each, sometimes more. It was an intriguing discovery: that the SS *Republic* had not only been carrying large quantities of gold coins for investors of the day, it had also been transporting pocket money — coins for the daily needs of the people of New Orleans. In 1865, after all, a $20 gold piece bought far more groceries than an ordinary person would need to pick up at the store.

Many of the silver coins looked as if they had just been struck. A sharp Lady Liberty sat on one side of each silver coin, an American eagle pranced on the other side. And many were marked with a little "O," meaning they had been minted in New Orleans and sent to New York in some money exchange without getting into circulation; after war's end, they were being shipped back to the streets of New Orleans.

The haul included two bank seals. Made of lead, engraved "Bank of New York," the seals were the size of two dimes welded together. They offered, for the first time, a clear indication of the origins of some of the money.

The night crew brought up 700 more silver half-dollars using the limpet and the lobster bucket. They had found a virtual waterfall of coins pouring from the decayed wood of a yet another keg. Now there were two sites the ROV was mining — one gold, one silver.

The ROV was back down next morning, picking up silver pieces. Cascading from beneath a beam, the silver hoard seemed even larger than it had the day before. The outlines of a wooden keg could be seen poking from the sand. The coins were in stacks, like Pringles potato chips. Peterson and the other ROV pilots were quickly gaining speed and dexterity with the manipulators and limpet. They were approaching a retrieval capacity of more than 1,000 individual coins a day.

But the weather was closing in again. The storm arrived with black purpose in the afternoon, and the wind whipped long streams of froth from the whitecaps that topped the huge swells. The ship plunged and rolled, and several men stayed prone in their cabins, their insides heaving along with the ship.

Greg wanted to head back to Jacksonville. A coin expert was going to meet the *Odyssey Explorer* at the dock to give advice on handling and maintenance. But in the distance, a rare, bright light seemed to bob at sea on the horizon as the ship dipped and rolled.

What was it? An interloper? Was it safe to leave the site unattended for a brief period?

Someone asked José Rodriguez, a Spanish technician and pilot who usually operated the ROV crane. "Fishing," he answered in his basic English.

"Yeah? What kind, José?"

Rodriguez, a slim 35-year-old man who claimed to be the best soccer player in the town of Bayona, in Galicia, reached down and pulled out an imaginary sword. He swashbuckled around the heaving deck. *Swish! Swish! Swish!*

"Swordfish boat."

He smiled and went off into the darkness. José didn't talk much. The mysterious light disappeared soon after.

Realistically, no one worried about poachers. "We have no real competitors," Greg said. "To protect this site, we put seventeen hundred feet of water over it and a five-knot current running through it! There are only a few companies in the world who could go down and get it, mostly ones that work with cable and oil. Only they're not going to go down there."

Deep in the hold, Neil Dobson sat by the blank monitor screen and tried to work out how the *Republic* sank. "I have a theory," he said. "As passengers were throwing things overboard, water came on deck and down into the hold. The water was slogging in the hold, from one side to the other, and lurching with a free-surface effect that affected the trim and stability of the ship. And eventually the old lady gave in.

"When she sank, she fell like an autumn leaf through the water. Now, depending on where the main bulk of cargo was, she tilted. The sinking ship was abeam to the current and was pushed north, the force of the water flushing objects out of it.

"She really careened to the bottom. And it wasn't a slow, but a rapid, violent sinking. The force of the water cracked the masts and pulled out cargo, and she crashed down violently on the bottom, her riggings and wires broken in the two- to three-knot current and the force of the fall. She started immediately to break up, with the light stuff falling away first, then the heavy.

"The coins may have shifted to the back because of the way the ship fell, and that's why we found them there. They may have been stored anywhere aft of the boilers. She was a well-traveled ship for her twelve years — an old lady already."

John Morris waited on the dock at Jacksonville, along with Rob Westfall, an expert assessor of coins from Tampa's National Gold

Exchange, Inc. The usual Customs crew was there as well, but this time they were joking with the Odyssey staff. Word had gotten out that the company had found gold. Suddenly the ship was legitimate.

Westfall's hand was shaking as he put his glass to the best of the *Republic* coins and saw the sharp edges on the engravings. "See the luster, the real rich white on them?" he marveled. "These are basically mint-state coins — never circulated. Nobody's ever seen such silver coins from America in such condition. And to my knowledge there's never been a hoard discovered of Civil War–era coins. This is just amazing."

Also visible on some coins were examples of "arrows" and "rays" — select markings sometimes used in the minting process. "These are rare types," said Westfall. "And you have all different types. The Seated Liberty with arrows, distinctive for that date. Rays on the back of a coin is another rarity."

Staff and visitors were all gathered in the *Odyssey Explorer's* "coin room," a single-entry space near the stern. The mood was a quiet euphoria, for the future of Odyssey had been assured. But they would have to be good conservators to get optimum value from the recovered artifacts.

"If you have a mint-state coin, you can't touch it," warned Westfall. "A lot of people will see corrosion on an item in their coin collection and wipe it off. They touch the coin and put it away. And a month later they take it out — and see a fingerprint on it. Oils from your hand make a change in the surface of the coin. It's amazing how little you have to do to change a fifteen hundred dollar coin into a ten dollar coin."

Were these coins being brought up from the *Republic* wreck site to be considered museum artifacts or salvage items for sale? Right then, to the Odyssey team in the small coin room, they looked a lot like much-needed capital. That evening, Neil and Roy lugged the heavy briefcases of coins to John Morris' car to be taken back to

Tampa; they looked for all the world like a couple of guys carrying bait buckets.

For the next six months, the giant ROV with its little limpet cup delicately mined the Gulf Stream to bring up more than 50,000 Civil War–era coins and other artifacts. About a tenth of the coins were gold, but to the continuing surprise of the recovery team, tens of thousands were silver half-dollars.

The coin world was in awe. Depending on how many coins would eventually be recovered of the reported "$400,000 in specie" said to have been shipped on the steamship, the find looked to be worth between 50 and 200 million dollars.

CHAPTER 10

A World of Gold

THROUGH THE SPRING OF 2004, Greg and John held their breath. The previous August, when Odyssey had "arrested" the shipwreck in a federal court, the judge had given other claimants, those who might also have some rights to the material in the wreck, thirty days to make their case.

After finding a wreck, the immediate question is: who legally owns any artifacts, whether cultural treasures or business cargo, which might be recovered from the sea? The short answer is: the owners . . . if they can be located. The long answer, however, is often complicated by the location of the wreck, in some cases by the ship itself (if a government warship), and by the nature of salvage rights.

In general, private companies or citizens who can prove ownership of wrecked ships and cargo are entitled to recovery of their possessions. It usually doesn't matter if the owners have not actively been pursuing their loss; neglect does not automatically constitute abandonment. The U.S. courts have found clear abandonment only in long-lost historical wrecks.

But in practical terms, those owners often cannot get their lost goods to the surface or even find a wreck without the help of salvage companies. So owners might find themselves facing a hefty fee for any salvage work needing to be performed.

The location of the wreck affects the legal question of which country's laws apply. The clearest situation lies within a narrow band off a country's shores. The United States, for instance, codified its laws of ocean salvage in the Abandoned Shipwreck Act of 1987. This regulated historic research for wrecks found within a three-mile zone.

In response to critics of commercial salvagers and to protect underwater heritage from unscrupulous treasure hunters, President Reagan expanded the three-mile zone to twelve in 1988. A little over a decade later, President Clinton moved it farther out, to 24 miles. But neither expansion had real teeth; neither one legally changed existing law.

There is some recognition of a 200-mile zone around countries. In the heat of the metallic-nodule boom of the 1980s, the international Convention on the Law of the Sea permitted nations to establish Exclusive Economic Zones (EEZ) reaching 200 miles offshore. These zones were meant to control fisheries and other natural resources of the deep ocean. They did not deal with cultural or historical wrecks, except to encourage their stewardship.

But other rights apply in certain cases, even close to shore. For instance, sunken government-owned ships or aircraft belong to their respective governments. In a recent landmark ruling by a circuit court in Virginia, Spain was able to reclaim ownership of two of its warships, *La Galga* and *Juno*, sunk in 1750 and 1802, respectively, in shallow waters off the American coast near Virginia. Sea Hunt, Inc., a maritime salvage company that discovered the wreck sites, was left without recourse.

So finding a wreck and "arresting" the find (taking an item from the wreck into a federal court) begins the process of claiming salvage rights and keeps competing salvors at bay. But it is just the beginning. It is not a finders-keepers situation. A salvage company must still navigate the morass of government rules, acts, extensions, zones, and obscure interests of past owners. Finding a wreck can be just the start of an intricate dance of legal maneuvers in the courts.

In the case of the *Republic,* the ship was found 100 miles off the U.S. coast, so it lay outside the direct jurisdiction of either the State of Georgia or the United States. The ship itself had been owned by a steamship company that no longer existed. But part of the cargo and the hull had been insured by the Atlantic Mutual Insurance Company, which was still in existence and had kept ample records of old claims in its corporate files.

Back in 1865, after the wreck, Atlantic Mutual had paid H.B. Cromwell and Company, the steamship line that owned the *Republic,* a claim for what had been insured: $45,000 in specie, $96,313 in general cargo, and $150,000 for part of the hull. This payoff transferred legal ownership of the hull and the cargoes to the insurance company, and it was in a position to seek all of the *Republic's* discovered remains.

But John Morris moved quickly to make the insurance company a substantial offer. To save everybody time and expense, he proposed, Odyssey would simply offer Atlantic Mutual an enticing lump-sum payment of 1.6 million dollars. The insurance company found it easy to agree to this windfall instead of going to court. The amicable agreement was a major victory for the project. Not only did the deal transfer all ownership rights to Odyssey, but as a bonus, the insurance company happily agreed to provide Odyssey with copies of all research and data that it had on the last voyage of the SS *Republic.*

"This is the first agreement of its kind reached in such a timely and efficient manner," said John, justly proud of the success of the bold move. "It's another milestone in our business plan — a wonderful example of the benefits of working cooperatively with property owners rather than going the route of litigation."

But one other potential claimant existed: the U.S. government itself. It was probing the background of the money, on the chance that some portion of it may have been federal payroll funds en route to New Orleans. Twice the government asked for and received extensions to the deadline for filing claims. But the same lack of shipping records that had thwarted Odyssey researchers also led the government researchers to a dead end.

On March 26, 2004, the partners could exhale. The federal judge for the Middle District of Florida, Tampa Division, awarded Odyssey a "default judgment" granting it the title and ownership to the SS *Republic* wreck and cargo. This included the hull, plus all artifacts and specie on board when the ship sank.

The remains of the *Republic,* with its treasure of coins and artifacts, now truly belonged to Odyssey. The final ruling came just a few months following the discovery. In comparison, the SS *Central America* team had been forced to wade through litigation for twelve years before their claim was ultimately cleared.

The 1989 excavation of the *Central America,* though, was a valuable prototype in other ways. It had established that a team of researchers, sitting comfortably in front of video monitors, could use robotics to successfully examine and excavate material from a shipwreck in 8,000 feet of water. It established in the courts that this "telepresence" in the deep sea was a basis for admiralty claims as legal as the human touch of a diver. But the *Central America* excavation was a unique exercise for the company that found her. The Columbus-America Discovery Group had been created by engineer Tommy Thompson for only one project, the recovery of the SS *Central America.* It has since disbanded.

In Odyssey's vision, the *Republic* was one of a dozen projects on the drawing board, one in a slate of potential shipwrecks that could sustain a growing company. In Greg's and John's minds, the *Republic* was the validation of a business plan, not a one-shot prize. Odyssey presented a brand-new paradigm to the world of ocean exploration. The venture was led by professionals, not adventurers or academics, working around the year as well as around the clock. And it had just notched its first success.

When the venerable George Bass introduced Greg Stemm to his class at Texas A&M more than a decade earlier, Bass had instructed them to pay close attention, that private ventures might be part of the future of deep-ocean archaeology. Now, Odyssey was demonstrating that commercial recovery could be both scientifically sound and financially viable. The company was refining its deep-ocean recovery techniques, intending to use them more efficiently in subsequent projects. As in any other endeavor, experience and practice develop skills, and the crew of the *Odyssey Explorer* was quickly figuring out a system that worked.

"Your guys make it look easy," a surprised Tom Dettweiler had said to Greg Stemm when he joined the *Odyssey Explorer* crew in February of 2004. By then the ROV team was routinely lifting more than 1,000 coins a day, one at a time, without seriously disturbing the site. Dettweiler, one of the best deep-ocean project managers in the business, had been on the team that led Bob Ballard to the wreck of the *Titanic* and had been the science officer with Jacques Cousteau aboard the *Calypso*. He came to the Odyssey team from Oceaneering International, the world's leading supplier and operator of ROVs for the oil and gas industry.

Tom's comment meant a lot to Greg. "It was one of the greatest compliments we felt we were ever paid," he reflected. "Tom Dettweiler is a legend in the deep-ocean business, someone we have always had utmost respect for. It was a real boost when he joined our team."

By summertime, *Zeus* with its eager limpet had cleaned out the first gold and silver caches on the wreck site. Those caches had been close to the surface of the mound of material, with no major obstructions. But days of further probing were failing to find what should have been the rest of the coins. To find the remaining kegs, Odyssey would need more serious excavations; *Zeus* would have to begin moving things around. The team had already recovered more than 51,000 coins: 2,620 twenty-dollar gold "double eagles," 1,496 ten-dollar gold "eagles," 47,094 silver half-dollars, and 2 silver quarters.

Some of the coins were unique. One 1858 half-dollar carried poignant graffiti: someone had hand-scratched "WAR" and "1861" on one side of the coin in an elegant serif script, and "EC" on the other, perhaps a person's initials. This someone, with idle time and a steady hand, had left his mark, as human beings have done for centuries, on something he probably considered to be a relatively permanent item, a silver coin, to commemorate what must have been a fearful and intensely traumatic episode in his life. Whoever he was, EC had left a piece of history that ended up on the *Republic,* reminding everyone on the project that they were unveiling a glimpse of personal histories lived in turbulent times.

In all, Odyssey found hundreds of different coins that carried similarly unique and historically significant inscriptions, everything from tiny crude drawings to numbers and stamped letters and dates. Ordinarily, an inscription on a coin is not especially significant, because there is generally no practical way to prove whether the addition was carved last week or a hundred years ago. With coins recovered from a shipwreck, however, there is no question — all are messages from the past, none inscribed later than 1865.

Besides the ship's bronze bell, the team had recovered a medley of small artifacts — everything from countless common lumps of coal to iron rivets, copper nails, pieces of horse tackle, a stoneware pot, a ceramic soap-dish, buttons, lace bobbins, shoes, tools, barrel staves, an oil lamp, canvas wrapping, several large portholes, pieces of copper sheathing, and some pintles and gudgeons (large brass fasteners that held the rudder to the ship). They found a large number of harmonicas — the poor man's accordion. *Zeus* had also brought up a collection of ceramic and milkglass candlesticks and an assortment of religious icons, including a number of delicate porcelain figurines.

By the end of summer in 2004, over 10,000 artifacts had emerged from the site. One of the most varied subsets of the growing collection of commercial objects were the thousands of bottles and jars, some whimsical and odd, in many colors and shapes.

Odyssey planned to make the most of these artifacts, both the commonplace and the unusual, the everyday and the poignant. The most significant would be placed in the company's own shipwreck attractions, the first planned to open in 2005 in New Orleans. George Becker, manager of the attractions program, had previously built and managed the operations of Sea World marine-life parks around the country. Now he was unveiling plans for shipwreck-heritage displays at weekly planning meetings in the company's Tampa office. Architects, filmmakers, and computer artists had been working to design state-of-the-art displays and interactive programs. Exhibits would include a large-format, high-definition film of the *Republic* recovery. Such exhibits had once been a dream of the old Seahawk company; now, in a testament to the tenacity of Greg Stemm and John Morris, the 15-year-old plans were finally coming to fruition.

For Greg and John, the possibilities of the story of the wreck, the science, and the market were finally blending together. Happily, they could look forward to a lot of merchandising spin-offs, from polished-coal jewelry to angel figurines. For those without deep pockets who yearned for the adventure story of the shipwreck, Odyssey would provide a range of more common artifacts from the *Republic* and inexpensive souvenir replicas. On the other end of the scale, for numismatists and coin collectors, they would offer what might be the largest and most valuable collection of rare American coins ever found.

As plans proceeded for the Odyssey attractions, in February 2004 another cache of sunken treasure became available via the auction block. Greg learned that most of the artifact collection of the Dry Tortugas wreck, which he and John had recovered from the sea as one of Seahawk's first projects, was up for sale in California. With a determined face, Greg traveled to the West Coast and bought the artifacts, along with a huge archive of videos taken of the wreck site. The collection had been sold earlier by the remaining managers of Seahawk for $2.5 million dollars, part of their attempt to keep the company solvent in the late 1990s. The next owner planned to build his own museum around the artifacts, but had not been able to accomplish that, and the collection had bounced around from Palm Beach to Idaho to California.

Greg and John now had it back — the fruits of their labor that they always felt had been wrongfully taken away. The Dry Tortugas find was still the deepest Spanish wreck ever recovered, and its artifacts would make a terrific display in the permanent shipwreck attraction that George Becker was planning.

To handle its fast-growing artifact collections, Odyssey hired Ellen Gerth, with degrees in cultural anthropology and museum studies, to head up the company's archaeology, research, and conservation department. Gerth quickly oversaw the opening of a conservation laboratory in Sarasota, in the same building as the Numismatic Guaranty Corporation where the *Republic* coins were being conserved, graded, and packaged. For her first year, she was given a substantial budget of more than half a million dollars.

Odyssey considered even the most mundane artifact from the *Republic* site worthy of conservation. In a large warehouse room in Sarasota, Gerth and NGC conservator Brian Silliman organized metal shelving to handle the desalinization process needed to stabilize the salt-saturated objects. Here, the old bell from the *Tennessee* hung suspended in a special solution — the exact formula a well-kept secret. Conservators, like chefs, have their personal recipes.

One tank held two axe heads whose metal had deteriorated into layers, like baklava. In the refrigerator were two intact bottles filled to the brim with berries — what looked like gooseberries and currants, perhaps brought along to make pies during the voyage; these were being kept cold to prevent the glass from exploding from fermentation pressure. A pair of metal hand-files hung in an electrolytic solution, along with screws, bolts, and a muleshoe. Other containers held clumps of silver coins embedded in hardened sand or wood. Some shipwreck-coin collectors, it turns out, actually prefer to own these clumps, rather than loose coins, as unique specimens from underwater finds.

In another part of the conservation laboratory, pieces of coal from the *Republic* were being boiled in an experiment to make jewelry. "Just watch," Greg had predicted. "People will want to touch a piece of history." Even the coal was valuable.

Once the smaller items were recovered, the larger items from the *Republic* — anchors, the immense walking-beam, the rudder — would be left where they lay. As Dobson noted, "The anchors may be badly corroded; they might not survive the lift from the sea bed. The walking beam would require special lifting frames and, of course, huge water-filled tanks to store it in. And it might be too large for the *Odyssey Explorer;* it might require a barge.

"The rudder would also need a special frame made to lift it. There are no guarantees that these large objects would survive the recovery."

The bulk of the *Republic,* in other words, would likely remain in her resting place. Of course, even that might have its economic potential. Greg has suggested plans to transport adventure tourists to the final resting place of the *Republic* in deep-water submersibles. This phase of the plan was being developed in partnership with Mike Macdowell, the entrepreneur who charges as much as $35,000 per trip to visit the *Titanic.*

The Odyssey team's surprise continued to grow for the amazing variety of bottles recovered from the site. The thousands of glass containers were a medley of color, size, and shape. There were green, bluish, and clear bottles for wine, beer, and gin, and beautiful amber pouring carafes. There were "cathedral" pepper-sauce and pickle bottles and "umbrella" ink-stands. There were small and large bottles of Lea & Perrins Worcestershire Sauce and a similar sauce bottled under the label Lord Ward's.

Among the samples that *Zeus* brought to the surface were many patent medicines of the day, such as bottles of Mrs. Winslow's Soothing Syrup ("soothing" meaning morphine-laced). There were "fluid extracts" and a bottle of "vermifuge," a substance to get rid of intestinal worms. Also rising from the deep were ceramic jars for Holloway's ointment, and jars embossed with: "J.B. Thorn Chemist, London, John A. Tarrant, New York, Sole agent for the United States."

The stamped jars and embossed bottles were fine examples of the early history of marketing and advertising. The "J.B. Thorn/John A. Tarrant" product, for example, its stentorian names ringing with reliability, was a balm to diverse ills, from gonorrhea to "incipient stricture and affections of the kidney" — claims later judged fraudulent. False claims about products were very common in the 1800s, particularly with the growth of newspapers and public literacy, allowing new forms of mass communication and marketing to emerge.

"The packaging," noted Dobson about the Thorn/Tarrant balm, "suggested that some erudite chemist from Great Britain — then regarded as the most advanced nation in the world — had exported a unique salve to be distributed by an important New York businessman. It was the kind of label intended to impress the consumer. So some very cheap — and often very dangerous — products were put into fancy-looking jars and sold all over at outrageous prices."

The stoneware jars for Holloway's ointment were similarly labeled. Englishman Thomas Holloway was one of the world's first patent-medicine hustlers. He made his fortune by selling products that became famous worldwide, though there was no scientific proof that the medicines — made mostly of tallow, myrrh, and saffron

— did anyone any good. Holloway began by going down to the docks to sell his products to sailors, who took them to every port around the world. In a subsequent sales blitz to build his markets at home, he toured the English countryside in a little buggy.

The range of diseases he claimed his cream could cure was astounding: "Apply it to bruises, burns, scabs, cuts, chilblains, chapped hands, boils, abscesses and wounds," read the directions. "It is an unfailing remedy. It promptly relieves and cures bronchitis, asthma, sore throat, and other affections of the throat and chest." Testimonials appeared in newspapers all over the British Empire, including India, Australia, and the North American colonies.

Holloway, as one of the world's first advertising executives, knew where people's vulnerabilities lay. "It is not generally known," one advertisement for his line of pills offered, "but such is the fact that children require medicine oftener than their parents. Three-fourths of the children die before they attain the age of eight years. Let their mothers, then, be wise, and give to their children small doses of these invaluable pills once or twice every week . . . the gross humors that are constantly floating about in the blood of children, the forerunners of so many complaints, will thus be expelled, and the lives of thousands saved and preserved to their parents."

The ointment found ready customers in America during the Civil War. "The horrors of war can be greatly mitigated by that sovereign remedy, Holloway's ointment," an ad in the *Milwaukee Daily News* of 1863 claimed, "as it will cure any wound however desperate, if it be well rubbed, around the wounded parts, and they be kept thoroughly covered with it. A pot should be in every man's knapsack. Only 25 cents per pot."

Charlatan or not, Thomas Holloway's ointments and pills made him very rich, and he ended his life as a philanthropist. He even founded a college for the higher education of women, Royal Holloway College, which later became part of the University of London.

The Odyssey team had also discovered, scattered on the ocean floor, several bluish flasks marked as Phalon's hair products ("Chemical Hair Invigorator" and "Magic Hair Dye"). Some had the substance still inside. Edward Phalon, known as Broadway's most fashionable barber, had opened an elegant hair-dressing establishment in 1852 on the ground floor of Manhattan's St. Nicholas Hotel. When the Civil War broke out, Phalon cleverly issued "hard times" tokens to customers in place of change, which they could use in his salon on their return visits.

A magazine of the period, *Gleason's Pictorial Drawing-Room Companion*, summed up the merits of a visit to Phalon's: "The American who visits New York and does not go to Phalon's Hair-Cutting Salon is in infinite danger . . . of departing this life without having had the slightest idea of what it is to be shaved." In that age, "infinite danger" appeared not to mean the same thing for a copywriter as it did for a Civil War colonel at Gettysburg or a steamship captain facing a hurricane.

Of course, the greatest monetary treasure of the *Republic* was her coins, those gleaming disks of gold and silver, many virtually untouched from government mints and bank vaults. Taken care of properly, those coins would enable Odyssey Marine Exploration to go on to other projects. Greg and John had to be careful; they had learned in watching Tommy Thompson's *Central America* experience how important it was to get a wide range of dealers and experts involved, each in his own specialty, for the coins to remain desirable.

They had also learned that a large cache of valuable coins could not be dumped into the coin market without disrupting the pricing regime, as other shipwreck recovery projects had learned the hard way. "We intend to make public the entire population of coins — how many we found of each and the condition," said Zajonc, the company lawyer. "We won't hold any information back, so there will be no surprises. And we'll follow the advice of coin dealers, some of whom felt blindsided by past shipwreck marketing efforts, to take our time and spread out the introduction of the coins through varied marketing channels and dealers. If we do this carefully, we won't lose ground in values over time."

Transparency and access would be the strategy, said Greg, "to make the dealers and buyers feel like they're part of the find. We will sell a group of coins to each dealer who we feel can handle the items with the care and credibility required of this type of find."

The *Republic* find was already firing imaginations and attracting offers from coin professionals. Odyssey was suddenly in the driver's seat. "We were advised that we could dispose of all of the gold coins at once," Greg said, as matter-of-factly as possible, considering he must have been grinning broadly inside. "Three dealers already have made significant offers for everything. They're ready to put down millions just to hold their places in line, but that's not how we're going to do it."

The face value of the 50,000 coins recovered to date represented only a quarter of the steamship's reported cargo of $400,000 in specie; it was still not clear whether more would be found or indeed were ever on the ship, despite the report attributed to the captain. Still, the 50,000-plus coins comprised a dazzling collection that made an immediate impact on the numismatic world. Seeking a team of top professionals to handle its *Republic* collection, Odyssey retained Donald Kagin, widely respected in the field, as the project's chief numismatist. John Albanese was chosen to direct the marketing of the collection. Albanese, founder of both of the world's two leading coin-grading services, was the ideal gatekeeper. He would be in charge of allocating the right mix of coins to the dealers he felt could best represent them.

To handle the exacting demands of conservation, Odyssey engaged Numismatic Conservation Services (NCS) of Sarasota. To certify and encapsulate the coins for long-term preservation, Odyssey retained Numismatic Guaranty Corporation (NGC), the world's largest coin-grading service, also the official grading service of the American Numismatic Association and the Professional Numismatists Guild. Mark Salzburg, founder of NGC, would direct the grading — the complex assessment of the condition of each coin, essential to determining a relative value.

Albanese estimated that the coins recovered from the *Republic* so far were worth more than $75 million in today's retail value to collectors; perhaps $50 million if sold to wholesalers. This meant that it was possible that coins worth another $150 million or more — the missing three-quarters of the specie — still lay somewhere in the Gulf Stream. Whether those additional specimens were scattered far from the wreck or buried too deeply to ever be discovered was not yet clear to the Odyssey partners. But from any viewpoint, the value of the coins recovered was staggering. Odyssey's stock (OMR) steadily rose on the American Stock Exchange, and new business plans were percolating in the dark-wood paneled headquarters on Swann Avenue in Tampa.

Albanese recommended that the company divide the coins into two types: "numismatic" coins and "shipwreck effect" coins. Numismatic coins were those that showed no signs of having been recovered from a shipwreck, but were of value to collectors because of their condition and rarity. Of course, they were documented to have come from the *Republic* site, which increased their conversational value, if not their technical merit in numismatic terms. Carefully conserved, they would be marketed to the worldwide fraternity of coin dealers and collectors. The collection included coins that were the finest examples ever seen in their categories; offers for individual coins rose as high as an astounding $550,000.

To kick things off, Odyssey's first "Featured Coin" was an 1854 gold double eagle minted in New Orleans. "The 1854-O double eagle is a tremendous rarity today," read the press release worded by NGC experts, "with no more than 25–30 examples known in

John Morris and Greg Stemm review side-scan anomalies and rate them as possible shipwreck sites. *Photo: Laura Lionetti Barton/Odyssey Marine Exploration.*

Project managers Andrew "Irish" Craig and Roy Truman at sea during operations. *Photo: Jonathan Blair/Odyssey Marine Exploration.*

The 251-foot *Odyssey Explorer* after a refit in Baltimore, ready for work on the SS *Republic* shipwreck site. *Photo: Jacques de Rham/Odyssey Marine Exploration.*

Alan Smith was dubbed the "Oracle of Zeus" for his amazing ability to troubleshoot and make repairs on *Zeus*, Odyssey's work-class ROV. *Photo: Jacques de Rham/ Odyssey Marine Exploration.*

Zeus, a seven-ton, 200-horsepower ROV, is launched from the deck of the *Odyssey Explorer* to dive to the shipwreck site nearly 1,700 feet below. *Photo: Jacques de Rham/Odyssey Marine Exploration.*

The ROV is controlled from aboard the *Odyssey Explorer*. One person pilots the vehicle (Jim Starr, in background), while another operates the manipulator arms and cameras (Ewan Basom, in foreground). *Photo: Jonathan Blair/Odyssey Marine Exploration.*

A photo-mosaic image of the walking beam, standing guard over the SS *Republic* shipwreck. Detail at left shows the walking beam in operation. *Photo: Odyssey Marine Exploration. Painting: courtesy Peabody Essex Museum.*

One of the 28-foot-tall paddle-wheels of the SS *Republic* sits upright on the ocean floor. *Photo: Odyssey Marine Exploration. Painting: courtesy Peabody Essex Museum.*

Greg Stemm (at right) studies the photo-mosaic of the site to plan a dive. *Photo: Laura Lionetti Barton/Odyssey Marine Exploration.*

Part of the photo-mosaic of the stern section of the SS *Republic*, marked in one-meter grids for precise archaeological mapping. A five-transponder acoustic array enabled the team to create this geographically accurate mosaic of the entire site. *Composite Photo: Gerhard Seiffert/Odyssey Marine Exploration.*

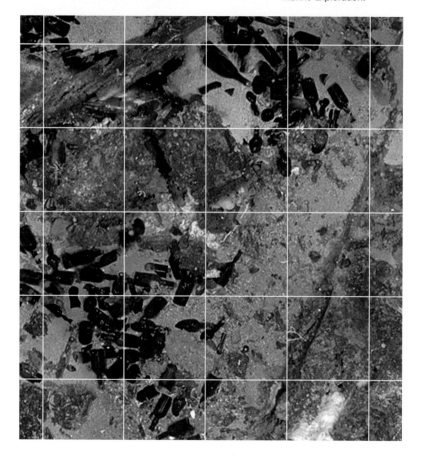

Early in the excavation, the ship's bell was found resting near the bow end of the site and was carefully recovered from the sea floor with *Zeus*'s rubber-tipped manipulator (above left). On board the *Odyssey Explorer*, a partial inscription could be seen on the bell's surface (below): the letters *S S E E*. The bell still bore the *Republic*'s original name — the *Tennessee* — confirming the identity of the wreck. *Photos: Jonathan Blair/Jacques de Rham/Odyssey Marine Exploration.*

After a first coin was discovered and some sediment was removed, a virtual carpet of gold was unveiled to the amazement of technicians and archaeologists watching on video monitors on the research vessel more than a quarter-mile above the site. *Photo: Odyssey Marine Exploration.*

A curious crab inspects the container used to collect coins.

In addition to thousands of gold coins, tens of thousands of silver coins were discovered on the shipwreck site. Some of the original barrels were nearly intact; others had disintegrated over the years, leaving the coins grouped in the outline of a barrel. *Photos: Odyssey Marine Exploration.*

Above and opposite: A "fourplex" unit is prepared for another trip 1,700 feet down to the shipwreck site. The ROV *Zeus* will place artifacts into numbered plastic baskets, which are then loaded into numbered sections of the fourplex for the trip to the surface. *Photo: Jonathan Blair/Odyssey Marine Exploration.*

Middle: A coin is delicately picked up with a soft silicone limpet. The ROV operator uses suction to secure the coin to the limpet. When the suction pump is disengaged, the coin falls into a collection container, cushioned by a specially formulated lubricant gel. *Photo: Odyssey Marine Exploration.*

Bottom: *Zeus*'s manipulator arms recover a porthole from the SS *Republic*. *Photo: Odyssey Marine Exploration.*

A single frame from the photo-mosaic reveals a portion of the cargo-hold of the SS *Republic* with a stack of slates. Believed to be bound for Southern schools, these items never reached their destination. *Photo: Odyssey Marine Exploration.*

A porthole provides an aquarium-like hiding place for sea life on the shipwreck site. *Photo: Odyssey Marine Exploration.*

A bottle of gooseberries is lifted with the limpet. A number of such bottles were found containing fruits, including rhubarb, blue-berries, and pineapple.

A fragile bun-comb is recovered after being submerged for nearly 140 years. Many Civil War–era items used in everyday life were recovered and conserved for future display in exhibits. *Photos: Odyssey Marine Exploration.*

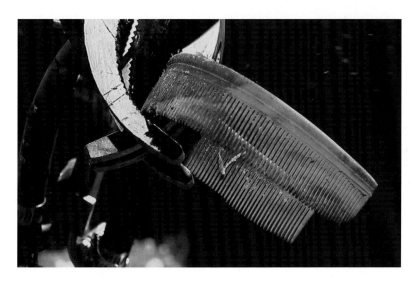

After recovery, every item goes through a conservation process. All coins were treated in this lab by Numismatic Conservation Services, while non-coin artifacts were processed by Odyssey's own conservation team. *Photo: Jonathan Blair/Odyssey Marine Exploration.*

Above: On board the *Odyssey Explorer*, archaeologist Neil Cunningham Dobson (at left), with Greg Stemm, inspects coins after recovery. *Photo: Jonathan Blair/Odyssey Marine Exploration.*

Right: Coins recovered from the ship-wreck site include silver half dollars, gold $20 double eagles, and smaller gold $10 eagles. *Photo: Odyssey Marine Exploration.*

Approximately 200 different bottle types were recovered from the SS *Republic*, providing a broad cross-section of medicinal, condiment, beverage, and cosmetic/perfume bottles. *Composite image: Rebecca Hagen/Odyssey Marine Exploration.*

Some of the most interesting artifacts recovered from the shipwreck site were religious in nature. Four different types of small angels, crucifix candlesticks, and statues of saints were found on the site. Amazingly, most of these delicate glass and porcelain pieces survived the shipwreck without damage.
Photos: Odyssey Marine Exploration.

Although scientific research and high-tech equipment made possible the discovery and recovery of many artifacts from the steamship, the most poignant elements are the personal tales and mysteries intertwined with the story of the steamship *Republic*.

This locket with a photo of Thyrza Nichols (above) was passed down through generations of the Nichols family. It is believed to be the same piece carried by Col. William Nichols as he endured the sinking of the *Republic* and two days in a lifeboat on the Atlantic, as detailed in a gripping account of the ordeal written later in a letter to his wife. *Photo: Jonathan Blair/Odyssey Marine Exploration.*

This remarkable half-dollar silver coin (above at right) recovered from the shipwreck has "WAR" and "1861" painstakingly hand-engraved on one side. On the other side are inscribed the letters "EC" (perhaps the engraver's initials). Although we may never know who was responsible for the etching, the emotion associated with the outbreak of the Civil War is captured in this graffiti-like reminder of the trauma of a country torn apart by war — and only slowly beginning in October 1865 to mend again. *Photo: Numismatic Conservation Services/ Numismatic Guaranty Corporation.*

For additional images of the SS *Republic* excavation
and artifacts recovered, visit www.lostgold.net.

all grades. The remarkable quality of the specimen presented here is thus a banner headline in American numismatics."

The press release delivered its punchline: "Having been recovered just recently from the wreck of SS *Republic*, it is previously unknown to the hobby and uncounted in any census. Its great rarity as a date, combined with its historic provenance, assures that it will receive a wealth of attention from the collecting community."

"Previously unknown to the hobby" was a thunderous statement. It was as if a new cache of Raphaels had been uncovered in Florence. But until the recovery operation was substantially completed and the populations of the numismatic coins of particular rarity were known, Albanese and Odyssey were cautious not to place such astounding coins on the market. They wanted to wait so that both Odyssey and collectors knew exactly what they had and how many of each.

By August 2004, the company was ready place on sale a few of the graded specimens, a first batch of 600 coins that were not as rare as the 1854-O but were still expected to command prices from $5,000 up to $75,000.

"Shipwreck effect" coins, on the other hand, were ungraded coins recovered from the *Republic* site. Their intriguing feature is that they show some evidence, albeit often almost imperceptible without the help of a microscope, of having spent nearly 140 years in the deep ocean. In many cases they have either tiny coral structures embedded in their surfaces or some minute traces of saltwater etching. These specimens were less rare in terms of numismatic grade or pure rarity as a coin; their primary appeal is that they came from the historic shipwreck.

NCS, the conservator company, encased each such coin in a certified tamper-resistant holder, placed in a rich-looking hardwood box with an engraved plate on the cover. The complete package, with an illustrated booklet, a DVD video of a National Geographic program about the *Republic*, and a certificate of authenticity, was priced at

$1,000 to $2,000 per coin. The sale of the coin boxes began on television on May 15, 2004, during a 24-hour "Coin Vault Marathon," a popular program on the Shop At Home Network. They sold like jars of Holloway's ointment, setting new records for single-day sales for the channel.

Greg's experience in the advertising and marketing world was paying off. He understood something about motivation, about what the public wanted. Some academics argue that shipwreck artifacts belong to the public as a whole and that selling any of them to private individuals is improper, that artifacts should be in a museum for everyone to see. But what is private and what is public?

Greg Stemm believes that artifacts belong to the public in a different sense: "At the end of the day, [these] resources don't belong to the archaeologists. Resources belong to the people. The archaeologists who are against what we do can make their case to the public. And frankly, it falls on deaf ears."

He strongly believes that individuals should be allowed to buy examples of artifacts — especially when the artifacts are documented thoroughly and examples are well represented in museum or accessible private collections. He believes that through private enterprise, Odyssey's work is bringing more artifacts into the public eye, not fewer.

Clearly, the public response to Odyssey's approach has been overwhelmingly positive. Greg pointed out: "We hear many people telling us, 'We love what you're doing because you're getting our kids interested in history.'

"It's ironic that we tell people to pay more attention to history, but then tell them that they can't have any — that they can't have an artifact to put on their mantel, that everything in the *Republic* should be gathered up and stuck in a museum storeroom, and God forbid that anybody take anything home. But the public sees right through that."

One of the fears some archaeologists have about the sale of artifacts is that they will never be properly studied. Perhaps that's true when fishermen take home ancient amphorae that they have snagged in their nets and use them to decorate their living rooms.

But in the case of coins, the argument is turned upside down. Coins of interest to collectors are carefully studied and recorded by professionals; perhaps no archaeologist has studied a coin as completely as a dedicated numismatic dealer, whose livelihood depends on interpretation of a coin's history. Even if the object later passes into private hands, the documentation is accessible to other collectors for reference and comparative evaluation.

Perhaps a fair comparison is the art world, where many important examples of art reside in private hands; most artists would not long survive if they had to rely only on museum acquisitions. But from private collections, works are often loaned out to special exhibitions and tours. The private/public mix allows key work to stay in private ownership, with public resources for exhibition and interpretation.

Not long after Odyssey's first strategy sessions for the sale of the *Republic*'s coins, Greg flew to California for the Long Beach Coin, Stamp, and Collectibles Expo. The country's top numismatists filled the cavernous Long Beach Convention Center. Individual dealers had set up long aisles of booths with displays, and all around was the brisk buzz of a marketplace. On white tablecloths in booths, collectors pored over rare coins, holding them beneath a battery of desk lamps, peering through loupes and magnifying glasses to detect nuances and flaws. Cash changed hands liberally around the hall.

Coin dealers are a cautious lot, wary of scams and overblown promises. "We're generally non–college educated, but smart people," said John Feigenbaum, president of David Lawrence Rare Coins. At the show, all the dealers knew about the coins from the *Republic,* and all had opinions.

"There's no one here who's not interested in these coins," said Steve Eichenbaum, president of NGC, which also had a prominent booth at the show. "People get the gold bug. The idea of holding a coin that no one else has held for 150 years adds to the mystery of it."

His first day at Long Beach, Greg walked from booth to booth with a $20 gold piece from the shipwreck in his pocket — one valued at $50,000. Always the showman and student of human behavior, he was interested mostly in the reactions of others at the show when he brought it out.

"Every time I showed someone the coin, they'd say, 'Oh, my gosh!' These people, many who had been looking at coins since they were fifteen years old, had a commonality of experience about coins — to react to it that way, without even a second of hesitation." The *Republic* coins were an instant sensation.

Greg was astounded at the attention to detail. "These guys can riff on one coin for an hour — a tiny file mark in the die here, a corner there. It was absolutely amazing! They were like little children when I showed them that coin. Tell me that the coins held by the public aren't being studied! Can you imagine anything being studied more carefully, and more documentation being generated, than these coins owned by private individuals?"

Arnold Saslow, an antiquities dealer from South Orange, New Jersey, is a man with an encyclopedic knowledge of coins, and lets you know it. He fairly bristles with authority. "The most fortuitous thing about the *Republic* is the incredible diversity of date, mint mark, and types that they found on the wreck," he said. "There's nothing comparable — nothing at the Smithsonian, nothing in the numismatic society, nothing in any major collection that could reflect the material being found on the ship.

"It's an absolutely unique occurrence because it was not a government shipment. It was put together by private bankers, who must have simply said something like, 'Joey, bring over ten kegs.' And that's what they did. They didn't know what was in the ten kegs. It's what was sitting around in the bank storage vaults at that time."

In the history of the lucrative American coin market, only two other shipwreck hoards from the mid-19th century have made a sizeable impact. One was the SS *Central America,* found in 1989; the other was the *Brother Jonathan,* discovered in 1995. These ships carried coins from the California gold rush, mostly 1857 gold double eagles minted in San Francisco. But when large quantities of the same coin flood the market, that can radically drive down their value. "Before the *Central America* collection came in," said Saslow, "that 1857-S was worth maybe $100,000. Now you can buy a fine one for about $8,000."

But that was an unusual case; hundreds of that particular issue in mint condition were recovered from the *Central America* wreck. In contrast, the *Republic's* wealth of dates, mints, and denominations could have an impact on nearly every serious collection. Thousands of individuals would be able to find something to fill in one or more of their empty slots, which is the collector's most powerful urge. Cost be damned when that one coin is missing.

But Tom Hawkins, a numismatist from Humble, Texas, put the find into cautionary perspective. "It could absolutely have a negative effect," he said, "because coins by and large don't get more rare, they get more common as other coins are found. That's a given in this market; you have to learn that early on. If I have a one-of-a-kind coin that someone needs, and all of a sudden there's five of them, I'm going to lose money on the sale."

Yet Hawkins had faith that the market would absorb most of the *Republic* coins: "Especially when you get back into Civil War coins. When dealing with individual customers, you look for overlays of interest — collectors, investors, Civil War buffs, shipwreck buffs, pirate buffs. There are lots of different markets coming in at different angles for different reasons. And they will overlap."

Some collectors specialize in coins from shipwrecks. Jeff Garrett, president of Mid-American Rare Coin Galleries, explained the special cachet of such coins. "They don't get socked away in museums," he said. "They get circulated among collectors. People may not really know old coins, but a coin with a story behind it is a lot more impressive.

"This is just like in the days of Egyptian archaeology. Odyssey has found a treasure that's been undisturbed for 150 years — it's amazing. And people want a piece of it. People are inherently fascinated by money. Four hundred thousand dollars was a king's ransom in 1865 — that's pretty fascinating. There will be thousands of people who buy one of these coins who may never buy another coin again. But they want one of these because of the history involved.

"The coin business is in a boom period right now. The nation has more interest in nostalgia, in our history, where we come from. This was the end of the Civil War, the beginning of Reconstruction and carpetbagging. It's a kind of time capsule of money from one hundred and fifty years ago."

Chris Karstedt, one of the few women prominent in coin-collecting circles, was excited about the narrative power in the objects from the *Republic.* "To hold that piece of history in my hand — whether it's a coin, a bottle, or a piece of wood from the paddlewheel — connects me to that time. I get to pass it on to my kids and say, 'This is a moment of history.'"

But gold, as archaeologist Neil Dobson likes to say, is only a yellow metal. For many who would come in contact with artifacts from the *Republic,* the real impact lay in the totality of the story, not the small pieces of the puzzle. From the mundane to the curious, from the tiny fragment to the spectacular, all were as tiles in the mosaic of that fateful day, October 25, 1865. The wealth of information locked in the deep ocean, the lost capsules soaked with narratives of triumph and tragedy, are as compelling as any gold.

The SS *Republic* and her passengers lived on the eve of Reconstruction in America and bore witness to some of the riveting movements of that boisterous era. It was a time of deep national sadness, yet also of opportunity and hope, a time when men could put aside their swords, as William Nichols did, and go make plowshares and screw-harrows. The steamship's discovery adds another chapter to the narrative of the Civil War and its immediate aftermath, and her rescued artifacts are rejoined to the tangible record of the nation. If the deep sea becomes addictive for men like Greg Stemm, it may be the haunting sirens of history more than the gold that brings them back.

For Greg the success can be illusory, because the next project is already percolating in his head, and because his triumph is tinged with regret that there are those who still don't approve of his philosophy or his methods. Even with money from the *Republic* securely funding the next round of endeavors for Odyssey, Greg never loses his intensity, spurred not only by the exhilaration of the hunt, but also by nagging doubts about his company's standing in the eyes of eminent marine archaeologists like George Bass. Although he tries, he can't let it go completely.

"I think we're beginning to bridge the gap between the commercial for-profit world and the archaeological world," Greg says. "In our time and culture, every discipline will suffer if you can't bring its science and its business potential together. We understand the position of the archaeologist at the Smithsonian, who may think we're a bunch of treasure hunters. And we talk to the salvagers at Blue Water Recoveries, an English company that has used grab buckets to rip apart wreck sites. We're there, positioned right in the middle, saying, 'Here's a new model. See, it *does* work.'

"Everyone out there has big dreams. We're just picking the best, the most successful things, from what they've done and can do."

Still, the SEC trial provides a bit of grounding for Greg and his long-time partner and steadfast friend, John Morris. That personal storm, barely survived, reminds Greg to look around constantly for warning signs.

"After all," he says, "you really only learn to pay attention when things are difficult. If everybody's doing well, home and happy, the tendency is to sit back a little bit. But my antenna is up. There's a line in a Grateful Dead song: 'When life looks like easy street, there is danger at the door.'"

History would agree. When a young boy is out fishing with his grandpa, who would expect the world to collapse around him? And when a ship full of gold, headed for easy street in New Orleans, steams confidently down the coast of Georgia, what passenger would expect to find himself thrown onto a heaving lifeboat with only a jar of peaches? But it happens. Hurricanes happen. Ships sink and languish, perhaps for centuries, on the dark bottom of the sea. And though we fear otherwise, what was lost can sometimes be reclaimed. What was broken can be mended, whether a country divided in war or a ship's voyage tossed on the waves of foul chance.

With its cast of shipbuilders and soldiers, tycoons and carpet-baggers, admirals and archaeologists, the drama of the *Republic* is an epic journey that's imbued with the enduring American spirit of resilience and perseverance. The lost gold is found. But in the tale of the discovery of a shipwreck, a broken, crushed ship that disappeared a century and a half ago far off the coast of Georgia, the real treasure, perhaps, is held in the ticking of the metronome of history, in that echo in which we hear our own voice returning from distant realms, in that glittering coin that joins time and memory, story and artifact, sunken wreck and treasure revealed.

Gods & Heroes

WHEN YOU FALL OFF a bike, says the old adage, you have to get right back on it to overcome the fear. When you tumble into the sea in a small but deadly shipwreck, as eight-year-old Greg Stemm did, you have to someday get back onto the waters to seal your courage. You can't let misfortune dictate your fears. Most of the surviving passengers of the star-crossed SS *Republic* bounced back from their ordeal and journeyed on. Even the two ragged castaways found on the makeshift raft, Martin and Noolan, the only sailors to live through the ordeal of those pitiful crew members who had clambered on that precarious platform eight days earlier, no doubt shook off their suffering and returned to sail another day.

Greg first saw the darkness and the finality of the sea through the shocked eyes of a little boy floating beside a dead grandfather. Several decades later he returned to the sea, to spend the rest of his life staring it down, looking deeply into its mysteries.

In the Greek epic poem by Homer, the *Odyssey*, the hero Ulysses suffers a similar, though more grandiose, misfortune. He escapes from captivity on an island where he had been held by the sea-nymph Calypso. Ulysses builds a raft, and nearly crosses the sea to safety when Neptune, god of the sea, decides to take revenge on the bold mortal who had gouged out the single eye of the Cyclops.

So Neptune "gathered his clouds together, grasped his trident, stirred it round in the sea, and roused the rage of every wind that blows till earth, sea, and sky were hidden in cloud, and night sprang forth out of the heavens. Winds from East, South, North, and West fell upon him all at the same time, and a tremendous sea got up, so that Ulysses' heart began to fail him."

And as Ulysses is lamenting his fate, "a sea broke over him with such terrific fury that the raft reeled again, and he was carried overboard a long way off. He let go the helm, and the force of the hurricane was so great that it broke the mast half way up, and both sail and yard went over into the sea. For a long time Ulysses was under water, and it was all he could do to rise to the surface again . . . but at last he got his head above water and spat out the bitter brine that was running down his face in streams."

To torment the mortal Ulysses, Neptune had created a perfect hurricane, a storm whose winds attack from all sides as they whirl around its baleful eye.

It does not spoil the metaphor to know that it was a passing yacht that capsized Greg and Papa Shell, not a raging storm. Both Ulysses and Greg Stemm were left clinging to a wreck, spitting out the bitter brine. Both survived to fulfill a greater purpose. And it does not ruin the story to realize that hurricanes as we know them do not form in the Mediterranean Sea, where Ulysses wandered for twenty years, pining for home.

In 2004, Neptune shook his trident and stirred up a string of four consecutive storms of devastation — Charley, Frances, Jeanne, and Ivan — the largest number of destructive hurricanes to hit one state in one season since 1885. Florida, where Odyssey Marine Exploration is based (in Tampa), and where its research vessels are berthed (in Jacksonville), was left flooded and at the edge of despair for months. The deluge of storms left meteorologists nervously pointing to the specter of global warming — for the more heat that generates above tropical waters, the more likely that hurricanes will develop.

In the *Odyssey*, Neptune traveled to Ethiopia, a land Homer describes as being at the end of the world. There the god looked over the edge of the sea and saw the tormented wraiths that rose from the bowels of Hades. To challenge the sea in a ship was to defy death.

By the 19th century, not much had changed. Men still set out, in their hubris and ambition, in small wooden or metal-sheathed vessels that could well become their coffins. In some sense, every long sea journey of that era was an act of courage and defiance. It rests within the larger narrative of our compulsion to harness the powers of wind and water, deceptively simple but potentially savage substances that have conceded only a little over the years to advancing science and technology. And the journey of the *Republic* reflects as well the greater desire of humans to risk much in search of better prospects elsewhere. The saga of the SS *Republic*'s last voyage ends with one of those epic confrontations between man and the sea, between human desires and the powers of nature challenged.

In 1865, when the *Republic* was lost, atmospheric science was still in its infancy. The full-blown industrial and scientific revolution of the United States was still a quarter century away. Ships sailed into a sea that sometimes seemed as dark and menacing as that ancient coast of Ethiopia. Radiowaves that could relay news were still unknown, and no weather satellites existed to create a heavenly image of the familiar white curl of a hurricane storming up from the Equator. Sea captains such as the *Republic*'s Edward Young depended on daily observation, intuition, and word-of-mouth. And sometimes they, too, fell off the edge of the sea.

Mariners through the ages, from Vasco da Gama to James Cook, have probed the unknown and met the unexpected on the sea. By the end of the 18th century they had largely defined the shapes of continents and islands, and learned to navigate the currents of the world's oceans. But even now, ninety percent of the deep ocean remains unexplored. Those who can reach that dark abyss, miles below the surface, who describe its mysteries and bring back its treasures, are the visionaries of today.

It's not surprising that Greg Stemm and John Morris named their marine exploration company Odyssey, and called their remote-operated submersible *Zeus* for the Greek king of the gods. Marine explorers have been inspired by the myths of ancient Greece for decades. Similarly, Cousteau named his ship *Calypso* after the sea nymph who held Ulysses captive. Ballard named his submersible vehicles *Jason*, *Hercules*, *Medea*, and *Argo*, after Greek gods and heroes. Homer's epic, after all, is the allegory for adventures of discovery, the story of a bold journey fraught with hardship and obstacles.

John and Greg struggled through their own gauntlet. Rejected by academics, tested by the SEC, beset by equipment failures, battered by the Gulf Stream and nor'easters, challenged by the Coast Guard — the two fought back. They punched back at the eye of the Cyclops.

In the fall of 2004, as the relentless line of hurricanes battered Florida, the *Odyssey Explorer* spent much of her time in dock. When the ship was able to slip out between storms, the crew found no new caches of gold or silver on the *Republic* site. But with a patience honed over years of methodical searching, Odyssey set out to carefully record and remove, piece by piece, every bit of shipwreck debris that had collapsed on the ship's hull. Each wooden spar, each lump of coal that had been stored for those steam engines, became an artifact to be considered and catalogued.

By year's end, project manager Tom Dettweiler and his crew had recovered some 13,000 artifacts, from horseman's spurs to delicate porcelain figures to implements for feminine hygiene — things rarely found on land sites. "Shipwrecks are events that are not supposed to happen," archaeologist Neil Dobson explained. "That's why you'll find such items of daily life. They are not passed down in families, or saved as valuable."

One great mystery remains: where is the rest of the treasure? The *Republic* was said to carry $400,000 in specie, yet only one fourth of that was found. As the Odyssey team continues to ponder that, they believe there are several possible explanations.

For starters, it is possible that, not for the first time in history, newspaper accounts were mistaken, despite the attribution of the report of the large amount of coinage on board to the seemingly most reliable source: the captain himself. But no one has yet found an actual cargo manifest for the *Republic*. Perhaps there was some monkey business, unbeknownst to the captain, that occurred in October 1865 when the ship was being loaded. If so, did this mischief involve the director of the Port of New York — the man who later committed suicide after being charged with corruption? If this were a novel, it would turn out that the specie intended for the cargo was diverted to some nefarious cause or evil cabal.

Other possibilities consider that a portion of the specie might have been lost on the high seas. Did the passengers or crew manage to throw it overboard with other pieces of cargo in the desperate attempts to lighten the load in the storm? Or did some take part of it with them as the ship was sinking? Both theories are highly unlikely. Heavy money kegs would have been impossible to handle in hurricane conditions aboard a lurching ship, and no substantial stash of such coins was reported to be present on any of the lifeboats. Passengers, including the Nichols brothers, could have stuffed only a few coins into their pockets in the melee.

Could the money still be somewhere on the wreck site? Despite the fine-tooth combing by the Odyssey crew, some areas of the wreck remain unexplored, because they are largely inaccessible. The ponderous iron boilers and walking-beam apparatus cannot easily be moved aside, even by the powerful *Zeus* ROV. It's possible that some money is buried beneath them or under the remaining tons of coal still present on the site.

As the Odyssey team reviewed the question, one other theory began to take wing. It was based in part on the fact that the recovery operation did not find any first-class passenger luggage. Nor did they locate the purser's safe, a standard feature on such vessels for storing important documents and valuables. The purser's office, and the first-class cabins, were located on the main deck of the ship, part of the superstructure above the deckline.

The emerging theory took note of an incident from an 1865 newspaper account of the disaster. In that report, Captain Hawthorne — an experienced steamer captain sailing as a passenger — reported that at about 4:00 P.M., the *Republic* "broke amidships and sank." But the Odyssey team found the keel of the SS *Republic* intact on the bottom of the sea, not broken in half.

Is it possible that Hawthorne was misquoted or misunderstood by a reporter? Or . . . perhaps he meant that the ship broke in two not vertically but horizontally.

After all, the main decks of ships depend a lot on gravity to hold them down; they are not always so firmly attached to their hulls. And on that baleful day of October 25, 1865, the superstructure of the *Republic* was being battered by powerful waves as the ship rolled from trough to trough. Weakened not only by this storm but also by another hurricane experienced the previous year off the coast of Texas, the main deck and fittings could have detached from the ship — looking, in the howling darkness, as if the ship split in two.

If that happened, everything stowed in the main deck would wash away into the sea immediately, since the deck had no true floor: its floor was the ceiling of the next deck down. As the lower half of the steamship corkscrewed through the water to its doom in one direction, objects from the main deck would have dispersed broadly, sinking according to their own density and size. Heavier objects would have plummeted quickly; lighter objects would have trailed through the water like confetti in the current, leaving a long debris field. The many mapping voyages of *Zeus* across the wreck site had already revealed that two trails of debris, like bread crumbs in a fairy tale, led from the site — one going southeast, the other northwest. These have not yet been fully explored.

Typically, valuables like coins would have been stowed in the purser's office, safe from prying eyes. But since that small office was limited in size, and given the large quantity of the shipment, part of the specie, the overflow, might have been placed in an aft compartment — exactly where *Zeus* found them. But this would have just been the extra portion of the coins.

The undiscovered coins, then, if this theory proves true, could be scattered in the debris field with other objects that fell out of the detached main deck. They may be lying hundreds of yards away from the main wreck site.

In November 2004, Greg considered plans to follow the debris trails of the *Republic* with high-resolution sonar and magnetometer.

By year's end, though, Odyssey was beginning to look ahead to the next grand story. As it wrapped up core operations on the Civil War steamship, the company had a dozen other shipwreck projects in the works, including plans to excavate the formidable HMS *Sussex*, the 17th-century English warship lost off the coast of Gibraltar. Other projects were under further review; among scores of research portfolios that Odyssey has examined from the Bahamas to Madagascar are ones named *Concepcion*, *Seattle*, and *Atlas*. Those are, of course, code names for real lost ships; the shipwreck business works on a constant high-security alert. New deep-sea exploration companies, emboldened by Odyssey's success, could be poised to poach.

Reports of riches have launched these research efforts, yes, but the real treasures are the human stories spinning from archives, old letters, and newspaper articles — tales of bold entrepreneurs and heroic captains, of mustache-twirling villains and damsels in distress, of ships carrying prostitutes and minstrel troupes with tycoons and bankers. Accounts describe violent storms and collisions at sea. They hint at suspicions of misread charts and sleepy watches, and deliver up flashes of foul instinct or of quiet grit — as in that remarkable moment on the *Republic* as dignified gentlemen stood by lifeboats "shaking hands and bidding each other adieu . . . calmly saying to each other, 'You go in this boat, and I will go in the next.'"

When most ships go down, chaos reigns. And seldom are there barrels of gold or silver rocking in the hold. Odyssey has found shipwrecks with less valuable cargos — trade china or amphorae of olive oil — but bearing hints of tales that may prove to be no less fascinating. In looking for the famed HMS *Sussex* in the Mediterranean, the side-scan sonar picked out a shadow on the ocean floor that looks to be a Barbary pirate ship. Will she yield pirate gold? Or will her treasures be the ghostly artifacts once used by real buccaneers, found lying in the darkness of a deep-water wreck, reflecting human actions in a moment of final disaster, suggesting stories of what led to that fateful last moment before the ship disappeared into the restless sea?

It may prove that indeed the images and tales are what people will remember long after any gold has been collected and catalogued. "Shipwreck effect" may be the Midas touch when it comes to stories as well as coins. In another stormy wreck, for instance, an observer on board, a thespian with a dramatic flair, gave the most sensational account to the tabloids. In the last moments, he related, crew members in lifeboats slashed with knives and oars at desperately swimming passengers who were attempting to climb into lifeboats with them. As night fell, many perished.

The next morning, the bedraggled actor washed ashore, half dead, and crawled to a nearby house to ask for a shot of brandy.

A shipwrecked thespian? What a story to tell! What a story!

Ideas were already flying from Greg's head like butterflies. John had his charts out, calculating where next around the globe to send a research ship and ROV from their growing fleet.

Neptune waited in the wings, sharpening his trident, wondering what to do with these men.

Timeline of the SS *Republic*

August 31, 1853	SS *Tennessee* launched in Baltimore.
February 7, 1854	*Tennessee's* maiden voyage, to Charleston.
August 19, 1855	*Tennessee's* first trans-Atlantic voyage.
January 8, 1856	*Tennessee* begins South American service.
October 6, 1856	*Tennessee's* first voyage for Charles Morgan's Nicara-guan service.
January 29, 1857	*Tennessee* leaves for Nicaragua with her final load of filibusters.
April, 1861	In New Orleans, Confederacy impounds all merchant vessels at outbreak of Civil War, including *Tennessee*.
January, 1862	Confederate Navy pays for seized *Tennessee*, plans to use her as a blockade runner.
April 25, 1862	Farragut's fleet captures the port of New Orleans; the *Tennessee* is at a wharf, disguised in vain with a French flag.
May 8, 1862	USS *Tennessee* commissioned into U.S. Navy.
July 4, 1863	Fall of Vicksburg; on the Mississippi River to the south, Farragut uses the SS *Tennessee* as his flagship as he directs the naval siege of Port Hudson. Port Hudson surrenders a few days later.

August 5, 1864	Battle of Mobile Bay; USS *Tennessee* leads rearguard patrol of five ships to bombard Fort Morgan, as main fleet under the command of Farragut enters the bay.
September 1, 1864	USS *Tennessee* rechristened USS *Mobile*.
October, 1864	*Mobile* damaged by storm in Gulf of Mexico; sent to New York for repairs.
December, 1864	*Mobile* decommissioned and anchored at Brooklyn Navy Yard, awaiting disposition.
March 30, 1865	*Mobile* purchased by Russell Sturgis for $25,000; outfitted as passenger ship.
May 3, 1865	Newly christened SS *Republic* back in service for William H. Robson's New York–New Orleans Line.
July, 1865	While on her third trip south, the *Republic*'s charter is switched to H.B. Cromwell & Co. Lines; she continues to serve the same route.
October 19	SS *Republic* leaves on final voyage from New York's Staten Island.
October 23	Gale storm hits *Republic* off the coast of North Carolina, increases over the day and night to hurricane strength.
October 24	Ship begins to leak in the morning. Men assemble in the early afternoon to throw portion of cargo overboard, then bail water in buckets for more than 12 hours.
October 25	Half past one in the afternoon, the bailing attempt is given up as futile. Raft is hastily built. Four lifeboats and raft are launched. Moments later, at four o'clock, SS *Republic* sinks.
October 26	Lifeboat No. 1, led by Capt. Young, is rescued by the brig *John W. Lovitt*. Passengers later delivered to Charleston.
October 27	Lifeboat No. 2, led by Captain Hawthorne, rescued by the schooner *Willie Dill*. Passengers later delivered to Port Royal, South Carolina.

	Lifeboat No. 3, led by Sarsfield Young and Capt. George McNear, with Nichols brothers on board, rescued by the barkentine *Horace Beals*. Passengers later transferred to SS *General Hooker* and delivered to Charleston.
October 29, 1865	Lifeboat #4, the captain's gig, led by Edward Ryan, rescued by schooner *Harper* and delivered to Hilton Head, South Carolina.
November 2	Raft, with only two survivors of 14–18 men originally on board, picked from sea by barkentine USS *Tioga* just 20 miles from Cape Hatteras.

May, 2002	Odyssey begins full-scale search for *Republic* wreck in *Polo Pony*.
July 25, 2003	Ernie Tapanes and crew, on RV *Odyssey,* finds side-scan sonar image of "Sailboat No. 1."
August 2	Closer inspection by ROV confirms sonar image is a side-wheel steamer.
August 12	Court names Odyssey "salvor in possession" of wreck site.
October 7	*Odyssey Explorer* begins initial survey work on site.
October 9	ROV *Zeus* finds ship's bell.
November 5	Jim Starr and crew find gold coins.
March 26, 2004	Court grants Odyssey title and ownership of the remains of the SS *Republic*.

Coins of the SS *Republic*

BY Q. DAVID BOWERS

Early treasures lost and found

Treasure gold! American history is spiced with stories of lost wealth. Now and then, sunken treasures and other hoards of pirate gold, doubloons, and pieces of eight have come to light to fascinate historians and please numismatists. However, most of the finds of early pieces in or near American waters have involved coins of Mexico, Central or South America, and other foreign lands. Important United States coins, whether gold or silver, have been conspicuous by their absence, for the most part, in recoveries of sunken treasures.

The plenitude of foreign coins and scarcity of U.S. coins in shipwreck finds is due partly to the time frame involved. Into the 18th century, losses of Spanish galleons at sea, one of the most lucrative sources of sunken treasure, occurred in an era before the United States even existed. Typically, these treasure-laden galleons were returning from lands of the New World conquered by the Spanish. Each year a harvest of silver and gold, much in the form of freshly minted coins, was gathered and sent back to Spain via a flotilla. On notable occasions, in particular in 1622 and 1715, the flotillas encountered the hurricanes of late summer and early autumn, which wreaked great destruction and sank many vessels, often close to the shore of what is present-day Florida. Although some silver and gold coins from these Spanish wrecks were recovered over time by exploration parties or by individuals finding stray pieces washed up on beaches, it was not until the 20th century that the lost coins, ingots, jewelry, and other artifacts from these Spanish ships were recovered in quantity.

Perhaps the most famous such find was made in the 1970s and 1980s under the direction of Mel Fisher, who found the wreck of the *Nuestra Señora de Atocha*, which on September 6, 1622, had been lost at sea with three other ships off Key West. Also publicized, but to a lesser extent, were other finds made by Kip Wagner and associates, working as a firm called the Real Eight Corporation, from wrecks of the 1715 fleet.

American Gold and Silver Coins

The Mint Act of April 2, 1792, provided for the establishment of a federal mint in Philadelphia, the cornerstone for which was laid on July 31, 1792, with Mint Director David Rittenhouse and President George Washington in attendance. The first significant production of U.S. coins for circulation took place in 1793 with copper cents and half cents, followed by silver coins in 1794 and gold in 1795. Coins of the latter two precious metals were made in quantity for years after, eventually including many different denominations.

From the earliest times of settlement, each year many ships were lost at sea, sometimes with no trace of what happened, in other instances documented by tales of woe — piracy, foundering in hurricane-whipped waves, or collisions with rocks or with other vessels. Surely just about every passenger vessel departing from a port such as New York City, Baltimore, New Orleans, Charleston, or Boston carried some silver and gold coins, if not in bulk shipments, then among the passengers' personal effects, since paper money was not wanted in distant ports of call. Although the wrecks of some of these ships have been found, there is no record of any significant recovery of numismatically important coins.

Beginning in 1849, large quantities of gold from the California Gold Rush arrived in the East. To facilitate the use of gold in coinage form, the Coinage Act of March 3, 1849, provided for two new denominations, the $1 coin (known as the gold dollar) and the $20 (known as the double eagle). These joined the $2.50, $5, and $10 values that had been produced since the 1790s. Gold dollars were first coined in 1849, double eagles not until 1850.

Production of the double eagle was quickly recognized as the most efficient way to convert bullion into coin form. The importance and significance of the double eagle is dramatized by the fact that from 1850 until 1933, the span that this coin was issued, more than 75 percent of the value of *all* metal coined by the United States — copper, nickel, silver, and gold — occurred in the form of double eagles. With its popularity and intrinsic value, the double eagle naturally plays a key role in shipwreck treasure losses from 1850 on.

Silver coins, minted in quantity since 1794, also figure in accounts of losses in disasters at sea. However, this metal is usually acted upon by salt water to the extent that the coins are completely dissolved or are rendered unidentifiable. Many of the silver half dollars recovered from the SS *Republic* are a surprising and remarkable exception.

American Treasure Shipwrecks in the Age of Gold

The marvelous finds of the "Forty-niners" in the streambeds of California inaugurated the Age of Gold, literally, with double eagles minted by the millions in the 1850s and 1860s, as well as a lesser amount of other denominations from the $1 coin to the $10 eagle. During these two decades a number of mints in addition to the main Philadelphia Mint were in operation, including branches at San Francisco (opened in 1854), New Orleans (1838), Charlotte (1838), and Dahlonega (1838). The last two mints, in North Carolina and Georgia, respectively, produced gold coins of values from $1 to $5, but did not have presses able to make higher denominations.

In this era, gold coins, particularly in the form of double eagles, were staples in national and international currency. Paper money of state-chartered banks was not trusted, and even when federal Legal Tender bills were circulated beginning in 1862, they were of depreciated value in relation to silver and gold. Beginning in 1854 when the New York Assay Office and Sub-Treasury opened for business, New York City became the most important trading center for gold. Vast quantities of coins from California, including double eagles (in particular) from the San Francisco Mint, arrived in the port on a regular basis. Usually the shipments traveled by steamships connecting from Panama, where the valuable cargo had been transferred overland from the Pacific side. From New York City, gold coins and ingots (rectangular bars) were reshipped to various ports in the United States as well as to foreign destinations, London in particular. To a lesser extent, silver was also shipped, especially to Atlantic Coast destinations.

Navigation was hazardous in an era in which most reckoning was done by sight, accurate weather forecasting did not exist, and many unforeseen hazards lay ahead. Shipwrecks were so numerous that no complete accounting of them exists today. Maritime annals tell of thousands of ships that were sunk, wrecked on rocks, or simply disappeared — over 8,000 in the Great Lakes alone. Of course, relatively few of those shipwrecks contained gold or silver; the majority carried lumber, ore, a variety of manufactured goods, and passengers.

Of the thousands of American ships lost, relatively few are known to have carried large amounts of treasure, and of these, only a handful have been found and valuable coins recovered. The SS *Republic* is the latest in this very exclusive series. Indeed, there are just two other confirmed and documented major finds from the "Age of Gold," the decades of the 1850s and 1860s, to which can be added a third possibility, information about which is sketchy.

The earliest documented major recovery is the treasure from the SS *Central America,* lost at sea off North Carolina on September 12, 1857. The ship carried to the ocean floor a vast treasure in gold coins and ingots headed from Aspinwall, on the Atlantic side of Panama, north to New York City. In the late 1980s the wreck was found in 7,200 feet of water by the Columbus-America Discovery Group. Recovered were about 7,500 gold coins, dominated by more than 5,400 mint-fresh 1857-S double eagles, plus more than 500 gold ingots. Originating in San Francisco, the cargo had been carried south to Panama City by the SS *Sonora*, after which it was transported 48 miles over land on the Panama Railroad to Aspinwall.

The gold coins and ingots, plus a small number of heavily corroded silver coins, were distributed mostly by the California Gold Marketing Group (led by Dwight Manley) and, reportedly, the recovered treasure yielded well over $100 million in sales.

Next in the short list of recovered shipwreck treasures from the Age of Gold is not documented, but is believed to have been from the SS *Yankee Blade,* a side-wheel steamer lost when it hit the rocky shore off Santa Barbara, California, on the foggy afternoon of October 1, 1854. About $152,000 in gold was reportedly lost when the ship sank. While researching *American Coin Treasures and Hoards* (1996), I was told that in 1977 divers found several hundred 1854-S double eagles in the wreck of that vessel. However, the recovery, if there was one, was shrouded in secrecy. From about that time and continuing into the 1980s, 200 to 300 examples of 1854-S twenties indeed came on the market through auction sales and private transactions. Each of these coins has "saltwater Uncirculated" surfaces, as they were designated. In other words, the coins show signs of the action of sea and sand in relatively shallow water. The total market value of these double eagles was probably in the range of $1 million.

The third and final U.S. shipwreck antecedent to the SS *Republic* is the treasure of the SS *Brother Jonathan,* lost in the Pacific off Crescent City, California, on August 30, 1865. The ship carried an unknown quantity of coins, but it yielded slightly more than a thousand pieces when the wreck was found in the 1990s. Most were double eagles of the 1865-S variety and a lesser number of 1864-S and 1863-S twenties, along with some other varieties. Most were sold at auction in 1999. The market value was in the $5 million range.

To the preceding shipwrecks of treasure coins — two confirmed plus one unconfirmed — can be added another golden treasure, one lost just off the shore in the vicinity of modern-day Fort Pierce, Florida, at the Indian River Inlet. This consisted of a $23,000 payroll in gold coins sent by sea aboard the *William and Mary* from Charleston, S.C., south to the army post at Fort Capron, in the custody of Major Jeremiah Yellot Dashielle, in the year 1857. Upon arriving near the fort, Major Dashielle took the payroll with him in a small boat and headed toward the shore. The vessel capsized in the surf, and the coins were scattered.

In the 1960s, an estimated 3,500 or so of the gold coins from that small capsized boat, from dollars to double eagles, were recovered. Most of the face value was in 1855-S and 1856-S twenties, each showing etched surfaces from the action of the sand, again called "saltwater Uncirculated." This find was incompletely reported, and today its exact contents are not known. Most of the coins apparently were of lower denominations. Mainly distributed into the coin markets in the 1970s, the market value of this find may have been in the range of $500,000 to $1 million.

These four instances constituted the significant U.S. gold coin treasures recovered from shipwrecks of the 1850s and 1860s that were known by early 2003. To this list can now be added the dramatic find in the autumn of 2003 of the SS *Republic* coins, totaling over 50,000 coins — more pieces than all of the earlier-mentioned treasures of U.S. shipwrecked coins combined!

Money during the Civil War

On October 17, 1865, the SS *Republic* left New York City and headed toward the open sea, en route to New Orleans. On board was a reported $400,000 in coins — some gold, but also thousands of silver half dollars, plus scattered other issues.

At the time, such coins were especially precious, as paper money was deeply depreciated. This situation dated back to the beginnings of the Civil War. In the second week of April 1861, Confederate forces in Charleston bombarded Fort Sumter in the harbor, reducing most of it to rubble and forcing the federal troops to surrender. President Abraham Lincoln declared war soon afterward. The conflict was envisioned as an easy win for the North, as Confederate troops were thought to be poorly equipped and trained. A call was issued for volunteer troops to enlist in the Union army for a period of three months, certainly enough time for an easy victory. Parades and parties were held as soldiers marched off to war.

The unexpected and overwhelming victory by the Confederate troops at the Battle of Bull Run in July dispelled any lingering thoughts that the war would end soon. By that time the Treasury Department, largely depleted of readily available funds even before the war began, was in serious financial straits. By issuing Demand Notes — currency redeemable in gold — additional money was secured. Loans arranged through the help of bankers added to the revenue. As the year progressed, however, and the outcome of the conflict became increasingly uncertain, the public turned toward the hoarding of "hard money." In late December 1861, banks in New York and elsewhere stopped paying out gold coins in exchange for bank notes, the latter consisting of bills issued by more than a thousand state-chartered banks.

In early 1862 the Treasury Department issued Legal Tender bills. These were not redeemable in coins but exchangeable only for other such bills and, on a limited basis, in satisfaction of money owed to the government. Public distrust of paper money deepened, and silver coins soon disappeared from circulation. By the second week of July, copper-nickel cents were gone as well. With no coins available for trade, business was conducted mostly in paper money and, for small transactions, in substitutes such as postage stamps, tokens, and privately printed bills.

In the meantime, gold and silver coins were still available but only from banks and exchange brokers, who charged a premium for them in terms of Legal Tender bills. In January 1862, at the outset of hoarding, it took $1,010 in bank bills to buy $1,000 face value in gold coins. By October it took $1,235 in bank bills or the new Legal Tender bills to do the same. As the war progressed, the differential continued to rise. The apex was reached in July 1864 — when $2,850 in bills was required to receive $1,000 in gold coins.

Over time, the situation for small coins eased, and in 1863 copper-nickel Indian Head cents were again seen in commerce, together with an immense quantity of copper Civil War tokens bearing patriotic legends or the advertisements of merchants. Encased postage stamps, consisting of stamps mounted in a brass frame faced with mica, were encountered as well. To aid in small transactions, the Treasury Department issued Postage Currency bills of small size, followed by Fractional Currency in values from three cents to fifty cents. In 1864 the bronze two-cent piece first appeared, and these circulated widely, followed by nickel three-cent coins in 1865.

In the meantime, in California and certain other West Coast areas, paper money was not used in commerce. The Constitution of California, adopted in 1850, expressly forbid the use of such bills, a measure intended to prevent losses from bank bills of failed institutions. Instead, commerce was conducted solely in coins, mostly gold, bolstered by a small supply of silver.

When the federal Legal Tender bills appeared in 1862, followed by National Bank notes in late 1863, this currency was exchangeable in California only at a discount, the amount being equal to the premium charged in the East. In San Francisco, gold double eagles were used at par to buy and sell goods. To settle a transaction in paper money, a higher price would be charged, equal to the exchange-rate difference. In New York City, paper bills were used to buy and sell goods at prices much higher than in San Francisco, and anyone wanting to pay in gold coins got a deep discount.

In early 1865, as the Civil War drew to a conclusion, it was widely anticipated that gold and silver coins would soon be seen again in commerce, exchangeable at par with paper money. However, because the financial condition of the federal government remained uncertain, with huge debts incurred in the conduct of the war, silver and gold were still hoarded, and paper money remained the basis of commerce. Not until after April 20, 1876, were silver coins on a par with paper in terms of usage, and not until after December 17, 1878, were gold and paper exchangeable.

Coins and Paper Money in Autumn 1865

In October 1865, the month that the SS *Republic* undertook its final voyage, the monetary situation in America remained in a confused state. In common circulation in the North were copper-nickel one-cent pieces and the new (since spring 1864) bronze Indian cents, along with bronze two-cent pieces and nickel three-cent pieces. Civil War tokens were also still seen with frequency, although they had not been made in quantity since early 1864.

Fractional Currency bills flooded commerce and continued to be printed in large numbers. Legal Tender notes served for larger transactions, to which were added bills with the imprint of various National Banks. Bills of state-chartered banks were plentiful and were valued the same as federal paper money, but were in their decline. On July 1, 1866, such bank bills became subject to a 10 percent tax in transactions; in anticipation of this, few new bills were issued. Hundreds of state banks converted to National Banks.

In the South, the Confederate States of America had issued paper money since 1861, but it had depreciated greatly and was nearly worthless by early 1865. By the end of the war in April 1865, it had no value at all.

Gold and silver coins were plentiful in bank vaults and in the hands of exchange brokers, but not a single piece was to be found in everyday business. These coins could be purchased only by paying a premium in federal bills, but the differential had fallen sharply since its high point in July 1864. In the West the situation remained the same: gold and silver coins were staples in commerce, while paper money was accepted only at a discount.

Although New Orleans, the intended destination of the SS *Republic,* had been captured by the Confederates in 1861 and repatriated by Union troops in 1862, the monetary situation there was uncertain, even after war's end. Throughout the former territory of Confederate States of America, the South was being infused with Legal Tender and National Bank notes, but they were not widely trusted. The citizens of the Confederacy had held paper money during the war and subsequently experienced complete depreciation of their wealth; they were not inclined to trust the new paper being issued.

Accordingly, in October 1865, although bank bills could be spent to buy goods and services in New Orleans, gold and silver coins were much more desirable, even at a sharp premium. Anyone with such coins to spend had a distinct advantage in commercial transactions.

Coins carried aboard the SS *Republic*

Throughout this period, the gold $20 double eagle was the largest denomination of coin produced in the United States. The other gold coin in use but less common was the $10 gold eagle. Gold $1 pieces were far less common; although they had been minted for a long time, by 1865 they were not readily available in bulk.

For silver, the half dollar was the largest denomination in common use. Silver dollars existed, being minted since the early 1850s, but they were intended for use in international commerce and were not seen in everyday transactions.

Accordingly, on its final voyage in 1865 the SS *Republic* carried half dollars as the main component of its cargo of silver coins, while double eagles were most common among the gold coins found, along with some $10 gold eagles.

No doubt the passengers carried a supply of other coins as personal possessions, or perhaps stored them in the purser's safe. At the time these would have most commonly included bronze and copper-nickel cents, bronze two-cent pieces, and nickel three-cent pieces. Anyone carrying silver coins, from three-cent pieces (called *trimes*) upward to half dollars or dollars, or gold coins of values from $1 to $20, would have bought these specially for the trip from an exchange office in New York City. Collectively, in shipwreck parlance, such coins are known as *passenger gold*.

In bulk, gold and silver coins were usually stored in one of two ways. For transactions within cities, and also for many shipments sent by sea, coins were often put up in sturdy canvas bags. Wooden kegs furnished a practical alternative and were included aboard the SS *Republic*. Although kegs were more expensive, they had the distinct advantage of allowing large quantities of coins to be easily handled at the destination, as heavy kegs could be rolled along the ground. No special handling equipment was needed, as would have been the case if wooden crates had been used. Moreover, a sealed wooden keg offered better security than a canvas bag. Surely those in charge had heard the many tales in circulation of small quantities of coins or other precious items on board a ship being switched or pilfered in transit, and knew that to steal and hide something as large and heavy as a keg was much more difficult.

Treasure Found

When Odyssey Marine Exploration, Inc., located the wreck of the long-lost SS *Republic,* hopes were that significant quantities of *gold* coins would be found. There was little expectation that anything worthwhile would be recovered in the way of silver coins. The few known recoveries from sunken ships carrying U.S. coins had included gold, but hardly anything in the way of silver coins, and almost nothing in minor issues. It was thus a delight, surprise, and numismatic sensation that tens of thousands of half dollars were found on the *Republic* site!

The recovery of the SS *Republic* coins commenced with vigor in late 2003. In February 2004, John Albanese commented that the treasure "is looking like it will be the biggest thing to hit the numismatic world, at least in the 25 years I have been in the business." By that time about 31,000 silver coins and 3,425 gold pieces had been brought up from the depths, amounting in face value to slightly less than 18 percent of the estimated coins lost. By late 2004 the count had crossed the 50,000 mark, mostly augmented by a silver cascade of half dollars.

An analysis revealed that the gold coins consisted primarily of $20 double eagles. A lesser number of $10 eagles were found, but no smaller denominations. The silver coins were nearly entirely in the form of half dollars. The find equated perfectly with the types of coins that would have been shipped in bulk for important transactions at New Orleans, the intended destination.

Many of the gold coins recovered were covered with grime and were discolored. Careful attention by the Numismatic Conservation Services served to restore the pieces to their 1865 appearance. As gold is the most inert and impervious of coinage metals, no harm had been done to them. If anything, the surface grime served to protect the original finish, including a frosty mint luster on some of the pieces.

John Albanese, a long-time professional who had also served as an advisor to the SS *Central America* project, was enlisted to bring the *Republic's* treasure coins to market. From 2004 to the present, he directed the process of dividing the pieces into categories of rarity, grade, and demand.

The Silver Coins

Among the half dollars, although the earlier Capped Bust design coins dating back to 1832 were represented, the lion's share consisted of Liberty Seated pieces. This design, by talented engraver Christian Gobrecht, features Miss Liberty seated on a rock, one hand holding a shield and the other a pole surmounted by a liberty cap, a symbol of freedom. Thirteen stars surround, with the date below. On certain issues of 1853 to 1855, small arrowheads are found on each side of the date. The reverse displays a perched eagle, wings downward, holding an olive branch and three arrows, with UNITED STATES OF AMERICA around the border and the denomination noted as HALF DOL. below.

Liberty Seated half dollars, minted continuously from 1839 onward, were the design in use at the time of the ship's demise. Most were produced at the Philadelphia Mint, but many had been produced at the branch in New Orleans and a lesser number at a facility in distant San Francisco. The branch mint coins are distinguished by a mintmark — O or S — on the reverse below the eagle.

The New Orleans Mint, which had opened for business in 1838, continued in operation under federal auspices until January 1861, at which time it was taken over by troops of the State of Louisiana, and later by Confederate forces. Half dollars continued to be produced there after the mint was seized, using regular 1861-O Liberty Seated dies and the silver bullion on hand.

Early in the war, the Confederacy contemplated making its own half dollars. A.H.M. Patterson, a local engraver, was commissioned to create a distinctive reverse die, with inscription CONFEDERATE STATES OF

AMERICA. This design was to be mated with the regular Liberty Seated obverse, the latter considered still appropriate as it bore no identification to either the federal or Union government. Four of these patterns were struck. By chance, the Liberty Seated obverse die selected to be used with the new reverse was one that had a tiny crack extending from the bridge of Miss Liberty's nose to the border at the left. This die had been used under Confederate authority to produce 1861-O half dollars with a regular UNITED STATES OF AMERICA reverse.

You can imagine my delight when, upon examining an "ordinary" 1861-O half dollar recovered from the SS *Republic*, in exceptional Mint State condition, shown to me by Odyssey partner Greg Stemm, I discerned that it had a tiny die crack at Miss Liberty's nose. Here, certainly, was an 1861-O half dollar that could be positively attributed to the Confederacy, a silver coin minted after control was taken from the United States government.

For the 1861-O half dollars manufactured at the New Orleans mint, 330,000 were struck first by the federal government early that year, followed by 1.24 million for the State of Louisiana, then 962,633 for the Confederacy. Many pairs of dies were used. However, as the die with the crack was used thereafter to make the distinctive Confederate A.H.M. Patterson patterns, it is likely that it was the die still in use toward the end of the 962,633 run of the regular 1861-O by the Confederacy.

Whereas some of the recovered half dollars from the SS *Republic* were conserved to reveal lustrous Mint State examples, most were kept in a state designated by the Numismatic Guaranty Corporation (NGC), which graded and encapsulated the pieces, as "shipwreck effect" coins. These coins are of bright silver, with surfaces that have microscopic evidence of their nearly 140 years in the deep ocean. In many instances, such coins retain all of the details of the Seated Liberty figure, stars, date, eagle, and lettering. All are of commanding interest and importance because of their historical connection with the famous SS *Republic* and the era in which that steamship played a role. Simply holding one in your hand evokes a sense of drama and adventure. Beginning in late summer 2004, many of these half dollars were distributed through television and print-media marketing channels, as well as by rare coin dealers, each coin encapsulated by NGC with a unique registration number and accompanied with documentation.

The higher grade, more valuable coins were reserved for specific auction and other offerings to the rare coin market, through which dedicated buyers are able to expand their collections. Significantly, the treasure find included over 100 examples of the first Liberty Seated half dollar struck in San Francisco — the 1855-S — considered to be a key variety in any grade. To these can be added other San Francisco coins, thousands of New Orleans issues, and many Philadelphia coins.

Until now, no shipwreck of the 1850s or 1860s has yielded quantities of silver coins; in comparison, only a few dozen half dollars, all extensively etched by seawater, had been found in the SS *Central America* treasure. As a result, the SS *Republic* half dollars have made possible a new specialty — the opportunity to add a single coin to a numismatic or cabinet display as a historical artifact, or to create a collection of multiple pieces selected by date, mint or origin, or grade. Surely, the half dollars now entering private collections will be mentioned in essays and studies in the *Gobrecht Journal*, official magazine of the Liberty Seated Collectors Club, for years to come.

Eagles from the SS *Republic*

Although the silver half dollars are extremely important and valuable, the gold treasure found in the wreck of the SS *Republic* is of incredible worth. Virtually all the specimens proved to be in excellent condition after their conservation, with many identified either as rarities or among the finest quality of their variety, or both.

Eagles or $10 gold coins were found of all dates from 1838 onward, from the date of the inception of the Liberty Head design, with dies created by Christian Gobrecht. (No $10 gold coins were made between 1804 and 1838). On the obverse, the head of Miss Liberty faces to the left, with LIBERTY inscribed on a diadem. Surrounding are 13 stars and the date. On the reverse is seen a perched eagle, wings upward (an orientation opposite to that of the wings on half dollars), with UNITED STATES OF AMERICA around and TEN D. below. Like the half dollars, most eagles were coined at the Philadelphia Mint, with additional pieces struck at New Orleans (bearing an O mintmark) and San Francisco (S).

By 1865, the largest quantity of any date of the $10 gold coin was the 1847, of which 862,258 were struck. Not surprisingly, coins of this year were the most numerous of those recovered from the SS *Republic*, with 221 conserved by NCS and graded by NGC by September 2004. By contrast, just one 1841-O eagle was found, a logical reflection of its rarity, as just 2,500 were made. The roster of other remarkably rare issues for which fewer than five coins were recovered from the *Republic* site includes 1838 (4 found), 1842 (4), 1852-O (3), 1857-O (3), 1858 (1), 1858-O (4), 1858-S (4), 1859-O (2), 1860-O (4), 1860-S (4), 1861-S (2), 1862-S (2), 1863 (1), 1863-S (3), 1864 (2), 1865 (1), and 1865-S (1).

Certain of these individual coins combine great rarity with remarkable condition. One of the most storied rarities in the eagle series is the 1858, of which just 2,521 were struck. The single SS *Republic* specimen is one of the finest known, with most of its original mint frost still remaining. As another example, the solitary 1865-S is of the curious variety with regular date over an *inverted* date. In other words, the date was first erroneously punched into the die upside down, then corrected!

In time, all of the $10 gold coins will be offered into the market. No doubt some of the more numerous examples, such as the 1847 pieces, will find appreciative owners who desire a single eagle from this remarkable historic site for their collections. The rarities and higher grade pieces will engender excitement and competition among specialists, dealers, and others who are secure in the knowledge that once sold, it may be a long time, if ever, until they become available again.

Double Eagles from the SS *Republic*

Double eagles, first minted for circulation in 1850, were firmly established as *the* gold coins of dominance in banking and commercial circles. These and other gold coins did not circulate in the East or Midwest in 1865, the year the SS *Republic* was lost, nor would they be seen in trade until late December 1878. However, banks, exchange offices, and the federal Sub-Treasury in New York City, as well as many companies and individuals, held such pieces as a store of value. As mentioned earlier, such coins were worth a premium in terms of Legal Tender notes and other paper money.

No doubt most of the reported $400,000 in coins carried on board the SS *Republic* were in the form of double eagles. Destined for New Orleans, the $20 coins were expected to command attention and serve to purchase anything offered.

Similar to the situation for the $10 coins, the double eagles found on the *Republic* site and conserved and graded by September 2004 were most numerous in those dates and mintmark varieties for which the greatest quantities had been coined. By 1865, the laurels in that category went to the 1861 Philadelphia issue, of which 2,976,519 had been struck. Reflecting this, most numerous among the treasure coins of the *Republic* were some 450 examples of the 1861.

In contrast, low-mintage varieties proved elusive, as would be expected. Of the legendary 1854-O double eagle, of which only 3,250 were struck, just a single coin was found. It was a remarkable example, however, with nearly full mint luster and quite close to Uncirculated condition. Of the many date and mintmark possibilities from 1850 to 1865, only one variety was *not* found, the 1856-O, of which 2,250 were made. Accordingly, from the SS *Republic* treasure, an advanced numismatist could, at least in theory, form a complete collection up to that point in time except for just one missing coin! The other New Orleans double eagles of the era range from scarce to rare and were found in lesser numbers than those of the Philadelphia and San Francisco mints.

Careful study by the experts at NGC revealed many interesting curiosities among double eagles (and some among eagles, as well). In the $20 series, some of the 1854 Philadelphia issue have the date in large numerals, these being scarcer than those with the date in slightly smaller digits. Of the 1855-S coins, some have a large S mintmark, while others have a small S letter, the latter being more numerous. Among those of 1860-S, 68 were found to have a small S mintmark, but one — just one — has a large S. Mintmark differences were also found with the 1865-S double eagles, with slightly more than 200 having a small S, while fewer than three dozen bear a large S.

For a short time in 1861 the San Francisco Mint used a special reverse die, made by engraver Anthony C. Paquet, with the words around the reverse in tall, heavy letters. Soon after, the director of the mint decreed that this style be discontinued, but not before 19,250 were struck. One of these was found among the *Republic*'s treasure, in sharp contrast to 97 examples with the regular reverse style.

Many of the double eagles are in Mint State (Uncirculated) grade, including some at the choice and gem levels. Undoubtedly, these will arouse great interest and excitement when offered to the collecting community.

I personally have a little collection of "treasure" double eagles from the shipwrecks mentioned earlier. The examples include an 1854-S (with "salt-water" surfaces) from the SS *Yankee Blade,* a heavily etched 1856-S from the Fort Capron find, a Mint State 1857-S from the SS *Central America,* and a Mint State 1865-S from the SS *Brother Jonathan.* Like all collectors fascinated by the sense of history embodied in artifacts recovered from wrecks at sea, I can now look to build my collection with a coin from the newest contribution to this unique field: the treasure of the SS *Republic.*

Q. David Bowers, of American Numismatic Rarities, LLC, of Wolfeboro, N.H., has been in the rare coin business since 1953, when he was a teenager. He also serves as numismatic director and writer for Whitman Publications, LLC. He has been president of the American Numismatic Association (1983–1985) and president of the Professional Numismatists Guild (1977–1979), and is the recipient of many awards and honors in the field. He has authored more than 40 books, hundreds of auction and other catalogues, and several thousand articles and columns for *Coin World, Paper Money,* and *The Numismatist.* Among his books are *Collecting Rare Coins for Profit, High Profits from Rare Coin Investment,* and *A Buyer's Guide to the Rare Coin Market.* He has also written books on the treasure ships SS *Brother Jonathan* and SS *Central America.* This appendix article is provided courtesy of Whitman Publishing.